THE GREAT CONVERGENCE

THE
GREAT CONVERGENCE

Information Technology and the New Globalization

Richard Baldwin

The Belknap Press of
Harvard University Press
Cambridge, Massachusetts
London, England
2016

Second printing

Library of Congress Cataloging-in-Publication Data

Names: Baldwin, Richard E., author.
Title: The great convergence : information technology and the
    new globalization / Richard Baldwin.
Description: Cambridge, Massachusetts : The Belknap Press of Harvard
    University Press, 2016. | Includes bibliographical references and index.
Identifiers: LCCN 2016017378 | ISBN 9780674660489 (alk. paper)
Subjects: LCSH: Globalization—Economic aspects. | Income distribution. |
    Economic geography. | Technological innovations—Economic aspects.
Classification: LCC HF1365 .B35 2016 | DDC 337—dc23
    LC record available at https://lccn.loc.gov/2016017378

Design by Dean Bornstein

DISCARD

Contents

THE GREAT CONVERGENCE

Introduction

This book aims to change the way you think about globalization. The central assertion is that revolutionary changes in communication technology fundamentally changed globalization around 1990. The logic of how the revolution in information and communication technology (ICT) transformed globalization and its impact on the world is simple, but understanding it requires some background. Let's start with some facts.

Globalization took a leap forward in the early 1800s, when steam power and global peace lowered the costs of moving goods. Globalization made a second leap in the late twentieth century when ICT radically lowered the cost of moving ideas. As Figure 1 shows, these two leaps—call them the Old and New Globalizations—had dramatically different effects on the world's economic geography.

From the early nineteenth century, falling trade costs fueled a cycle of trade, industrialization, and growth that produced one of history's most dramatic reversals of fortune. The ancient civilizations in Asia and the Middle East—which had dominated the world economy for four millennia—were displaced in less than two centuries by today's rich nations. This outcome, which historians call the "Great Divergence," explains how so much economic, political, cultural, and military power came to be concentrated in the hands of so few.

From 1990, the trend flipped; a century's worth of rich nations' rise has been reversed in just two decades. Their share is now back to where it was in 1914. This trend, which might be called the "Great Convergence," is surely the dominant economic fact of the last two or three decades. It is the origin of much of the anti-globalization sentiment in rich nations, and much of the new assertiveness of "emerging markets."

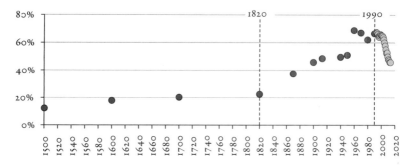

FIGURE 1: Globalization changed around 1990: the "shocking share shift" (G7 share of world income).

Modern globalization, which started around 1820, was associated with the rapid industrialization of today's rich nations—represented in this chart by the Group of Seven nations, or G7 for short (United States, Germany, Japan, France, Britain, Canada, and Italy). This triggered a self-perpetuating spiral of industrial agglomeration, innovation, and growth that produced an epic shift in the world economy. From 1820 to about 1990, the G7's share of global income soared from about a fifth to almost two-thirds.

The upward spiral was checked from the mid-1980s and reversed around 1990. For the last couple of decades, the G7 share has been torqueing downward at a mighty pace. Today it is back to the level that it first attained at the very beginning of the nineteen century.

This shocking share shift suggests that the nature of globalization changed radically around 1990.

DATA SOURCE: World Bank DataBank (GDP in U.S. dollars) and Maddison-project data pre-1960 (with author's calculations), http://www.ggdc.net/maddison /maddison-project/home.htm; the 2009 version is used since 2013 version does not update world GDP (2009 version hereafter noted as Maddison database).

Accompanying Figure 1's "shocking share shift" was a changeover in manufacturing. Today's rich nations—which had seen their share of world manufacturing slip slowly since 1970—witnessed an accelerated decline from 1990 (Figure 2).

Curiously, the G7's share loss showed up as share gains in very few nations. Only six developing nations (called the I6 in the chart, short for the Industrializing Six) saw their share of world manufacturing

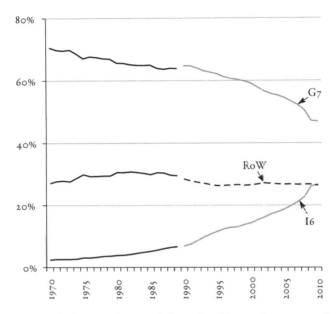

FIGURE 2: The decline in rich nations' share of world manufacturing translated to gains by just six developing nations.

The shift in global manufacturing shares was almost as stark as the "shocking share shift" in Figure 1. From around 1990, the slide in the G7's share accelerated and its share is now below 50 percent.

Just six developing nations—which I call the Industrializing Six, or I6 for short (China, Korea, India, Poland, Indonesia, and Thailand)—accounted for almost all of the G7's decline. The manufacturing share of the rest of the world (RoW in the chart) was largely unaffected by these changes. Note that China is a real standout. Its share of world manufacturing (not shown separately) rose from about 3 percent to almost a fifth.

DATA SOURCE: UNSTAT.org.

rise by more than three-tenths of one percentage point since 1990. The curiosity lies in the fact that the effect is so concentrated.

Why should the impact of globalization be so narrow geographically when cheap transportation and communication are so broadly available? Answering this question requires a broader view of globalization.

A Broader View of Globalization

When transportation involved wind power by sea and animal power by land, few items could be profitably shipped over anything but the shortest distance. This fact made production a hostage of consumption since people were tied to the land. Production, in other words, was forcibly bundled with consumption.

Globalization can be thought of as a progressive reversal of this forcible bundling. But the bundling was not enforced by shipping costs alone. Three costs of distance mattered: the cost of moving goods, the cost of moving ideas, and the cost of moving people. It is useful to think of the three costs as forming three constraints that limit the separation of production and consumption.

One of this book's core assertions is that understanding the evolving nature of globalization requires a sharp distinction among these three "separation" costs. Since the early nineteenth century, the costs of moving goods, ideas, and people all fell, but not all at once. Shipping costs fell radically a century and a half before communication costs did. And face-to-face interactions remain very costly even today.

Thinking about why the sequence matters is facilitated by a new view of globalization—what I call the "three cascading constraints" perspective. The new view is best explained by lacing it onto the back of a quick gallop through history.

The Pre-Globalized World and Globalization's First Acceleration

In the pre-globalization world, distance isolated people and production to such an extent that the world economy was little more than a patchwork of village-level economies. Things started to change when the cost of moving goods fell. Transport technologies improved in a process that fostered and was fostered by the Industrial Revolution.

With easier international shipping, more people bought faraway goods. Middle-income Britishers could, for example, afford to dine on bread baked with U.S. wheat while sipping tea brewed from Chinese leaves and sweetened with Jamaican sugar—all set on a tablecloth made of Indian cotton. Oxford economist Kevin O'Rourke and Harvard economist Jeff Williamson date the start of this process to 1820. In my 2006 paper, "Globalization: The Great Unbundling(s)," I refer to this separation of production and consumption as globalization's first unbundling.

While shipping got cheaper, the costs of moving ideas and people fell much less. This unbalanced reduction of separation costs triggered a chain of causes and effects that eventually produced enormous income differences between today's developed nations (called the "North" for short) and today's developing nations (the "South"). First, markets expanded globally but industry clustered locally. As history would have it, industry clustered in the North. This Northern industrialization fostered Northern innovation, and since ideas were so costly to move, Northern innovations stayed in the North. The result was that modern, innovation-fueled growth took off sooner and faster in the North. In just a few decades, the resulting growth differences compounded into the colossal, North-South income asymmetries that define the planet's economic landscape even today. In short, the Great Divergence was produced by the combination of low trade costs and high communication costs.

Globalization's Second Acceleration (the Second Unbundling)

Globalization accelerated again from around 1990, when the ICT revolution radically lowered the cost of moving ideas. This launched globalization's next phase—call it the "second unbundling" since it involves the international separation of factories. Specifically, radically better communications made it possible to coordinate complex activities at distance. Once this sort of offshoring was feasible, the North-South wage gap that had arisen during the first unbundling made it profitable.

The offshoring of production stages to low-wage nations changed globalization, but not just because it shifted jobs overseas. To ensure that the offshored stages meshed seamlessly with those left onshore, rich-nation firms sent their marketing, managerial, and technical know-how along with the production stages that had been moved offshore. As a consequence, the second unbundling—sometimes called the "global value chain revolution"—redrew the international boundaries of knowledge. The contours of industrial competitiveness are now increasingly defined by the outlines of international production networks rather than the boundaries of nations.

A sports analogy helps explain how this could so thoroughly transform globalization's impact. Imagine two soccer clubs sitting down to discuss an exchange of players. If a trade actually occurs, both teams will gain. Each gets a player of a type they really needed in exchange for a type of player they needed less.

Now consider a very different type of exchange. Suppose on the weekends, the coach of the better team starts to train the worse team. The outcome of this will surely make the league more competitive overall and it will surely help the worse team. But it is not at all sure that the best team will win from this exchange—even though their coach will profit handsomely from being able to sell his know-how to two teams instead of one.

The parallels with globalization are plain. The Old Globalization can be thought of as swapping players. The New Globalization is more like the cross-team training with the offshoring firms playing the coach's role.

Putting it differently, ICT-enabled offshoring created a new style of industrial competitiveness—one that combined G7 know-how with developing-nation labor. Because this high-tech, low-wage combination turned out to be a world beater, the easier movement of ideas sparked massive North-to-South flows of know-how. It is exactly these new knowledge flows that make the New Globalization so different from the Old Globalization.

Curiously Concentrated Effects and the Commodity Super-Cycle

Importantly, G7 firms own this know-how, so the new North-to-South knowledge movements should not be thought of as some enormous "Kumbaya moment." Rich nations are not sending their know-how to poor nations in a burst of caring and sharing. G7 firms work hard to ensure that their offshored knowledge stays within the confines of their production networks. According to the three-cascading-constraints view, this is why the manufacturing miracle happened in so few developing nations. To use the sports analogy, the New Globalization only boosted the manufacturing fortunes of the "teams" that the G7 coach decided to "train." But why was the training so curiously concentrated?

The answer, in my view, turns on the cost of moving people, not goods or ideas. Airplane fares have fallen, but the time-cost of travel has continued to rise with the salaries of managers and technicians. Since it is still expensive to move people—and international production networks still need people to move among facilities—offshoring firms tend to cluster production in a few locations. Again to economize on the cost of moving people, these locations tend to be near the G7 industrial powerhouses, especially Germany, Japan, and the United States. India is an exception, but mostly because India has engaged in international production networks primarily via the types of services for which frequent face-to-face interaction is less of an issue.

While the second unbundling's impact on industrialization was hyper-concentrated, the Great Convergence was a much broader phenomenon due to knock-on effects. About half of all humans live in the developing nations that are rapidly industrializing, so their rapid income growth created a booming demand for raw materials. Booming demand, in turn, created the "commodity super-cycle," which subsequently sparked growth takeoffs in many commodity-exporting nations that were untouched by the emergence of global value chains.

Globalization's Next Big Thing: Globalization's Third Unbundling

The three-cascading-constraints narrative—which is summarized graphically in Figure 3—plainly admits the possibility of a third unbundling, if face-to-face costs plunge in the way coordination costs

---

FIGURE 3: Summary of the "three cascading constraints" view of globalization.

When horse carts and sailing ships were high-tech, goods, ideas, and people mostly stayed put. For the vast majority of humanity, economic life was organized at the village level (top panel).

Steamships and railroads radically lowered the cost of long-distance trade, allowing production and consumption to separate in what could be called globalization's first unbundling (middle panel). But relaxing the shipping constraint did not make the world flat since the communication and face-to-face constraints were still in evidence. Indeed, even as production moved away from consumption, manufacturing gathered into factories and industrial districts—not to economize on trade costs, but rather to save on communication and face-to-face costs.

This microclustering spurred innovation in industrializing nations, and the innovations stayed local due to the high cost of moving ideas. The result was that know-how-per-worker rose much faster in the North than it did in the South. Ultimately, this is what created the great North-South income divide known as the Great Divergence.

Globalization's second unbundling (bottom panel) became economical when revolutionary advances in information and communication technology made it possible to organize complex production processes even when they were separated internationally. When this technical possibility became a reality, low wages in developing nations enticed G7 firms to offshore some labor-intensive stages of production. Since the production stages that were offshored still had to fit flawlessly with those left onshore, the offshoring firms sent their know-how along with the jobs. In this way, the flows of knowledge that used to happen only inside G7 factories became a key player in globalization (light bulbs in bottom panel).

These new information flows allowed a handful of developing nations to industrialize at a dizzying pace—resulting in a massive shift of industry from the North to the South. This Southern industrialization—together with the commodity super-cycle it launched—propelled emerging market income growth rates to unprecedented levels. The result was the "shocking share shift" shown in Figure 1.

In a nutshell, this is how the ICT revolution transformed globalization and its impact on the world economy; up to 1990, globalization was mostly about goods crossing borders; now it is also about know-how crossing borders.

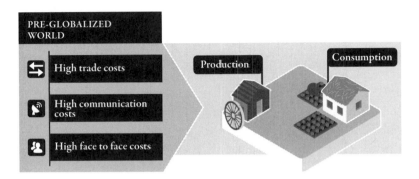

PRE-GLOBALIZED WORLD

High trade costs

High communication costs

High face to face costs

Production

Consumption

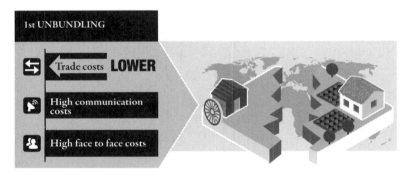

1st UNBUNDLING

Trade costs **LOWER**

High communication costs

High face to face costs

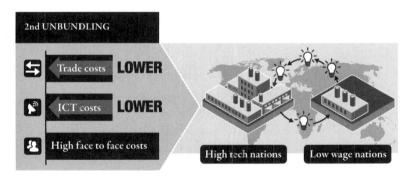

2nd UNBUNDLING

Trade costs **LOWER**

ICT costs **LOWER**

High face to face costs

High tech nations

Low wage nations

have since the 1990s. Two technological developments might provoke such a plunge. Really good substitutes for people crossing borders to share "brain services" is the first. Such technologies, known as "telepresence," are not science fiction. They exist today but they are expensive. The second would be the development of really good substitutes for people traveling to provide manual services. This is called "telerobotics" and it involves people in one place operating robots that perform tasks in another place. Telerobotics exists, but it is still expensive and the robots are not very flexible.

Taken together, these developments may dramatically change the nature of globalization in coming decades. Both allow workers from one nation to perform service tasks inside another nation without actually being there. Such "virtual immigration," or international telecommuting, would radically expand the range of jobs that are directly subject to international competition. Many menial and professional tasks in rich nations could be performed (remotely) by workers and professionals sitting in poor nations. It would also allow rich-nation professionals to apply their talents on a much wider basis. For example, Japanese engineers could repair Japanese-made capital equipment in South Africa by controlling sophisticated robots from Tokyo. Some people would win from this new competition / opportunity; others would have to find something else to do.

Thus globalization's third unbundling is likely to involve workers in one nation providing services in another nation—including services that today require physical presence. Or to use the unbundling theme, globalization's third unbundling is likely to allow labor services to be physically unbundled from laborers.

What Is New about the New Globalization?

The changed nature of globalization also means that nations are affected in many new ways. Six of them stand out.

The New Globalization affects national economies with a finer degree of resolution.

Twentieth-century globalization produced greater national specialization at the level of sectors. Lower trade costs thus tended to help or hurt whole sectors of the economy and the people working in them. Twenty-first century globalization, by contrast, is not just happening at the sector level; it is also happening at the level of production stages and occupations. As a result, globalization's impact is more unpredictable.

Under the Old Globalization, nations could identify their "sunrise" and "sunset" sectors. No longer. Now we have sunrise and sunset stages and occupations in almost all sectors. As it turns out, one cannot accurately predict which stages and jobs will be affected next in a world where the contours of industrial competitiveness are defined by offshoring firms.

The New Globalization's impact is also more individual in the sense that the winners and losers are no longer mostly grouped by sectors and skill groups. Globalization's impact can vary across workers who possess the same skill sets and work in the same sectors. "Kaleidoscopic globalization" is how Columbia University economist Jagdish Bhagwati describes it. No matter what job you have and no matter what sector you work in, you cannot really be sure that your job won't be the next to suffer or benefit from globalization.

The finer degree of resolution also has important policy implications. Many nations have policies aimed at helping declining sectors and disfavored skill groups, but globalization's finer resolution means that such policies are insufficiently nuanced to distinguish among today's winners and losers.

The New Globalization's impact is more sudden and more uncontrollable.

The passage of time on the Old Globalization "clock" was marked in years, since that is how long it took for tariff cuts and transportation improvements to take effect. The New Globalization, by contrast, is more sudden due to the fact that it is driven by the doubling of transmission, storage, and computing capacity every year or two. As we have seen repeatedly in the last couple of decades, exponential ICT improvements can turn implausible things into commonplace things in a matter of months.

The technical nature of ICT also means that national governments have less control over the New Globalization. The laws of physics make it easier to control the flow of goods than it is to control the flow of ideas. And politics reinforces the physics. The ideas are, after all, flowing out of G7 nations whose voters have embraced openness. Staunching the massive "knowledge arbitrage" that is now driving globalization would be next to impossible.

The New Globalization denationalized comparative advantage.

G7 firms are leveraging their firm-specific know-how by combining it with labor in low-wage nations. With firms mixing and matching different nations' sources of competitiveness, nations are no longer the only natural unit of analysis. Increasingly, the boundaries of competitiveness are controlled by firms who run international production networks.

To put it differently, the first unbundling was all about allowing nations to better exploit their comparative advantages. The second unbundling is much more about allowing firms to boost their competitiveness by recombining national sources of comparative advantage.

The New Globalization partly ruptured the compact between G7 workers and G7 firms.

When technology was national, international wage gaps adjusted to international technology differences. For example, German wages rose when German technology advanced. The second unbundling partly disables this wage-technology equilibration process. The New Globalization means that German workers are no longer the only beneficiaries of German technological advances. German firms can now exploit improved German technology by combining it with, say, Polish labor. Similar things could be said about firms and workers in all the G7 nations.

The New Globalization changed the role of distance.

Standard thinking characterizes globalization as being mostly about goods crossing borders. Doubling the distance between markets is thus naturally thought to roughly double the trade costs. Applying this logic today is a misthinking of twenty-first-century globalization for a very simple reason.

Cartographical distances affect the cost of moving goods, ideas, and people in very different ways. With the Internet, the cost of moving ideas is almost zero and varies little with distance. For people, however, there is a big difference between destinations that can be reached with a day trip and those further out.

This may help explain why so few developing nations have been able to industrialize rapidly, despite having adopted all the right pro-business policies. To put it bluntly, they may simply be too far from Detroit, Stuttgart, and Nagoya compared to other developing nations.

The New Globalization should change how governments think about their policies.

Vast swaths of economic policy are based on the notion that competitiveness is a national feature. In rich nations, policies ranging from education and training (preparing workers for the jobs of tomorrow) to research and development tax breaks (developing the products and processes of the future) are aimed at bolstering national sources of competitiveness. In developing nations, policies ranging from tariff levels (protecting domestic production) to development strategies (moving up the value chain) are founded on the idea that the sources of national competitiveness are national.

All these policy presumptions need to be rethought in the light of the New Globalization. For example, denationalized competitive advantage changed the options facing developing nations. Instead of building the whole supply chain domestically to become competitive internationally (the nineteenth- and twentieth-century way), developing nations now join international production arrangements to become competitive and then industrialize by getting more good jobs inside international value chains.

The flip side of this transfigured the competitiveness options facing rich nations. Globally competitive firms knit together national competitive advantages to make things in the most cost-effective locations. Firms and nations that eschew this new school of mix-and-match competitive advantage struggle to compete with those that have embraced it.

In short, the changed nature of globalization killed old-style development policies just as it killed naively nationalistic industrial policies in developed nations.

Roadmap for the Reader

The rest of this book is presented in five parts. The first takes a short look at the long history of globalization using the concept of bundling and unbundling as the organizing principle. This history is covered in Chapters 1 through 3.

Part II, Extending the Globalization Narrative, comprises two chapters. Chapter 4 presents the three-cascading-constraints view in greater detail. Chapter 5 expands on what is really new about the New Globalization.

Part III, Understanding Globalization's Changes, has two chapters. Chapter 6 lays out the boot-camp economics of globalization, and Chapter 7 then uses this information to make sense of why globalization's impact changed so radically between the first and second unbundling.

Part IV turns to the implications of the New Globalization for policymaking. Specifically, Chapter 8 looks at what the changes mean for G7 globalization policies and Chapter 9 does the same for developing nations.

Part V, entitled Looking Ahead, does exactly that by presenting a small number of conjectures about what the future holds for globalization and vice versa.

The Long History of Globalization in Short

Part I looks at 200,000 years of globalization. Why go so far back? The reason is aptly expressed in this 1957 quote:

> Since we are all too much affected by the times in which we live and are too prone to generalize from transitory circumstances, we are not likely to gain a clear understanding of [globalization] if we simply start with existing conditions and attempt to disentangle the major factors currently at work.

This first sentence in the book *Economic Development* (written by my father Robert Baldwin and Gerald Meier) originally had "economic development" in place of "globalization," but the thought rings true all the same.[1]

Today's discussions on globalization are indeed "all too much affected by the times in which we live." Globalization's impact on the world economy was fairly steady for the past 170 years—a fact that led many observers to view it as immutable. U.S. president Bill Clinton, for example, called globalization "the economic equivalent of a force of nature, like wind or water." This is wrong.

Globalization has changed radically in recent decades, as argued in the Introduction. Part I goes way back to show that the magnitude of globalization's recent change is not out of line with historical experience.

Organizing Principle

With a couple of hundred millennia to get through in a couple of dozen pages, the narrative shall, to say the least, be skipping some less important details. In such cases, it is best to be clear—right from the start—about what "important" means. Here, the classic definition of trade is the organizing principle.

Trade happens when production and consumption are separated geographically. The important thing is to watch how the production / consumption relationship changes. Using this organizing principle—and the three-cascading-constraints view of globalization mentioned in the Introduction—four phases of globalization emerge.

For readers who are not worried about being influenced by transitory circumstances and thus wish to skip the history in Chapters 1, 2, and 3, here is a quick summary of the phases.

Globalization Divided into Four Phases

For most of human history, globalization meant something quite different than it does today.

Phase One: Humanizing the globe (200,000 BCE to about 10,000 BCE)

For something like 190 of the past 200 millennia, "production" mainly meant food that was tied to particular locales and seasons. Production and consumption were spatially bundled since prehistoric transportation made it easier to move people to food rather than food to people. Little trade occurred. In Phase One, globalization meant a burgeoning human population traveling to exploit ever-more-distant production sites.

Phase Two: Localizing the global economy (10,000 BCE to 1820 CE)

In Phase Two, production and consumption were bundled as before, but with one absolutely critical difference. Thanks to the Agricultural Revolution, food production was brought to people rather than vice versa. The world economy was, in other words, "localized" in the sense that production and consumption occurred in fixed locations. Trade was still difficult and thus rare.

This phase also saw the rise of cities and the ancient civilizations in today's Iraq, Iran, Turkey, Egypt, China, India / Pakistan, and

Greece / Italy. While trade emerged among these production / consumption clusters, globalization in the modern sense had not yet begun. Prices inside nations were determined primarily by local supply and demand conditions, not international ones.

Phase Three: Globalizing local economies (1820 to about 1990)

The steam revolution gave humans the ability to concentrate and control previously unimaginable amounts of energy. In an intricate, century-long waltz, the steam revolution and the Industrial Revolution completely transformed mankind's relationship with the environment in general—and distance in particular.

Radically better transportation made it economical to consume goods that were made in faraway places. As a result, production patterns shifted and international trade volumes skyrocketed as nations started to "do what they do best and trade for the rest."

Production microclustered in advanced-nation factories even as it dispersed internationally. Productivity surged in the North and this sparked a cycle of industrialization, agglomeration, and innovation that yielded a huge North-South knowledge gap. This knowledge imbalance, in turn, led to an unprecedented divergence of incomes known as the Great Divergence.

Phase Four: Globalizing factories (1990 to present)

The revolution in information and communication technology (ICT) was to the second unbundling what the steam revolution was to the first. By relaxing the constraints that had underpinned the vast imbalances in the global distribution of knowledge, the ICT revolution unleashed a historic transformation that might be called the Great Convergence. The North deindustrialized while some nations in the South industrialized. The world experienced a shockingly large shift in world GDP shares that has made a big step toward reversing the Great Divergence.

The rest of Part I considers the four globalization phases in more detail. Chapter 1 covers the first two phases, leaving Chapter 2 and Chapter 3 to cover the third and fourth phases, respectively.

CHAPTER I

Humanizing the Globe and the First Bundling

Modern humans appeared about 200 millennia ago in Africa. As the population rose and fell, the search for additional food expanded and contracted humanity's geographic range. For seventy-five millennia or so, this consumption-moving-to-production happened only in Africa.

This chapter first relates the story of how humans hunted and gathered their way across the globe in Phase One. It then turns to explaining how the nature of globalization changed radically when a large share of humans got "stuck" in certain locales after the invention of agriculture.

Phase One: Humanizing the Globe

The detailed timing of modern humans moving beyond Africa is not fully understood, but it was certainly not linear. Given the close ties between climate, food, and population—and the vast climate change going on during this period (Figure 4)—humanity's dispersion quite naturally waxed and waned.

Archaeological evidence shows that one group exited Africa during the last really warm period—something like 125,000 years ago. They left via the Egyptian route and entered the Fertile Crescent. Contemporary DNA evidence, however, tells us that they did not survive.

A team of scientists led by Vincent Macaulay used evidence from mitochondrial DNA to prove that all non-African humans

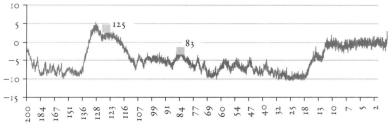

Thousand years, before present

FIGURE 4: Climate change since the first *Homo sapiens* (temperature difference to today, degrees centigrade).

Humans evolved 200 millennia ago when climatic conditions were similar to those of modern times. The planet cooled for 70,000 years before temperatures jagged up about 128,000 years ago. The subsequent hundred millennia saw a bumpy, downward trend that inverted from 20,000 BCE—first warming and then stabilizing around 10,000 BCE.

Globalization's Phase One (humanization of the globe) was triggered when modern humans left Africa around 83,000 BCE following a millennia-long spike in the planet's average temperature. Phase Two was triggered when the climate warmed and stabilized 12,000 years ago. With the climate warm and relatively stable, humans were able to master food production. Local food production could be expanded to match local population expansions. This change, known as the Agricultural Revolution, enabled the rise of civilization.

Modern "global warming" is the upward tick at the far right.

SOURCE: J. Jouzel et al., "Orbital and Millennial Antarctic Climate Variability over the Past 800,000 Years," *Science* 317, no. 5839 (2007): 793–797; based on Arctic Dome C ice cores.

are related to a small group that left Africa across the Red Sea route some fifty-five to eighty-five millennia ago during another warm spike. Humans then spread rapidly (by prehistoric time scales).[1]

The DNA and archaeological data suggest that about forty millennia ago, humans were continuously present in Africa, Asia, and Australia (Figure 5). Northern Europe was settled somewhat later, say, 35,000 years ago. Around fifteen millennia ago, people entered the Americas; by 12,000 years ago they had reached Patagonia. This

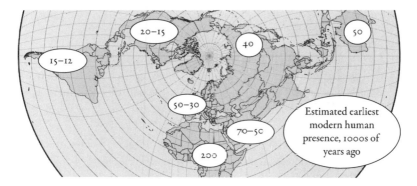

FIGURE 5: Globalization of the human race.

The human race dispersed across the Middle East, Asia, and Australia over a span of tens of thousands of years. Europe, which was much less hospitable to human life, was populated tens of thousands of years later sometime after 30,000 years ago. Much later, modern humans reached the Americas by crossing over an ice bridge that connected Asia to North America. By about 10,000 BCE, the globe was fully humanized.

SOURCE: Dates of earliest continuous settlement based on contemporary DNA (mitomap.org, accessed March 2014).

phase of globalization—within Africa and then out of Africa—lasted about 185 millennia.

The dates are very rough, but they serve to illustrate a fact that dominated history until quite recent centuries. East, South, and West Asia are particularly amenable to human life, and they are relatively well connected by land and sea.

There is incontestable archaeological evidence of long-distance trade during this period. One example is obsidian (black volcanic glass) from southeast Turkey that was exchanged among hunting and foraging groups around the Fertile Crescent in prehistoric times. Pack animals had not been domesticated, so long-distance trade in obsidian literally meant people carrying rocks. Obviously, this severely limited trade volumes.

BOX 1: SUMMARY OF PHASE ONE

For most of the 200 millennia that modern humans have been on the planet, production meant getting enough food to keep body and soul together. Food production was left to happenstance, so survival meant finding a food-abundant locale and then finding another once the food was exhausted.

To put it differently, production and consumption were spatially bundled—thus there was little trade—but since moving people to food made more sense than moving food to people, the bundles of production and consumption were continuously shifting in a way that hindered the development of civilization.

Essential Outcome

Globalization in this epoch meant "humanizing" the globe. The rising world population drove humans to inhabit every inhabitable corner of the planet by about 15,000 years ago. The Agricultural Revolution ended Phase One and opened the door to Phase Two.

Phase Two: Agriculture and the First Bundling

For scientific reasons that are still unclear, the climate warmed twenty millennia ago and stabilized about 12,000 years ago (Figure 4). Prehistoric population density was limited by food, and food was limited by climate, so this "good" climate change triggered a transformation of human society. This, in turn, transformed globalization.

Population density rose in regions with long growing seasons and reliable water sources. With lots of people and lots of food clustered in proximity, humans gradually learned how to reverse the mobility balance. Food production was moved to people rather than people to food. This was the Agriculture Revolution (also called the Neolithic Revolution). Jared Diamond's *Guns, Germs, and Steel* offers fascinating conjectures on how it might have happened.[2]

With climate and population density so closely linked, it is no surprise that all the early Eurasian production / consumption clusters lay in a narrow range of latitudes—roughly 20 degrees to 35 degrees north (Figure 6). River valleys were favored since the runoff from annual flooding solved the problem of soil exhaustion—a problem that locked most of humanity into nomadic patterns that prevented agglomeration and large-scale civilizations. (Land farmed for more than a few years loses its ability to nurture crops, so the farmers had to move to new land.)

Phase Two is made up of the dozen or more millennia that saw the rise of cities, civilizations, industry, and planet-wide travel.

Phase Two in Three Stages

A few thousand years of history is a difficult thing to organize. History, after all, is just one damned thing after another. Here ancient Rome's *omne trium perfectum* (rule of three) comes to the rescue. According to the rule, there are three good things about dividing a complicated matter into three: it makes the subject easier to explain, easier to understand, and easier to remember. Phase Two is therefore sliced into three stages: the Rise of Asia, Eurasian Integration, and the Rise of Europe. The dividing line between the first two stages is the rise of the Silk Road. The Black Death separates the last two stages.

This organization of Phase Two was inspired by historian Ian Morris's *Why the West Rules—For Now*.[3] However, the Middle East (and Egypt) are classed as part of Asia rather than as part of the West, as in Morris's worldview. This means that Asia rises first, with Europe catching up only at the end of Phase Two.

Stage 1: The Rise of Asia, 10,000 to 200 BCE

In terms of the organizing framework, the Agriculture Revolution meant that production and consumption were still bundled, but with one decisive difference. The production / consumption bundles were

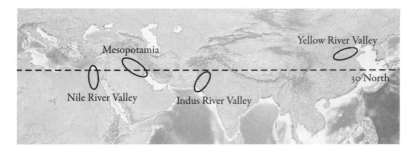

FIGURE 6: Earliest consumption / production clusters.

The earliest civilizations arose at latitudes favorable to agriculture and in river valleys since seasonal flooding helped keep the soil fertile. Mesoamerican civilization
arose in similar latitudes and was also clustered around river valleys to start with but
its beginnings came a couple millennia after the rise of the Middle Eastern clusters.
SOURCE: Background map from Wikicommons.

now in fixed locations. This economic "localization" had three momentous implications.

Agriculture, Food Surpluses, and the Rise of Civilizations

If nine workers, for example, can produce enough food to feed ten
people, the tenth person can focus on "civilization services" (building
monuments, creating religions, writing, collecting taxes, etc.) as well
as military services (defending the surplus or stealing that of others).
For practical reasons, such services tended to be grouped in cities.
Indeed, the connection between cities and civilization is ancient and
inevitable (the word "civilization" stems from the Latin word for city,
civitas).

The cities slowly grew in size and sophistication over a period of
centuries thanks to the snowball effect of innovation, agglomeration,
and population growth. That is, the physical concentration of many
people boosted the reward to innovation, as more people could benefit from the same invention. At the same time, denser clusters of
people lowered the cost of innovation, as invention often comes more

easily when many people share ideas about a problem. Because much of this innovation was related to food production (coming up with irrigation, for example, and the domestication of grains, fruits, and animals), innovation led to rising population density. In a process that lasted centuries, cities slowly spawned civilizations.

The Fertile Crescent and Mesopotamia are where the rise of cities and civilizations happened first, followed by the Nile River valley, the Indus River valley, the Yellow River valley, and Mesoamerica.

Agriculture and Rapid Population Growth

With food more abundant and reliable, the number of humans jumped between 10,000 and 8000 BCE (Figure 7). It leaped again with the beginning of the Bronze Age from about 3500 BCE.

Bronze is an excellent metal, but one of its ingredients, tin, is scarce in areas near the civilized river valleys. The constraining aspects of this scarcity ended with the spread of ironmaking. As the most plentiful metal on earth, iron is much more of a "people's metal." Due to its high cost, bronze had mostly been reserved for weapons and trinkets for the elite. Iron's abundance meant that it was cheap enough to be used in agriculture and everyday tools. This raised farm productivity while simultaneously making agriculture possible on less favorable land. Both trends boosted population growth.

Soon after the beginning of the Iron Age the world had a clear demonstration that there is nothing automatic or linear about human progress. In his book *1177 BC: The Year Civilization Collapsed,* historian Eric Cline describes how cities in the Eastern Mediterranean were destroyed violently within a few decades—throwing the whole region into a centuries-long dark age. In Greece, for example, writing disappeared for hundreds of years. When writing did return to Greece in the eighth century BCE, it was based on a new alphabet derived from letters imported from the Middle East. The connection with Bronze Age Greek writing was so completely broken that even today some

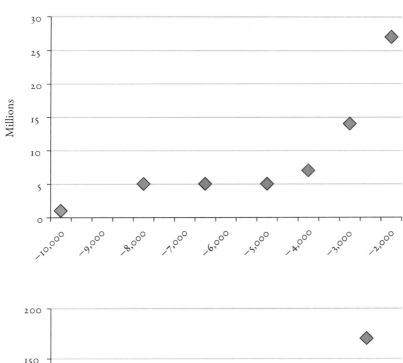

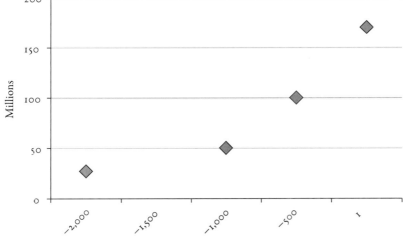

Minoan and Mycenaean writing cannot be deciphered. For unrelated reasons, the early Indus valley civilization collapsed in the second millennium BCE and the subcontinent entered a period of ten centuries without writing.

These civilization collapses did nothing to slow world population growth (Figure 7). As it turned out, iron made it possible to feed a growing population with or without highly organized civilizations.

By 500 BCE, civilization had spread westward beyond its Asian heartland to Greece, Italy, and North Africa (Figure 8). The Indian subcontinent had reemerged as an independent civilization and its center of economic activity had shifted toward the Ganges River plain. Chinese civilization had spread southward to include the Yangtze River basin, westward to the Hengduan Shan Mountains, and northward to the Korean Peninsula.

While the Asian political geography experienced innumerable twists and turns, its economic geography was remarkably stable. The four Asian centers of civilization continued without interruption as economic focal points for the next thousand years. Trade was the third momentous implication of this first "bundling" of consumption and production in fixed locales.

FIGURE 7: Ancient population estimates, 10,000 BCE to year 1.

The human population went through three growth phases in ancient times. The first came as humans mastered agriculture (the jump from 10,000 to 8500 BCE), the second as they mastered bronze (the jump from 5000 to 2000 BCE), and the third as they mastered iron (from about 1000 BCE).

Bronze helped humans shape their environment, but it required tin, which is scarce. Iron is far more common but turning it into tools and weapons required more advanced metallurgy skills. These skills probably developed first in today's Turkey.

Note the big change in the vertical scale (population in millions) between the two panels.

DATA SOURCE: Public data from U.S. Census estimates (www.census.gov).

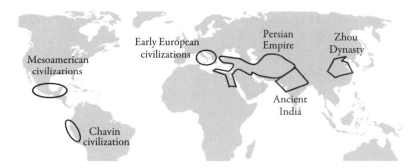

FIGURE 8: Production / consumption clusters, circa 500 BCE.

The global economy that emerged during Phase Two was dominated by clusters of bundled production and consumption in the Middle East, Egypt, India / Pakistan, and China. While the political organization changed frequently, the economic organization was stable since at least 2000 BCE—although by 500 BCE, expansions brought three of the hubs (Egypt, the Middle East, and India / Pakistan) into direct contact.

Other hubs arose in Latin America, but they remained insular until the fifteenth century.

DATA SOURCES: Ian Morris, *Why the West Rules—for Now* (London: Farrar, Straus and Giroux, 2010); Ronald Findlay and Kevin O'Rourke, *Power and Plenty* (Princeton, NJ: Princeton University Press, 2007).

Trade among Fixed Production / Consumption Clusters

Trade as it is conceived of today—namely, made-here-sold-there goods moving among fixed regions—rose during this stage. The game-changing innovations were the domestication of the camel (around 1000 BCE), refinements of sailing technology, and advances in coastal navigation. Archaeological finds and literary sources shine some light on which goods were traded. For example, a fourteenth-century BCE shipwreck discovered off the western coast of Turkey contained copper and tin ingots (the ingredients of bronze), glass beads, ebony wood, ivory, tortoise shells, ostrich eggshells, ceramic jars filled with resin, and some weapons and tools as well as Egyptian jewelry. Trade,

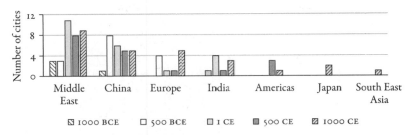

FIGURE 9: Asian dominance: evidence from cities with over 100,000 inhabitants. City populations are easier to estimate than overall populations or economic output. The preponderant share of large Asian and Middle Eastern cities in the world's total provides direct evidence of these regions' ascendency in the global economy throughout Phase Three. Note that in this chart, Egypt is included in the Middle East.

SOURCE: Author's coding of city lists in George Modelski, *World Cities: −3000 to 2000* (Washington, DC: FAROS, 2003).

in other words, was limited to things that were unavailable locally such as essential raw materials and luxury items.

Geographically, Mesopotamia was the hub. It was close to the Indus River valley by sea and close to the Nile River valley by land. China, which was separated from the others by vast mountains, deserts, seas, and jungles, did not participate in this West Asian trade in the Iron Age. The early American clusters were isolated and would remain so for another two and a half millennia.

Maps like Figure 8 hide Asia's dominance during the whole of Phase Three. There are really no reliable regional population or income figures for the Iron Age, but there are archaeological-based sources of data on the number and size of cities (Figure 9).

Large cities tend to leave written records across cultures thus making it more likely that some information survives to today. They also leave physical evidence that can be excavated. The political scientist George Modelski, for example, uses estimates of city areas

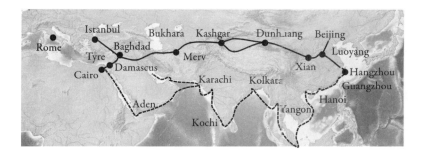

FIGURE 10: Trade connects all four clusters: Silk Road by land and sea, circa year 1.

The Silk Road was the first sustained connection between the economic clusters at the East and West ends of Asia. Trade flowed by land and by sea. It opened around 200 BCE, reached its zenith around 1300 CE, and shut down with the fall of Constantinople in 1453 CE.

SOURCE: Background map from Wikicommons, with routes added by author based on various sources. Note: The map uses modern city names where possible.

in hectares and applies various population-density coefficients to estimate the number of inhabitants. The results, shown in Figure 9, illustrate the basic Asian-dominance point. China and the Middle East were the most prominent regions in the ancient cityscape. Even in 500 BCE, there were twice as many large cities in India and China as there were in Europe.

Stage 2: Eurasian Integration, 200 BCE to 1350 CE

While the three westernmost cores of civilization had regular contact since the earliest times, China was much less integrated until the Silk Road opened around 200 BCE. The overland route passed just north of the Tibetan Plateau connecting the Han Dynasty to the Roman Empire. This road was complemented by a sea route from China and Southeast Asia to India, the Middle East, and Southern Europe (Figure 10).

The integration of the Eurasian civilizations constitutes the next stage in globalization's long march. For the next seventeen centuries, the Silk Road connected the same basic production / consumption clusters, although the western edge of highly organized civilization retreated back to Turkey and Egypt when the Western Roman Empire collapsed around 450 CE.

While the world's economic geography was remarkably stable in this era, the political organization of the production / consumption clusters shifted in a kaleidoscopic panoply of kingdoms, dynasties, and empires. Two particularly notable political reorganizations came with the Golden Age of Islam and the rise of the Mongolian Empire.

The Mongolian Empire, which still holds the record for the largest land empire, brought the entire overland Silk Road under a single authority for about 160 years, starting from 1200 CE or so. The period is known as Pax Mongolica. The spread of Islam from the seventh to thirteenth centuries advanced trade by integrating much of the southern, sea-based part of the Silk Road. This reduced trade costs over territory that stretched from Southeast Asia to southern Spain.

There is abundant evidence that Silk Road trade had important effects on certain cities and on the elite in most nations. However, because of rudimentary transportation technology, it was physically impossible for trade to have a major impact on the average person's consumption.

Some rough calculations serve to give an idea of Silk Road trade realities. Consider the length of the daily camel train that would have been required to supply a given number of kilograms of Chinese goods to each of the 45 million people living in the Middle East and Europe in 1000 CE. A camel can carry something like 400 kilograms and is about three meters long, so a camel train of almost a kilometer long would have to arrive every day to deliver a kilo of goods per Westerner per year. A kilo per person per week would require a daily camel train that is 52 kilometers long. Since camels can travel something like 25 kilometers a day, the Silk Road would have had to have been more like a dual carriageway than the dusty track it actually was.

While many goods certainly arrived by sea, this sort of illustrative calculation suggests that Silk Road trade could not have materially altered life for the masses. Even when the Silk Road was integrated under the Mongolian Empire in the North and Islam in the South, the quantities of trade that would be necessary to change the average person's consumption were still unthinkable. For example, when the Roman Emperor Elagabalus, who ruled around 220 CE, first sported clothes made entirely of silk, silk was a hundred times dearer in Rome than China. It cost as much per ounce as gold, according to William Bernstein's engaging account of Silk Road trade in his book *A Splendid Exchange.*[4]

One clear example of ancient mass shipping was Rome's "wheat fleet," which brought grain for the Roman masses from Sardinia, Sicily, and Egypt. A vivid account can be found in the Christian Bible. In the Book of Acts, Chapter 27, we learn of the Apostle Paul's voyage from Egypt to Rome in the year 67 on a wheat-fleet ship. The danger and difficulty of trade is clear from the account of how his vessel was caught for many days in a terrible storm that eventually wrecked the ship, resulting in the loss of all cargo. Paul survived.

While important to historians, trade in this era did little to change the basic reality facing most people. The average person—never far from starvation—was bound to consume locally made products when trade was this difficult. While statistics for East–West trade are missing, the goods shipped seem to have consisted mostly of elite goods and locally scarce raw materials. Insights can be gleaned from a ninth-century CE shipwreck of an Arab vessel off the coast of Indonesia. Archaeologists recovered Chinese ceramics, cast-iron vessels, copper-alloy bowls, grindstones, lime, gilt silverware, silver-covered boxes, a large silver flask, Chinese bronze mirrors, and spices.

Even as late as the 1700s, imports remained difficult, slow, and uncommon. The Dutch East India Company accounted for about half of Europe-to-Asia trade from 1500 to 1800, as Angus Maddison writes in his masterful book *Contours of the World Economy, 1–2030 AD.*

The company had a standing fleet of about a hundred vessels, each of which could do four round-trips in its ten-year lifetime. Each voyage brought less than a thousand tons of cargo to Europe. During the entire seventeenth century, only 3,000 European ships sailed to Asia. The number was little more than twice that for the whole of the eighteenth century.[5]

Stage 3: The Rise of Europe, 1350 to 1820

The boost in trade that Pax Mongolica enabled had the unintended effect of globalizing the bubonic plague. While the disease had caused havoc several times in history, the waves of epidemics from 1350 onward were truly transformative. Moving East to West along the Silk Road, the Black Death arrived in Europe in 1347.

The disease wiped out between a quarter and half of all Europeans in just three years. Norman Cantor, in his book *In the Wake of the Plague*, notes that the effect on the Islamic World was at least as severe. The impact on China and India, by contrast, seems to have been less marked.[6]

Black Death: Rebooting the Ancient World

The Black Death can be seen as a watershed event—setting in train several truly historic shifts. The massive population losses transformed European societies in ways that triggered progress, but had the opposite effect on the Islamic world.

Economic historians have various theories about this differential impact. In their book *Power and Plenty*, Ron Findlay and Kevin O'Rourke provide an engaging discussion of how such a shock could have helped the West but hindered the Middle East. One explanation rests on the fact that Western Europe had been stagnating in an equilibrium dominated by rural nobles, while Islamic civilization was flourishing via its urban centers. Since the disease hit cities harder, the shock may have shifted Europe from a bad equilibrium to a good one, while having the opposite impact on the Islamic world.[7]

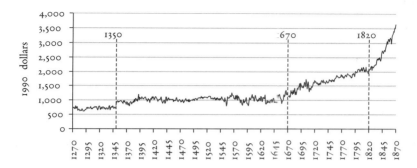

FIGURE II: The Black Death's impact on British incomes.

After stagnating near subsistence levels for thousands of years, per capita incomes in England got a one-off boost from the Black Death. While growth was unsteady and setbacks frequent, English living standards progressed modestly—gaining by 26 percent over the three centuries from 1370 to 1670. During the century and a half after 1670, annual growth doubled to 0.2 percent yearly, implying that incomes were 13 percent higher in 1820 than they were in 1670. This growth, while hardly remarkable today, was the beginning of the persistent growth that would transform the human condition in the nineteenth century.

DATA SOURCE: GDP per capita from Stephen Broadberry, "Accounting for the Great Divergence," Economic History Working Papers 184-2013, London School of Economics, November 2013.

In his 2013 paper, "Accounting for the Great Divergence," economic historian Stephen Broadberry ascribes the divergent impacts to differences in the type of agriculture, the age of first marriage of females, the flexibility of labor supply, and the nature of state institutions.[8]

Regardless of the economic mechanism that explains it, the impact is clear to see in Figure 11's depiction of British incomes. There is a jump in gross domestic product (GDP) per capita and a hint of faster growth right around 1350, although the obvious acceleration doesn't take place until the late seventeenth century.

A second watershed event came in the fifteenth century with the shutdown of the Silk Road due to the fragmentation of the Islamic world, the policy-driven closing of China by the Ming Dynasty, and

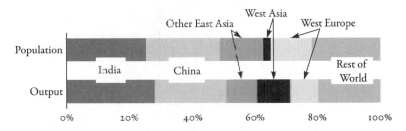

FIGURE 12: World output and population shares: dominance of Asia in 1500 CE.

Per capita incomes were not radically different across the globe in 1500 CE. The distribution of population and GDP (output) were thus quite similar, so Asia, especially India and China, dominated the world economy in 1500. West Europe's economic output and its population amounted to only 18 percent and 13 percent, respectively, of the planet's totals.

West Asia had a much larger share of output than population because its per capita incomes were quite high during this period known as the "Golden Age of Islam."

DATA SOURCE: Maddison database (2013 version).

the fall of Constantinople (which allowed the Ottomans to cut off trade with Europe).

Chinese civilization flourished in these centuries, reaching new heights in art, science, and manufacturing under the Yuan and Ming Dynasties. This was also when Chinese ships roamed the high seas. As the historian Edward Dreyer recounts in his book *Zheng He: China and the Oceans in the Early Ming Dynasty*, the Chinese Admiral Zheng sailed from China to Southeast Asia, India, Persia, and Africa in ships that dwarfed European seagoing vessels in size and sophistication.[9]

The Silk Road closure isolated Europe and the Middle East from these Chinese advances.

Economic Dominance by Middle East and Asia

When Silk Road trade stopped in the fifteenth century, Asia dominated the world economy. Angus Maddison has guesstimated GDP and population shares back to the year 1, and his estimates for the nearest date, 1500, are shown in Figure 12.

The key point is that Asia was the focal point for human civilization during this era—a fact that is often overlooked in many North Atlantic discussions of globalization. Economically and geographically, Europe was "a small promontory of Asia," as historian Felipe Fernández-Armesto puts it in his 1995 book *Millennium: A History of the Last Thousand Years*.[10]

Proto-Globalization, 1450 to 1776

The opening of the Silk Road proved to be a key stage in globalization's long history. Its shutting in 1450 was equally notable. It launched a period described by historian Anthony Hopkins as proto-globalization—a preparatory stage for the dramatic shift that was to come in Phase Three.

Proto-globalization rested on three pillars: the Renaissance and Enlightenment, the Age of Discovery, and the Columbian Exchange.

Renaissance and Enlightenment

In the fourteenth century, Europe started transforming itself from the western periphery of Asian civilization into the world's leading economic and military power. John Hobson, Ferdinand Braudel, and Ian Morris argue that much of the European revival was based on ideas, institutions, and technologies borrowed from the advanced civilizations in the Middle and Far East—much of which had been preserved, integrated, and extended by Islamic scholars during the Golden Age of Islam. In particular, Europe got a boost from Islamic commercial practices, mathematics, and cartography as well as from Chinese innovations, including iron and steel production methods, the printing press, new agricultural methods, navigational technologies, gunpowder, and much more.

The Renaissance (1300s to 1600s) moved into high gear with Michelangelo, Galileo, Luther, da Vinci, Machiavelli, Copernicus, and many more. The Enlightenment (1600s and 1700s) furthered the rise of Europe by adding the thinking of Descartes, Locke, Voltaire,

Hobbes, Hume, Kant, Newton, Smith, Rousseau, and others. Europe was also marked by keynote developments in banking, finance, and markets.

The economic thought foundations were laid during this period for trade and what would later be called globalization. A key text was Adam Smith's 1776 tome *The Wealth of Nations,* which built on thinking by French writers of the physiocratic school.

European Age of Discovery: Putting the Global in Globalization

The global economic and manufacturing center of gravity was still in Asia at the beginning of the 1400s. The demise of the Silk Road greatly raised the economic rewards in Europe to finding a way to the riches of the East around the Middle Eastern blockage. The search started in earnest when the Portuguese Crown financed a series of trips whose goal was to find a route to Asia around Africa. These trips put the "global" in globalization.

The Portuguese started by exploring the West African coast in 1419. They soon discovered that prevailing winds (the South Atlantic Gyre) made it easier to travel south by going far to the west. The wind movements and currents took them so far west that they sighted South America, although they didn't bother to follow up on this discovery at the time.

The first key breakthrough as far as globalization is concerned came when Portuguese ships rounded the Cape of Good Hope in 1488. Four years later, Columbus landed in Central America in his futile pursuit of a western passage to Asia. Ten years later, Portuguese ships reached India around Africa and returned to tell the tale. Just two years after that, Brazil was claimed for the Portuguese Crown.

By the end of the 1500s, Portugal had trading posts that connected Lisbon to Nagasaki via the west and south African coasts, the Middle East, India, and Southeast Asia. Spain had colonies throughout Central America and the west coast of South America—most notably in Peru and Bolivia.

From the start of the sixteenth century, Europeans dominated Europe-to-Asia trade, playing "king of the hill" among themselves. The Dutch knocked off the Portuguese, and were in turned knocked off by the British.

In addition to altering Asian–European trade routes, this so-called Age of Discovery is associated with Europeans' colonization of North and South America—an event that would help reverse ten millennia of economic dominance by Eurasian civilizations.

The Columbian Exchange: Food Crops for Epidemics

The shift of the planet's economic center of gravity to the North Atlantic was based in part on the so-called Columbian Exchange. Imported food crops from the Americas—especially potatoes and maize—were imperative in allowing Europe to gain critical levels of population density. In exchange, Europeans brought new diseases that depopulated the New World and almost erased the ancient civilizations in Mesoamerica and the Andes. Both effects are illustrated in Figure 13.

The Industrial Revolution Begins

The gray area between proto-globalization and Phase Three is marked by the start of the Industrial Revolution in Britain. The term "revolution" refers to the outcome, not the pace. It was a century-long sequence of incremental technical, organizational, social, and institutional changes that completely transformed the human condition.

Economic historian Nick Crafts would argue that any precise year is misleading given its accretive nature, but 1776 provides as good a landmark as any, since this is when he finds a structural break in British industrial growth. Conveniently, it is also the publication date of Adam Smith's *The Wealth of Nations*.

The Industrial Revolution was directly linked with improved transportation. Inland water and road transportation networks densified in the last decades of the eighteenth century. Water

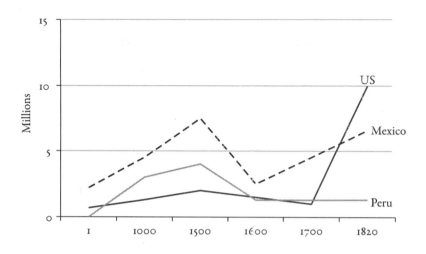

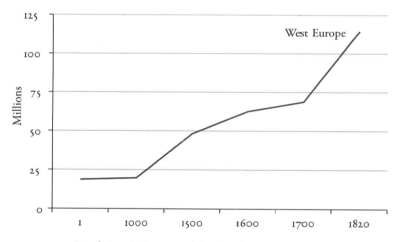

FIGURE 13: Populations in Europe and the Americas, year 1 to 1820.

The Columbian Exchange boosted European populations via the introduction of new food staples. It also decimated New World populations via the introduction of Old World diseases like smallpox, measles, and typhus. This set up a situation where the Old World had too many people and not enough land—an imbalance mirrored by the opposite imbalance in the New World. Note the scale for the Old World chart is about ten times that of the New World chart.

DATA SOURCE: Maddison database (2013 version).

transportation advanced with new types and layouts of sails, new shipbuilding techniques, and big advances in navigational technology. By the 1700s, Europeans had mapped the world and were navigating the seas with ease. Colonialism continued to be developed—especially by the British, French, and Dutch. The independence movements in North and South America did nothing to disrupt trade and economic development in the Atlantic.

The whole process was fostered by the rapid development of financial intermediation (centered on London). As a result, the British economy was reoriented from agriculture to manufacturing and the population shifted from rural to urban.

The big changes were at first limited mostly to Britain, as the French Revolution of 1789 and decades-long Napoleonic Wars delayed the Industrial Revolution's spread to the Continent. As David Landes puts it in his famous 1969 book *The Unbound Prometheus,* technological advances hit roadblocks on a continent suffering "capital destruction and losses of manpower; political instability and widespread social anxiety; the decimation of the wealthier entrepreneurial groups; all manner of interruptions to trade; violent inflations and alterations of currency."[11] In particular, trade was directly dampened during the Napoleonic Wars by competing trade blockades imposed by France and Britain.

Stagnating Asian Economy and Rising Atlantic Economy

Ending a millennium and a half of Middle Eastern monopoly on East–West trade had momentous effects on the global distribution of economic, political, and military power. As Figure 14 (top panel) shows, during the first millennium BCE, the ancient civilizations were ahead. Indeed, per capita incomes were above the starvation-avoidance minimum only in the ancient civilizations: Egypt, India, Iran, Iraq, China, Turkey, Greece, and Italy as well as some Roman colonies such as Portugal, Spain, and France. The North Atlantic economies and Japan were still close to subsistence levels of income.

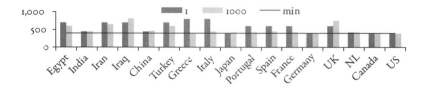

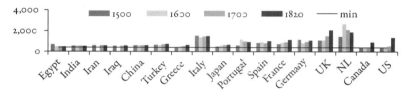

FIGURE 14: Per capita income, year 1 to 1820 (1990 dollars).

Incomes in most of the world were at near-starvation levels, the so-called Malthusian level that Angus Maddison estimates to be $400 a year at modern price levels. Before 1000 CE, only the ancient civilizations enjoyed income above this level, and even then not by much. During the proto-globalization phase, incomes in Western Europe and its offshoots in the New World climbed while those of the ancient civilizations stagnated.

DATA SOURCE: Maddison database (2009 version).

By the end of the millennium, Rome and its colonies had stumbled badly, while the Islamic civilizations surged ahead, along with the Byzantine Empire.

From 1500, things started looking quite different (Figure 14, bottom panel). Apart from Italy, which led the Renaissance, all the ancient civilizations stagnated while Western European incomes grew. Progress was especially marked for the big European imperialists—the United Kingdom, the Netherlands, Spain, and Portugal. The rising European incomes reflected massive economic and political transformations as feudalism's rural / agrarian focus evolved toward a more urban and market-based economy—a change known as the commercial revolution.

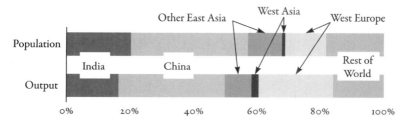

FIGURE 15: Asia's world economic dominance in 1820 (shares of world income).

By 1820, Atlantic incomes were well above those of Asia, but the preponderance of Asia's population meant that Asia was still the planet's economic center of gravity. China experienced a demographic boom during the Qing Dynasty due to the introduction of new food crops. As a result, its share of the planet's population rose from about 25 percent in 1500 to almost 40 percent when modern globalization took off in 1820.

DATA SOURCE: Maddison database (2013 version).

Population versus Per Capita Income

While a per capita income gap opened between the Atlantic economies and Asia during Phase Two, Asia's global economic dominance continued. As Figure 15 shows, Asia's massive population far outweighed the Atlantic economies' income advantage.

The World Set to Change

Phase Two established the world's distribution of population. By the year 1, about two-thirds of humanity lived in East and South Asia. The proportion today is roughly the same for the very simple reason that Asia is just very amenable to human life. Big changes, however, were afoot. The shift in the distribution of per-person output that started to percolate just at the end of Phase Two would eventually turn the world's economy on its head. The story of Phase Three is the subject of the next chapter.

BOX 2: SUMMARY OF PHASE TWO

Since the beginning, our species has been knocked about by climate changes that make today's global warming look like a spring rain (see Figure 4). Phase Two started when the earth's climate settled into a more "civilized" pattern about 12,000 years ago.

Production and consumption were bundled as before, but thanks to the Agricultural Revolution, production came to consumption instead of consumption going to production. Globalization in this phase meant "localizing" the world economy.

Essential Outcomes

If the modern world were a house, Phase Two would be its foundations. All the trappings of civilization took their modern forms during this Phase—everything from writing and worship to governments and gunboats. The foundations were built in three stages.

The rise of Asia (10,000 to 200 BCE) came with climate change.

After the climate warmed and stabilized, production was first localized with consumption in four river valleys that were in the crop-growing sweet zone (about 30 degrees north) and subject to annual flooding that solved the bane of ancient farming—soil exhaustion. The presence of lots of people and lots of food in the same place for thousands of years eventually led to the rise of the ancient civilizations in Egypt, Mesopotamia, India / Pakistan, and China. Some trade happened among the three western clusters, but it was limited to missing raw materials and elite goods.

Eurasian integration (200 BCE to 1350 CE) came with the rise of the Silk Road.

Regular trade arose among all four clusters even though volumes were severely limited by high transport costs.

The rise of Europe (1350 to 1820) began with the traumatic disruptions caused by the Black Death.

Western Europe, which had always been a primitive backwater (apart from the Greco-Roman civilization during a few glorious centuries), transformed itself into an economic entity that would soon bestride the world economically, militarily, and culturally. The keys to this reversal of fortunes were the Renaissance and Enlightenment, the Age of Discovery, and the Columbian Exchange. The Industrial Revolution, which was a small English bushfire at the end of Phase Two, became a global firestorm in Phase Three.

CHAPTER 2

Steam and Globalization's First Unbundling

One of the greatest dramas in human history was played out in Phase Three. It was an astounding reversal of fortune.

Since civilization first saw daybreak, the consumption / production clusters in Asia and the Middle East presided over world affairs in every sense of the word. Writing, cities, organized religion, government, laws, full-time armies, ethics, arithmetic, literature, poetry, and just about every other aspect of human society was invented in the production / consumption clusters to the east, south, and west of the Tibetan Plateau. The ancient civilizations also dominated the planet's economic activity. All the other areas in the world put together accounted for less than a third of global economic output. By the end of Phase Three, all this was turned upside down.

This world-changing drama can be told as a three-act play.

Act I: 1820 to 1913.

The setup in Act I introduces the viewing public to the "hero" (falling trade costs) and other main characters (trade, industrialization, urbanization, and growth). Act I lasts almost a century.

Act II: 1914 to 1945.

The confrontation—which comes in Act II as the classic rules of drama tell us it should—sees the hero faced with daunting setbacks that leave theatergoers wondering whether globalization is doomed. The Act, which lasts a mere thirty years, lashes the hero with two world wars and the Great Depression. Audiences gasp as protectionism raises its ugly head and war forces a rebundling of production and consumption.

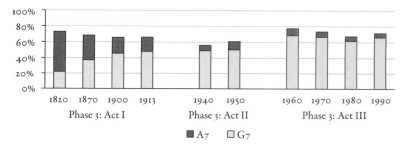

FIGURE 16: Ancient Seven and Group of Seven shares of global GDP, year 1820 to 1990.

Shifts in global GDP shares illustrate the massive reversal of fortune that took place in Phase Three. The "Three Act" structure is also obvious when comparing two groups of nations: the seven ancient civilizations (China, India / Pakistan, Iraq, Iran, Turkey, Italy / Greece, and Egypt) called the A7 for short, and the nations that eventually came to be called the Group of Seven (G7)—the United States, Japan, Germany, France, Italy, Britain, and Canada (Italy is moved from the A7 to the G7 circa 1500, so in this chart Italy is in the G7 not the A7).

GDP shares shifted away from the A7 and toward the G7 quite suddenly in Act I but stagnated in Act II, only to surge ahead even further in Act III. Note that the sum of A7 plus G7 shares remains at approximately 80 percent throughout all three acts.

DATA SOURCE: Maddison database (2009 version).

Act III: 1946 to 1990.

The "resolution" comes in Act III when the trade-cost hero regains her aplomb and triumphs over adversity. For forty years, trade costs are reduced by trade liberalization and transportation innovations. The unbundling of production and consumption advances as never before.

This three-act structure is not just an organizational convenience— it is obvious in data, as Figure 16 shows.

The technological breakthrough that started this reversal was the steam revolution. Steam power allowed humans to conquer intercontinental distances and reshape the world in ways that were unimaginable with horse, wind, and water power. Before continuing the historical narrative, it is important to delve into this shock that defined the transition between Phase Two and Phase Three.

Breakthrough: The Steam Revolution

Trade costs of all stripes fell dramatically during Phase Three by magnitudes that dwarf post–World War II reductions that are routinely described as revolutionary. Figure 17 (top panel) shows that trade costs varied greatly up to the early nineteenth century when they jumped on a century-long downward slide. This initial decline was reversed between World War I and World War II, but resumed thereafter. The consequences for trade volumes are apparent in the bottom panel.

The primary driver of lower trade costs in the eighteenth and early nineteenth centuries was the phenomenal drop in transport costs. But cost reductions came not through better shipping alone. Economic historians Alan Taylor, Antoni Estevadeordal, and Brian Frantz find that the spread of the gold standard also greatly facilitated international commerce.

The initial spark was steam power. The first steam engine in commercial use came online in 1712. This Newcomen engine was massive, consumed vast quantities of fuel, and was not particularly powerful. But it could perform a task, pumping water out of coal mines, that had previously required a team of 500 horses. The next century and a half brought forth design improvements that made steam engines economical for many industrial uses.

The concentrated power promoted industrialization, which raised incomes and stoked the demand for transportation. The booming demand for better transport options was richly rewarded with breakthrough innovations—first in sailing ships, inland waterways, and road transport. By the early nineteenth century, commercial steam engines had been put on boats and wheels.

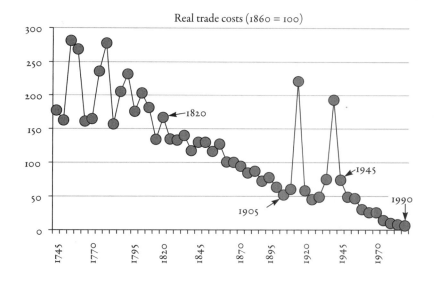

Real trade costs (1860 = 100)

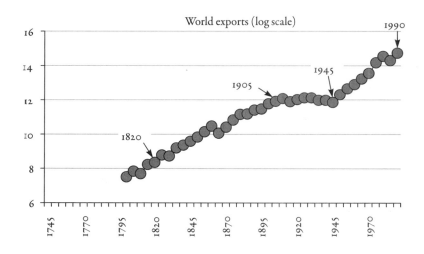

World exports (log scale)

Railroads radically reduced the cost of moving bulk goods across land and this development opened up the interiors of continents to the global economy. The big advances started in the 1840s. In a few decades, railroads had completely recast land transportation. Britain got out with a head start, but the United States and Germany rapidly surpassed it in terms of kilometers of rail per capita. Japan joined the race only in the late nineteenth century, although like Britain, Japan could rely far more on the sea for domestic transportation.

Steamships likewise revolutionized ocean travel, although the transition was not as abrupt (Table 1). The year 1819 saw the first steamship cross the Atlantic. It was a wooden ship and combined wind and steam power; fueling problems prevented sole reliance on steam power for decades. Just as the lack of recharging stations today hinders the spread of electric cars, the scarcity of coal sources constrained the use of steamships until coaling stations were established around the world in the late 1800s.

FIGURE 17: World trade costs and trade volume, 1745 to 1990

As with the world GDP shares shown in Figure 16, the three-act structure of Phase Three is plain to see in the evolution of trade costs (shown in the top panel) and trade volumes (in the bottom panel). Trade rose rapidly up to WWI, spurred on by the extraordinary reductions in barriers to trade that stemmed from the steam revolution and Pax Britannica.

Income growth is a powerful pro-trade stimulus, so the growth takeoffs that accompanied the Industrial Revolution in Europe, Japan, and European offshoots like the United States also fueled the trade bonanza. After a pause between the world wars, trade volumes continued their ascent.

DATA SOURCES: Trade volume (exports) from David S. Jacks, Christopher M. Meissner, and Dennis Novy, "Trade Booms, Trade Busts, and Trade Costs," *Journal of International Economics* 83, no. 2 (2011): 185–201, augmented by pre-1870 data provided in private communication with authors. Trade costs, pre-1870, from Knick Harley, "Ocean Freight Rates and Productivity, 1740–1913: The Primacy of Mechanical Invention Reaffirmed," *Journal of Economic History* 48, no. 4 (1988): 851–876. Remainder from Saif I. Shah Mohammed and Jeffrey G. Williamson, "Freight Rates and Productivity Gains in British Tramp Shipping 1869–1950," *Explorations in Economic History* 41, no. 2 (2004): 172–203.

TABLE 1

British steamship capacity in tonnages, 1825 to 1860.

	Iron Steamships	Wooden Steamships	Total
1825	0	4,013	4,013
1830	0	3,908	3,908
1835	3,275	22,192	25,467
1840	20,872	30,337	51,209
1845	33,699	8,268	41,967
1850	70,441	52,248	122,689
1855	478,685	34,414	513,099
1860	389,066	12,174	401,240

Steamships revolutionized ocean travel but the revolution took decades. Using British data to track the developments, the table shows that things started modestly in the early 1800s. There were big jumps in the first half of the 1830s and again in the second half of the 1840s. The biggest leap, however, came in the late 1850s when the number of steam-powered ships increased almost fivefold in just five years.

From the middle of the nineteenth century, steam ruled the waves until they were replaced by diesel-powered ships in the 1930s. Most of the World War I battleships, for instance, were steam powered, but by World War II, most were diesel powered.

DATA SOURCE: Jonathan Hughes and Stanley Reiter, "The First 1,945 British Steamships," *Journal of the American Statistical Association* 53, no. 282 (1958): 360–381, table 367.

The impact of steamships was momentous. In the late 1830s, a top-class sailing ship from Liverpool could make it to New York in forty-eight days or so. Favorable winds made the return faster, reducing it to about thirty-six days. By the 1840s, steamships brought the normal voyage to a reliable fourteen days in either direction.

The 1870s saw further advances, with the introduction of steel hulls that were lighter, stronger, and more fuel-efficient. By 1870, a combination of ship, engine, fuel, and propulsion technology made steam king of the seas and master of intercontinental distances. By the end of Phase Three, steam engines were pushed aside by diesel engines.

Just as steam transformed trade in goods, the telegraph transformed communication. The first transatlantic telegraph cable started operation in 1866, which was followed by the cabling of all major nations in a few decades. While the volume of information was trivial by today's standards, the telegraph revolutionized communications. Previously, intercontinental messaging involved weeks, if not months. The telegraph reduced this to minutes.

With these facts in hand, it is time to return to the historical narrative.

When Did Globalization's First Unbundling Begin?

In their extremely influential article "When Did Globalization Begin?" Kevin O'Rourke and Jeff Williamson argue that the best way to define economic globalization is as the integration of markets across space—especially as measured by international price convergence. Based on their statistical findings, they start the clock on modern globalization around the year 1820. They argue that this was when domestic prices—at least in Great Britain—were being set by the interplay of international supply and demand rather than domestic supply and demand.[1]

This international convergence of prices produced a divergence of national production profiles as local consumption was no longer a slave to local production. Instead, nations started to specialize in what they did best and import the rest. This was the beginning of globalization's first unbundling, which unfolded in three acts.

Act I: Pre–World War I Unbundling

The 1820 date does not line up precisely with any technological shock. It corresponds roughly to the end of the Napoleonic Wars

(1815) and the follow-on peace agreed at the Congress of Vienna. This arrangement launched a century of peace where Britain, as the world's unrivaled naval power, created Pax Britannica and trade flourished globally.

Trade Volumes Soared

In addition to the transport costs discussed, import taxes (tariffs) formed a separate deterrence to trade. Indeed, as transportation became less of a constraint, trade policy became more of a constraint. This is why trade policy becomes a major part of the globalization narrative in Phase Three.

One of the grandest of the old-school economic historians, Paul Bairoch, distinguishes three periods when it comes to tariff setting.[2] In the first period, Britain shuffled toward lower tariffs from 1815, finally taking the leap to free trade in 1846 with its hallmark legislation known as the Repeal of the Corn Act. Governments in Continental Europe attempted to mimic Britain's industrial success by embracing free trade. For three decades, liberal trade policy reigned triumphant (1846 to 1879); this was Bairoch's second period. Protectionism in the modern sense stepped into the picture in period three (1879 to 1914); Bismarck led the protectionist parade.

Having completed Germany's unification and lowered internal trade barriers, Bismarck restored high external tariffs, declaring: "The surfeiting of Germany with the over-production of other lands . . . depresses our prices and checks the development of our industry."[3] Continental tariffs doubled or tripled from 1879 to 1914. These tariffs, in modern parlance, were "infant industry protection" in that they were meant to shield Continental manufacturers from British industrial competitiveness.

Looking beyond Europe, nations that controlled their own trade policies (that is, nations that were not colonies) kept tariffs high throughout. For example, U.S. tariffs remained eight to ten times higher than those of core Europe. Colonies that were not self-ruling typically had liberal policies imposed, at least for imports from their "mother" country. Table 2 puts some numbers to these trends.

Northern Industrialization and Southern Deindustrialization

Napoleon's defeat opened the door to Continental industrialization. Belgium was the first to follow Great Britain, developing rapidly between 1820 and 1870. France, Switzerland, Prussia, and the United States followed in the 1830s and 1840s. Industrialization eventually spread to Canada, Russia, the Austrian-Hungarian Empire, Italy, Sweden, and much of the rest of Europe by the end of the 1800s.

As the nineteenth century entered its second half, new industries and production methods emerged around advances in chemistry, electricity, and the internal combustion engine. This so-called Second Industrial Revolution marks the years where the United States surpassed the United Kingdom in terms of industrial prowess. Industrialization in the North produced concentrations of factories in industrial districts. This proximity fostered innovation that triggered a dynamic of lower costs and further local concentration in the nations that started ahead (the North Atlantic economies and Japan). The flip side was a downward spiral in the ancient manufacturing consumption / production clusters. This industrialization of the North and deindustrialization of the South is one of the most striking aspects of Phase Three's reversal of fortunes.

As Simon Kuznets wrote in *Economic Growth and Structure*, "Before the nineteenth century and perhaps not much before it, some presently underdeveloped countries, notably China and parts of India, were believed by Europeans to be more highly developed than Europe."[4] During the eighteenth century, the Indian cotton textile industry was the global leader in terms of quality, production, and exports. Eighteenth-century India and China also produced the world's highest-quality silk and porcelain. Before the eighteenth century,

TABLE 2

Tariffs on manufactured goods, 1820, 1875, and 1913 (in percent).

	circa 1820	1875	1913
Austria-Hungary	prohibition	15–20	13–20
Belgium	n/a	9–10	9
Denmark	30	15–20	14
France	prohibition	12–15	20–21
Germany	n/a	4–6	13
Italy	n/a	8–10	18–20
Portugal	15	20–25	n/a
Russia	prohibition	15–20	84
Spain	prohibition	15–20	34–41
Sweden (Norway)	prohibition	3–5	20–25
Switzerland	10	4–6	8–9
Netherlands	7	3–5	4
United Kingdom	50	0	0
United States	45	40–50	44

Once Britain set the free trade precedent with its 1846 liberalization policy, protectionism waxed and waned. European powers followed its lead from 1860, but the period of liberal intra-European trade was short lived. Most Continental nations reversed the liberalization from 1880 or so. The exceptions, such as Belgium and the Netherlands, were nations that had long traditions of overseas trade.

Non-European nations (not shown in the table) that controlled their own trade policy mostly kept tariffs high to shield their industry from British competition. The United States flirted with tariff liberalism in the 1850s, but soon returned to its usual protectionist stance along with Continental Europe.

NOTES: "Prohibition" means manufactured imports generally prohibited; "n/a" means information not available; note that Belgium was part of the Netherlands in 1820; Prussian data is used for Germany in 1820 (Germany became a nation only in 1871).

SOURCE: Richard Baldwin and Philippe Martin, "Two Waves of Globalization: Superficial Similarities, Fundamental Differences," NBER Working Paper 6904, National Bureau of Economic Research, January 1999, table 8.

these manufactured goods were exported to Europe in exchange for silver, since European manufactures were uncompetitive in the East.

By the end of the nineteenth century, however, more than 70 percent of Indian textile consumption was imported and India had moved down the value chain to become an exporter of raw cotton. A matching, but less dramatic, story can be told for the Indian ship-building and iron industries.

Figure 18 shows the evolution of per capita industrialization and deindustrialization. Note that all nations and regions started at similar levels. Taking Britain's level of per-capita industrialization in 1900 as equal to one hundred, levels for European countries were between six and ten in 1750. The levels for China and India were at seven or eight, and the U.S. level was at four.

By 1860, Britain had an industrial lead over all other nations that was so dominant that it is easy to understand how this small island was able to enforce Pax Britannica across the planet. It was three times more industrialized than its nearest challengers, the United States and France, four times more industrialized than Germany, and nine times more so than Japan. Britain's lead over China in per capita industrialization in 1860 was simply enormous.

The per capita numbers, as always, misrepresent the global distribution. The similar levels of per capita industrialization across economies, combined with Asia's dominant population, meant that Asian industry dominated world production in the eighteenth century. Using global population figures to roughly translate the per capita figures into total figures suggests that China and India / Pakistan accounted for 73 percent of world manufacturing output in 1750. They continued to account for over half of global output even as late as 1830. By 1913, however, their share had dropped to a mere 7.5 percent.

Divergence "Big Time"

Nineteenth-century growth takeoffs in G7 economies created what Lant Pritchett calls "income divergence, big time" and Ken

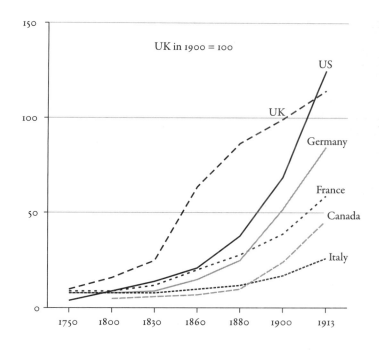

UK in 1900 = 100

US

UK

Germany

France

Canada

Italy

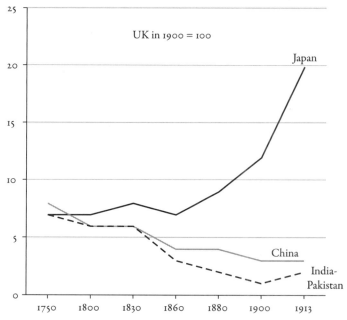

UK in 1900 = 100

Japan

China

India-
Pakistan

Pomeranz calls the "Great Divergence" in his book of the same title.[5] While the Industrial Revolution did not entirely bypass the ancient civilizations, their growth rates were less than half those of the North (Figure 19).

Due to the magic of compound growth, even small growth-rate differences produce shockingly large differences over a few decades. For example, U.S. income, which was about three times higher than China's in 1820, rose to almost ten times higher than China's by 1914. The gap between the ancient South and the rest of the "advanced industrialized nations" was almost as large.

The North's rapid industrialization is closely connected to its per capita growth for two reasons. First, shifting workers from agriculture to manufacturing produces big step-ups in productivity per worker for the simple reason that agriculture work involves large amounts of relatively unproductive time (between planting and harvesting). This shift, for as long as it is ongoing, boosts national growth rates. While transitional, this growth boost can last decades. Second, manufacturing is better suited to the incremental improvements that raise workers' productivity year after year. Boosting the share of workers in manufacturing thus lifts the economy-wide average rate of innovation and productivity growth and thus income growth.

The growth in the North Atlantic economies, however, was different on the two sides of the ocean. In Europe, population growth

---

FIGURE 18: Per capita industrialization levels, 1750 to 1913.

Britain was the first industrializer and maintained a massive lead until 1900, when it was surpassed by the United States. The other European G7 nations took off in the mid- to late-1800s. Japanese industry hit its growth acceleration around 1860.

As the chart shows, G7 industrialization was accompanied by deindustrialization in China and the subcontinent. Note that the vertical scale on the top panel goes to 150 while that of the bottom panel goes up to only 25.

DATA SOURCE: Paul Bairoch, "International Industrialization Levels from 1750 to 1980," *Journal of European Economic History* 2 (1982): 268–333, table 9.

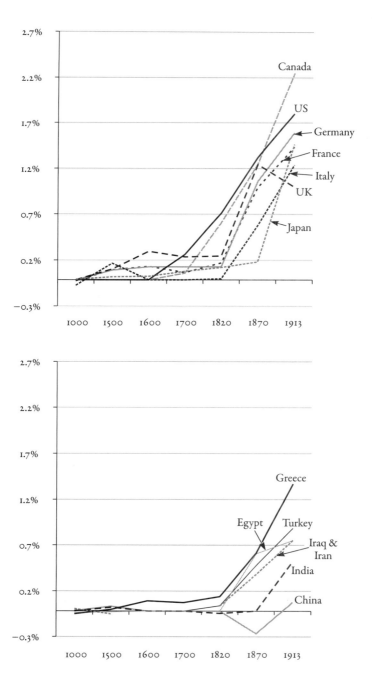

and limited arable land had pushed down labor productivity in agriculture. European farming was up against diminishing returns; income growth came mainly from industrialization.

In the New World, by contrast, agriculture offered important unexploited opportunities. Vast tracts of land were uncultivated— much of it quite similar to European farmland. With such high land-to-labor ratios, farm labor productivity was elevated. Given this situation, the massive transatlantic labor migration during the 1880 to 1914 period (Table 3) raised average productivity in both sending and receiving regions.

This triggered what are called "Kuznets cycles." As the dramatic drop in transport costs—especially the construction of railroads and

---

FIGURE 19: Growth takeoffs in the nineteenth century, G7 versus Ancient Seven (annual growth, %).

The income growth rates of G7 nations took off sooner and faster than those of the Ancient Seven (A7) economies that had so thoroughly dominated the world economy for millennia. For Europeans and Japan, the takeoff was clearly propelled by the industrialization shown in Figure 18. The story for the United States and Canada is somewhat different. The New World's relatively high agricultural productivity (lots of good land per farmer) meant that North American average incomes rose as immigrants expanded the amount of land under cultivation.

By World War I, all the G7—which can be thought of as "emerging markets" of the nineteenth century—enjoyed what was then considered good annual growth of one or two percentage points.

Many of the A7 also saw a sharp change in growth rates around 1820. The Mediterranean members of the A7 experienced positive growth takeoffs, with Greece's performance being particularly good. By 1914, Greece had clearly joined the high-growth club and was rapidly distancing itself from the rest of the A7 (Italy can be thought of having left the A7 in the mid-second millennium). The Asian A7 nations, by contrast, fared poorly. The Chinese economy shrank and India's stagnated.

Note that the two panels use the same scale to permit direct comparison. Even though the growth rate differences seem small by today's standards, the fact that the G7 rates were all above 1 percent growth while the ancient economies' rates were below 1 percent made a huge difference. Growth-rate differences of this size compound into massive income gaps in just a few decades.

DATA SOURCE: Maddison database (2009 version).

TABLE 3

Nineteenth-century mass migration from Europe to the New World.

% of own population		1880s	1890s	1900s
Senders:	U.K.	−3.1	−5.2	−2.0
	Italy	−1.7	−3.4	−4.9
	Spain	−1.5	−6.0	−5.2
	Sweden	−2.9	−7.2	−3.5
	Portugal	−3.5	−4.2	−5.9
Receivers:	U.S.	5.7	8.9	4.0
	Canada	2.3	4.9	3.7

Europe in the nineteenth century was overpopulated while the New World was underpopulated. The partial evening out of this state of affairs was one of the most remarkable economic aspects of Act I of globalization's Phase Three. As the figures show, there was an enormous population shift across the Atlantic from the 1880s.

The numbers are staggering by modern standards. Emigration flows of between 2 percent and 5 percent of the population per decade were entirely normal during this period. The impact on U.S. society was even more momentous. A large share of U.S. twentieth-century leaders in fields ranging from science and poetry to politics and the military were immigrants or children of immigrants.

DATA SOURCE: Baldwin and Martin, "Two Waves of Globalization," table 16, which is based on Alan Green and Malcolm Urquhart, "Factor and Commodity Flows in the International Economy of 1870–1914," *Journal of Economic History* 36 (1976): 217–252, table 2.

canals—opened U.S. frontier areas to staple production, the United States experienced a sequence of fifteen- to twenty-year booms driven by migration and capital flows that were responding to the newly opened land.

Urbanization

During Phase Three, urbanization was heavily biased toward the Atlantic economies, taking cities with more than a million inhabitants as the metric (Figure 20). When it comes to the number of these big cities, Europe was behind China and tied with Japan in 1800. By 1900, however, Europe had more million-plus cities than

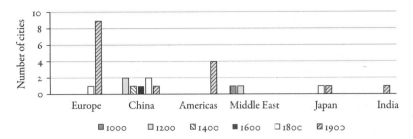

FIGURE 20: Reversal of fortune: evidence from the number of cities with over a million inhabitants.

From the first day of the second millennium right up until about 1800, all large cities in the world were located in the ancient Asian and Middle Eastern civilizations—defining "large" as over a million inhabitants. The sum of such cities rose and fell as the first millennium progressed, but it saw a pronounced jump when the world's economic center of gravity shifted toward the North Atlantic economies.

By 1900, all but two of the million-people cities were in Europe or the Americas, and one of the other two was in Japan—a clear testament to Phase Three's dramatic "reversal of fortune." Quite simply, the world urban landscape shifted from one that was dominated by A7 large cities to one dominated by G7 large cities.

The driving force behind this "changing of the guards" was the rising income gaps shown in Figure 19 (there is a very strong association between a nation's urbanization and its per capita income).

DATA SOURCE: George Modelski, *World Cities, -3000 to 2000* (Washington, DC: FAROS, 2003).

the whole rest of the world combined. And the Americas were in second place.

Moving forward to 1950, the trend strengthened. The average G7 nation had over 60 percent of its population in urban centers while the average in the ancient civilizations was under 30 percent. This suggests that the first unbundling promoted urbanization worldwide, but that by 1950, the North Atlantic economies were far ahead. This surely reflects the very strong correlation between urbanization and incomes teamed with the North Atlantic's massive income advantage.

Act II: Rebundling, 1914–1945

As far as globalization is concerned, Act I of the first unbundling ended badly, with the end coming first as a whimper and then as a bang. It was what economic historian Harold James calls "the end of globalization" in his 2001 book of the same title. War was the proximate cause.

War is almost always bad for trade, and World War I and World War II were no exceptions. They made commercial shipping risky and thus expensive. The result, seen clearly in the two wartime trade-cost spikes in Figure 17, forced a rebundling of production and consumption.

Just as transport costs were descending from their combat-related peaks, savage hikes in tariffs kept production and consumption from resuming their century-long unbundling. As Figure 21 shows, tariffs fell during the wars, but rose between them. The wartime tariff reductions were largely unintentional. Tariffs at the time were often set in nominal terms (for example, at $100 per ton of bananas), so wartime inflation eroded the tariffs as a percent of the consumer price of imports. In any case, most nations strictly controlled imports, so tariffs were often not the main hindrance.

The tariff hikes between the wars, by contrast, were quite purposeful—driven by a political backlash against globalization. The resolution of World War I, the Versailles Treaty in particular, generally ignored the health of the world trade system, despite the fact that President Woodrow Wilson listed global free trade as one of his famous fourteen points. Protectionism gained ground in Europe and elsewhere in the late 1910s and 1920s in a disorganized, erratic fashion.

The basic problem was that—unlike in Act I (1820 to 1913)—Britain was unwilling and unable to unilaterally support the world trading system. "With British hegemony lost and nothing to replace it, international relations lapsed in anarchy" is how the economist Charles Kindleberger of the Massachusetts Institute of Technology phrased

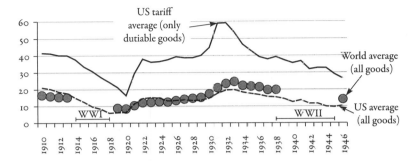

FIGURE 21: World and U.S. average tariffs, 1910 to 1946.

Act II saw big changes in tariff levels. Wartime inflation brought down tariff percentages but policy-driven tariff hikes between the wars continue to hinder trade. The most remarkable development was the Smoot-Hawley Tariff Act and the retaliation it provoked worldwide.

Berkeley economist Barry Eichengreen argues that the resort to protectionism was fostered by adherence to the gold standard. His famous book *Golden Fetters: The Gold Standard and the Great Depression* (Oxford University Press, 1992) explains how the lack of the exchange rate adjustment mechanism forced governments to turn to tariffs.

NOTE: Average tariff rates are the tariff revenue collected divided by the value of imports. The bottom line shows the average for the United States where the numerator excludes U.S. imports that enter duty-free (e.g., many raw materials).

DATA SOURCES: U.S. tariffs from United States International Trade Commission; world tariffs from Michael Clemens and Jeffrey G. Williamson, "Why Did the Tariff-Growth Correlation Reverse after 1950?" *Journal of Economic Growth* 9, no. 1 (2004): 5–46.

it in his 1989 article "Commercial Policy between the Wars." The straw that finally broke the back of the world trading system was the infamous 1930 hike in U.S. tariffs known as the Smoot-Hawley Tariff Act.

The Tariff Act of 1930, the legislation's formal name, found its origin in the protectionist campaign promises made by presidential candidate Herbert Hoover to U.S. farmers in the fall of 1928. A special congressional session, held in early 1929 to frame the bill, tumbled into an isolationist / protectionist spiral. The scope of tariffs was broadened to include industry, Democrats joined Republicans, and by the end, as Kindleberger describes it, "both Republicans and Democrats were ultimately pushed from the committee room as lobbyists took over the task of setting the rates."[6]

Foreign retaliation did not wait for the bill's final passage in June 1930. Italy, France, and others reacted forcefully in late 1929 and early 1930. Great Britain finally abandoned free trade, devalued sterling, and instituted a system of imperial preferences a couple of years later.

This outcome is plain to see in the data. Figure 21 shows two tariff averages for the United States and one for the world. The lower U.S. rate is the full average—that is, it includes all goods. The higher figures are for goods that are "dutiable"—that is, goods where the tariff is not zero. This difference is important since the United States had zero protection on the imports of things like mining and mineral products where there was no local production to protect. The dutiable goods were things like manufactured goods and food. Because of a lack of data, the Figure shows only the world tariff averages for all goods, but for comparability it also shows the U.S. numbers for the "all goods" average.

By the end of the 1930s, the world had broken into trading blocs. Germany, Italy, and the Soviet Union maintained systems of bilateral trade arrangements with explicitly autarkic aims and dreams of global domination. Britain, the dominions, and colonies were linked by the British Imperial Preference system, and Japan carved out a trade bloc called the Greater East Asia Co-Prosperity Sphere.

The breakdown of the trading system surely hastened the world down the path toward World War II. It fostered acceptance of the autarkic trade philosophies expounded by fascists in Germany, Italy, and Japan. Historian Gerhard Weinberg, for instance, argues in his essay "The World through Hitler's Eyes" that the closing of trade provided Hitler with a powerful justification for his territorial ambitions known as *lebensraum,* or living space. Hitler knew he needed goods made outside of Germany, but his solution was to turn international trade into domestic trade by expanding the borders of the Third Reich from the Atlantic to Moscow and from the Arctic Sea to the Black Sea.[7]

This was the darkest period for trade in modern times—the period when the association between protectionism and really bad things first took hold in policymakers' minds. Dawn, however, was on the way.

Act III: Post–World War II Unbundling

The history of post–World War II trade liberalization begins before itself, as so often happens with historical narratives. Regretting the burst of protectionism it sparked in the late 1920s, the United States Congress passed the Reciprocal Trade Agreements Act of 1934. This flipped the United States from a unilateral tariff setter to a reciprocal tariff cutter. To avoid a spaghetti bowl of tariffs, the 1934 Act imposed the concept of "most favored nation" status—known as MFN to experts. This principle—which became a cornerstone of global trade governance after World War II—meant that any tariff cut made bilaterally by any partner had to be automatically extended to all partners.

Figure 21 shows the outcome. From the mid-1930s right up to the end of World War II, U.S. tariffs fell as did world tariffs—a fact that many modern accounts of globalization miss since they start in 1945.

While tariff cutting started in Act II, establishment of a global system of trade governance had to wait for the war's end. This was a truly remarkable innovation. For the first time ever, global trade was governed by the rule of law instead of the rule of the gun.

GATT Establishes International Rules Governing Trade

At the end of Act I, the world trade system had virtually no institutional support. Indeed it was not really a "system"—it was just the fallout from Pax Britannica. In a sense, the Bank of England ran the international financial system (the gold standard, back then) as the International Monetary Fund does today. The British Navy was, at the time, playing roles similar to those now played by the United Nations, the International Court of Justice, and the World Trade Organization (WTO)—all with a particularly English twist.

Act III started out very differently. When it became clear who would win World War II, the Allies—especially the United States and United Kingdom—started designing the postwar architecture and they were dead set on avoiding the kind of international governance vacuum that had emerged after World War I. One of the key institutions they set up to avoid this was the General Agreement on Tariffs and Trade—or GATT, as it came to be known universally.

The GATT's mission was to foster rising living standards and sustainable development. Its members set out to accomplish this by establishing some basic "rules of the road" for international trade. They also committed themselves to negotiate reciprocal and mutually advantageous reductions in tariffs.

While the GATT rules are complex, they were absolutely essential in fostering modern globalization, so it is worth distilling the GATT's essence into one general principle and five specific principles. (Note the GATT rules morphed into rules of the WTO in 1995.) The general principle—what might be called the constitutional principle of the GATT / WTO—is that the world trade system should be *rules-based,* not *results-based.* This is why the GATT and WTO focus on things like the design, implementation, updating, and enforcement of procedures, rules, and guidelines rather than on quantitative outcomes like relative export growth or market shares.

The first specific principle is *nondiscrimination.* This has two aspects. The first is nondiscrimination at the border, which is basically the MFN principle mentioned above. MFN means that a tariff applied to any should be applied to all. Being a practical document, the GATT / WTO rulebook allows exceptions, especially for free trade agreements. The second aspect is nondiscrimination behind the border, which is called "national treatment" in GATT parlance. National treatment means that domestic taxes and regulations have to be applied to imported goods in the same way they are applied to domestic goods.

The second specific principle is *transparency,* which means trade restrictions have to be written down and made public. The third is *reciprocity,* which has a positive and a negative facet. The positive one says that nations that cut tariffs in the context of a GATT trade negotiation can expect other nations to reciprocate. Note, however, GATT had a huge loophole for developing nations. During tariff-cutting negotiations—called "rounds" in GATT jargon—developing nations did not have to reciprocate with tariff cuts of their own. The negative facet allows nations to retaliate against other nations that renege on tariff deals.

The fourth specific principle is *flexibility.* The GATT's founders knew that members would occasionally be subject to irresistible domestic pressure to impose new trade barriers, so they put in some "safety values" that allow new tariffs subject to various strictures. Finally, the last principle is *consensus decision making.* Most GATT / WTO decisions are arrived at by consensus.

Understanding the GATT's Success

The GATT was very successful at facilitating the reduction of tariffs—at least among developed nations. But before continuing with the historical chronology, it is useful to describe the two political-economy mechanisms, or sleights of hand, that account for GATT's success. The first mechanism—which can be called the *juggernaut effect*—rearranged the politics of tariff cutting inside each nation in a way that made liberalization a self-sustaining cycle. The key—as will become clear—is the GATT's reciprocity principle.

To understand this, step back and think about who likes and who dislikes tariffs. Domestic firms that compete with imports tend to like high domestic tariffs since these restrict imports, raise local prices, and thus boost their profits (or at least minimize their losses). Domestic firms that export, by contrast, dislike high foreign tariffs as these reduce their exports and profits.

These two sets of tariffs (domestic and foreign) are not intrinsically linked. Each nation, after all, gets to set its own tariffs. But the two sets become linked during GATT/WTO rounds due to the reciprocity principle. That is, foreign tariffs will fall only if domestic tariffs also fall. This then sets up a political fight within each nation. Exporters—who care little about domestic tariffs per se—know they must fight import-competing firms in their own nation if they are to win lower tariffs abroad.

From a political perspective, the linchpin of the juggernaut effect is the way that the reciprocity principle allows each government to counterbalance its protectionist lobbies with its pro-liberalization lobbies. Before the reciprocal talks, the government listens mostly to domestic pro-tariff pressure groups. During the reciprocal talks, the government also listens to pro-liberalization pressure groups (i.e., exporters). As a result, GATT/WTO reciprocal tariff-cutting talks realign the political-economy forces inside each nation in a direction that favors lower tariffs.

As an aside, note that consumer interests should, in principle, be factored into the political equation. Consumers, however, are rarely engaged politically in tariff choices, so their voices on tariff matters are muted in most nations.

The tariff cutting that results from a single GATT round is not the end of the juggernaut's tariff-cutting effect since the cuts trigger a "snowball" effect. The lower domestic tariffs let in more imports, which in turn lead to the downsizing of import-competing industries. At the same time, the foreign tariff cutting boosts output, employment, and profits of exporters. As political influence follows economic clout, the upsizing of export interests and the downsizing of import-competing interests conspire to tilt future political calculations toward more tariff cutting.

In short, the reciprocal tariff cuts agreed at one GATT round alter national political-economy landscapes in a way that fosters continued liberalization. "Juggernaut effect" is an apt term since, once the tariff-cutting ball starts rolling, it creates political-economy momentum that keeps it rolling until all tariffs in its path are crushed.[8]

The second sleight of hand is what enabled a handful of rich nations to run the GATT despite the consensus principle. The key is the huge loophole that existed in the reciprocity principle; developing nations were not obliged to reciprocate with tariff cuts of their own even though their exporters benefitted from rich-nation tariff cuts. When rich nations cut their tariffs, they were obliged by the MFN principle to extend the tariff cut to all GATT/WTO members—even those that did not reciprocate.

This loophole made developing nations into free riders in the tariff-cutting negotiations, but they were a special kind of free rider. Due to the MFN principle, they had a stake in making sure that the rounds succeeded so that their exporters could benefit from the rich-nation tariff cuts.

This fudged rather than solved the consensus problem by turning membership into a "don't obey, don't object" proposition for developing nations. In fact, many developing nations did not even attend the GATT negotiations. Why should they? They had nothing to defend due to the loophole. Moreover, since they had no tariff cuts on the bargaining table, they had no say in which tariffs the rich nations would cut.

Turning from political-economy logic to real events, Figure 22 is useful in structuring the narrative. It shows average tariff rates for a collection of poor and rich nations from 1950 to 1994 (top panel). The four years before 1950 were critical to understanding GATT tariff cutting, but systematic international data is not available, so

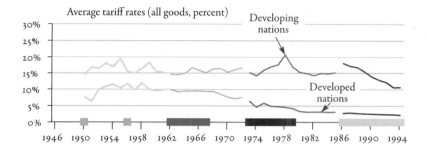

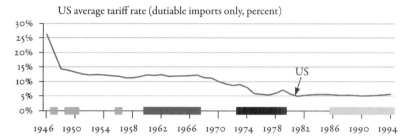

FIGURE 22: Average tariff rates, developed and developing nations, 1950–1994.

The first "T" in GATT stands for tariffs, and one of GATT's main accomplishments was to bring down tariffs from quite high levels after World War II to quite low levels by the early 1990s. These cuts were orchestrated in multilateral negotiations called "rounds" (the bands on the horizontal axis show when the various rounds were ongoing; see Table 4 for their names). But as the top panel shows, poor nations started with higher tariffs and did not reduce them in the rounds. As a result, developing nations had much higher tariffs throughout globalization's Phase Three.

The developed-nations tariff cutting came in three major phases. The first coincided with the inaugural 1947 GATT round, which cut tariffs quite a lot (data only available for the United States, bottom panel). The next two stages came as a result of the Kennedy round (1963–1967) and the Tokyo round (1973–1979).

NOTE: In the chart, "developed nations" comprise the EU nations plus Switzerland, Norway, Japan, and Australia; "developing nations" comprise Argentina, Brazil, China, Egypt, Indonesia, India, Kenya, Korea, Mexico, Malaysia, Nigeria, Pakistan, Philippines, Thailand, and Turkey. Average tariff rates are calculated as the dollar value of tariff revenue collected divided by the dollar value of imports. The bottom chart shows the average rate for the United States where the numerator excludes U.S.

the bottom panel shows the figures for the United States from the full period as a proxy for what was going on in rich nations.

The GATT started off with a tariff-cutting bang that can be thought of as a multilateralization and extension of the U.S. efforts since 1934. The first GATT round came in 1947 and it reduced tariffs substantially (Table 4). The next four rounds did little tariff cutting. They focused instead on setting up new rules and on the difficult negotiations that led to GATT membership for Germany in 1951 and Japan in 1955.

The GATT got back into the tariff-cutting business with the "Kennedy Round" (1963 to 1967). As Figure 22 shows, rich-nation tariffs fell substantially while the negotiated tariff cuts were phased in over five to ten years. Poor-nation tariffs did not fall, however, thanks to the "don't obey, don't object" mechanism.

The next turn of the juggernaut came in 1973 when the so-called Tokyo Round was launched. In addition to lowering tariffs (see Table 4), this round tackled important nontariff issues such as subsidies, regulations, and government procurement. As before, developing nations were free riders. Indeed, since developing nations were free to do pretty much whatever they liked in the GATT years, poor nations' tariffs spiked during the economic crises of 1973 and 1979.

After a few years, the juggernaut's impact paved the way for more tariff cutting. Most nations' anti-liberalization forces had become weaker and their pro-liberalization forces had become stronger, so more trade opening became politically optimal—on the multilateral and regional levels. As history would have it, GATT members

---

imports that enter duty-free (e.g., many raw materials); this gives a better overall picture of the level of the tariffs that could conceivably be cut in GATT rounds.

DATA SOURCES: Top panel: Clemens and Williamson, "Why Did the Tariff-Growth Correlation Reverse after 1950?"; bottom panel: "U.S. Imports for Consumption, Duties Collected, and Ratio of Duties to Value, 1891–2014," Office of Analysis and Research Services, Office of Operations, U.S. International Trade Commission, http:\\dataweb.usitc.gov.

TABLE 4
Tariff cuts in the GATT rounds and GATT membership, 1947 to 1994.

Name of round	Start	Tariff cut (%)	Number of members	Number of developing nations
Geneva Round I	1947	26	19	7
Annecy Round	1949	3	20	8
Torquay Round	1950	4	33	13
Geneva Round II	1955	3	35	14
Dillon Round	1960	4	40	19
Kennedy Round	1963	37	74	44
Tokyo Round	1973	33	84	51
Uruguay Round	1986	38	125	88

GATT multilateral negotiations (called "rounds" in the jargon) were held frequently in the institution's early days—five rounds in thirteen years. Apart from the initial round (Geneva Round I), the early rounds dealt mostly with new rules and the admission of new members. From the Kennedy Round onward, the rounds returned to tariff cutting, but also touched on increasingly complex trade barriers—things like technical barriers to trade, investment rules, government purchases, and the like.

The GATT was quite successful at lowering the tariffs of Japan, Europe, and North America, but developing nations were allowed to keep their tariffs high under a provision called "Special and Differential Treatment" that was aimed at allowing poor nations to industrialize behind tariff walls (as many advanced nations had done before World War II).

As part of the Uruguay Round final agreement, the GATT became the WTO in 1995. Apart from changing the name, the deal institutionalized the GATT's judicial role in dispute settlement and added some basic "rules of road" for international investment, regulations, intellectual property, and services.

DATA SOURCE: Will Martin and Patrick Messerlin, "Why Is It So Difficult? Trade Liberalization Under the Doha Agenda," *Oxford Review of Economic Policy* 23, no. 3 (2007): 347–366.

launched the Uruguay Round in 1986, the same year that some of the leading GATT members also started massive regional trade liberalization exercises.

Specifically, three liberalization initiatives were launched in 1986. The United States and Canada started talks on a free trade agreement that finished in 1989 (this eventually turned into the North American Free Trade Agreement, or NAFTA). The year 1986 also saw the Europeans both deepen and widen their trade liberalization club, which was by then called the European Union (EU). Spain and Portugal were admitted as new members, and the EU embarked on a deep liberalization of many other economic barriers in the context of the so-called Single Market program.

The Uruguay Round lasted from 1986 to 1994. As Figure 22 shows, the really original element in this phase was the rapid tariff cutting by poor nations. It is important to note, however, that this developing-nation liberalization had nothing to do with the GATT since the "don't obey, don't object" principle was still in operation. Instead, these reductions were the beginning of a revolution in developing-nation attitudes that are really part of Phase Four and the effort by poor nations to attract offshore factories and jobs (as will be discussed in Chapter 3).

The Uruguay Round finished in 1994, and as part of the final deal, the GATT became the WTO and acquired important adjudication responsibilities. Establishment of the WTO was truly historic, but the continued reduction in shipping costs in Act III was probably even more important in keeping world trade volumes on their upward trajectory.

Containerization Lowers Shipping Costs

Continuous technological improvements in ships, trains, and trucks reduced the cost of moving goods, but failed to overcome the age-old problem of loading and unloading. A big breakthrough on this front—called "containerization"—came in the 1960s and grew exponentially in the 1970s and 1980s.

Before containerization, ships were loaded by hand and this situation could mean that imported goods stayed for weeks in port. Worse yet for anyone running an international production network, the actual time in port was highly uncertain and this uncertainty, in turn, made shipping schedules unreliable.

Containerization revolutionized shipping by putting most traded goods into standard-size steel containers. The impact was momentous for many reasons, as Marc Levinson relates in his 2006 book *The Box*. For one thing, containers made shipping cheaper and more reliable. Filling the containers is usually done by the company sending the goods and unloading is usually done by the customer. This is typically faster and cheaper since these organizations know what is in the "box" and how to handle it. Getting the goods on and off ships is also cheaper, faster, and more predictable because it can be done with giant cranes. The advent of containers reduced the amount of labor required and—by undermining dockside labor unions—reduced the delays that had in the past been caused by strikes.[9]

Moreover, the standardization that came with containers meant that ports and train terminals all over the planet could optimize cranes and other machinery around these standard-size boxes. This also made it easier to "connect the dots" in the transportation network. A container full of, say, high-tech parts could be shipped by truck from its Californian factory, put on a container ship in the port of Los Angeles, and transferred to a truck or train in Nagoya, Japan for the journey to its final customer—all without the container ever being touched by human hands.

The result was a miraculous drop in the cost of moving goods. Economists have estimated that containerization boosted trade far more than all the tariff cutting shown in Figure 2.2.

BOX 3: SUMMARY OF PHASE THREE

If Phase Two can be thought of as laying the foundations of human society, Phase Three can be thought of as building the house that history came to call "the modern world."

For most of human existence, the strictures of distance limited most people's consumption to goods that were produced within walking distance. Phase Three started when the dictatorship of distance was overthrown. The key to the coup was steam power.

The steam revolution, like the Agricultural Revolution before it, triggered a "phase transition" that eventually launched modern globalization (or more precisely, what we have been calling Old Globalization, or the first unbundling). As the nineteenth century progressed, steam displaced wind and animal power before being displaced itself by internal combustion and electric engines. But the development of steam power is what started the sequence.

These breakthroughs in transportation technology made it economical to consume goods that had been made far away. Globalization in this phase meant the geographical unbundling of consumption and production on a massive scale.

Mastery of intercontinental distances opened the door to three interconnected phenomena—trade, agglomeration, and innovation—which conspired to turn the world economic order on its head. In one of history's most dramatic reversals of fortune, the Asian core became the periphery and the North Atlantic periphery became the core.

The drama unfolded in a three-act play; globalization advanced before World War I, and then retreated between the wars, before surging ahead further than ever after World War II.

Essential Outcomes

The key impacts of this first unbundling were:

- The Atlantic economies and Japan (the "North") industrialized while the ancient civilizations in Asia and the Middle East (the "South") deindustrialized (especially India and China).
- Growth takeoffs occurred everywhere but sooner and faster in the North than in the South.
- The Great Divergence appeared.
- International trade boomed.
- Urbanization accelerated, especially in the North.

At the base of all these gigantic changes was a very uneven distribution of productive know-how. The innovations developed in the North stayed in the North and thus drove Northern wages and living standards far beyond those of the South. Chapter 3 recounts the great transformations that came in Phase Four when information technology opened the sluicegates that have helped to even out the global imbalance in know-how.

CHAPTER 3

ICT and Globalization's
Second Unbundling

The New Globalization is not your father's globalization; it is really something quite different. A blessing for some and a bane for others, twenty-first-century globalization is affecting people in radically new ways. For Santiago de Querétaro, a colonial-era town in North-Central Mexico, the New Globalization has been a miracle-size blessing.

A magnet for offshore production facilities, Santiago de Querétaro and the surrounding region have attracted activities ranging from data centers to aircraft manufacturing. In 2006, for example, only two aerospace firms were present employing about 700 workers between them. Eight years later, there were thirty-three aircraft companies and over 5,000 jobs, according to Paul Gallant, writing for *Canadian Business*.[1]

As suggested by the title of Gallant's 2014 article—"How Bombardier's Experiment Became Ground Zero for Mexico's Economic Revolution"—one key company in all this was the Canadian company Bombardier. The firm first moved technologically unsophisticated, labor-intensive stages to Querétaro. Tasks such as the assembly of wire harnesses for aircraft were done in Querétaro, after which the subassemblies were shipped back to Quebec to be installed in aircraft assembled there. But increasingly sophisticated stages followed the offshoring of wire harnesses. For example, Bombardier's Querétaro facility now makes tails for business jets.

More recently, Bombardier Recreational Products (BRP), which builds watercraft like the Sea-Doo, opened a facility that makes sophisticated composite hulls. Bringing such innovative production stages to Mexico was unusual. Gallant explains this by quoting the director of BRP Querétaro, Thomas Wieners: "Normally you bring something that you completely know how to do and you want to leverage some labor content. But we believe we've found a strong talent pool here."

A large measure of Querétaro's achievement comes down to the knowledge that Bombardier moved from Canada to Mexico. This was not easy. As Gallant notes, "Bombardier was faced with the dilemma of how to transfer the know-how from French-speaking veterans to Spanish-speaking newbies." To overcome the hurdles, the company invented a system of pictograms that Mexican operators could follow without knowing a word of French.

This miracle for Querétaro's "Spanish-speaking newbies" has been rather less happy for the "French-speaking veterans" in Quebec. Bombardier can now make airplane tails using Mexican manufacturing engineers who get about $60 a day instead of Canadian aerospace engineers who get $35 an hour.

This personal perspective provides a mere hint of the New Globalization's impact. From a planetary perspective, it is hard to exaggerate how radical the effects have been. A glance at the evolution of national incomes over the last thousand years makes the point. (See Figure 23.)

This chapter starts with a closer look at the revolution in information and communication technology (ICT) that produced the transition from Phase Three (Old Globalization, or globalization's first unbundling) to Phase Four (New Globalization, or its second unbundling). It also relates the facts on the development of air cargo, which, like ICT, help reduce the cost of managing complex activities internationally.

The chapter then turns to documenting how the New Globalization's impact differs from that of the Old Globalization. Given how recent Phase Four is, the discussion is organized around topics like

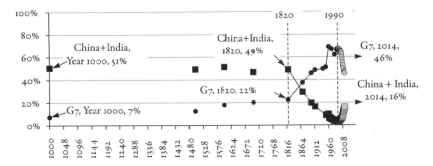

FIGURE 23: Spot the phase transitions: World GDP shares, year 1000 to 2014.

Before the Industrial Revolution, only a narrow slice of humanity lived above subsistence levels, so national shares of gross domestic product (GDP) lined up closely with national population shares. Given the sheer weight of numbers, Indians and Chinese dominated right up to the early nineteenth century when Phase Three initiated the 170-year crash shown in Figure 23.

The crash turned into a climb when the New Globalization started around 1990. Since then, the two Asian giants' share of world GDP has risen sharply—far faster than they fell in the preceding centuries. The share today is nothing like their historical standard of 50 percent, but they are well on their way. This is the Great Convergence.

DATA SOURCES: World Bank DataBank (GDP in U.S. dollars) and Maddison database (2009 version), pre-1960 with author's calculations.

economic activity, trade, and poverty rather than the historical narrative. The final section gathers the facts into four key features of New Globalization.

Breakthrough: The ICT Revolution

Revolution is a word that is often used carelessly. When it comes to ICT, however, the "R-word" is well deserved. Readers over fifty years of age will not have to be reminded of the revolutionary impact of advanced information and communications technology. They grew up in a world where conference invitations went by airmail, international calls cost five dollars a minute, and sending a single document by overnight courier could cost fifty dollars or more. Faxing was faster but the quality was horrible.

Even younger readers will have lived through dramatic changes. To them, email is a clunky ancient technology that is only useful for some things, while Facebook (since 2004), Twitter (since 2006), and Snapchat (since 2011) are much better adapted for instant communication and group organization.

The revolution can also be understood in the numbers. Between 1986 and 2007, world information storage capacity grew at 23 percent per year, telecommunications at 28 percent, and computation power at 58 percent per year. Such growth rates can be transformational in as little as a decade. For example, the amount of information transmitted by telecommunications during the whole of 1986 could be transmitted in just two-thousandths of a second in 1996. The *increase* in the volume of information between 2006 and 2007 was vastly greater than the sum of all information transmitted in the previous decade. (More precisely, the increment is 1.06×10^{36} times bigger than the sum.)

The computing power growth rate is even more fabulous. If you try to project the growth out more than a dozen years in Excel, you can't. Excel cannot handle numbers that large, even with scientific notation. One soon runs out of adjectives to describe the magnitude of the changes wrought by the increase in the ability to collect, process, and transmit information, but *transformative, revolutionary,* and *disruptive* are all apt.

The Laws Underpinning the ICT Revolution

The ICT revolution is made up of three interrelated strands. The "I," which stands for information, was driven by computing and data storage costs. The "C," which stands for communication, was driven by transmission advances. The "T," which stands for technology, should probably be an "R" for reorganization since the economic impact of the "I" and "C" were greatly amplified by new working methods and workplace organizations.

The law that impels the "I" in ICT is called Moore's Law after its originator Gordon Moore. This law asserts that computing power grows exponentially—with, for example, computer chip performance doubling every eighteen months. The propulsion behind the "T" part is described by two laws: Gilder's Law and Metcalfe's Law. George Gilder observed that bandwidth grows three times more rapidly than computer power—doubling every six months. This allows transmission advances to help relax computing and storage constraints. Advances in data transmission, processing, and storage amplify each other. This is the economic basis of "the cloud" and its various uses.

Robert Metcalfe asserted that the usefulness of a network rises with the square of the number of users. When the number of network users is, say, 100,000, the number of possible new connections created by adding one more user is 100,000. When there are 200,000 users, adding one more creates 200,000 new connections. In other words, the incremental number of new connections does not rise in a straight line. The size of each increment grows with each new increment, so growth feeds on growth.

Long-distance information sharing was revolutionized as these developments in computing power and telecommunications were complemented by the rise of the Internet—first email and then web-based platforms. And it didn't stop there.

Revolutions are never just one thing (to paraphrase Audre Lorde). The ability to send ideas down cables for almost nothing to almost anywhere triggered a host of reformations in work practices, management practices, and relationships among firms and their suppliers and customers. Working methods and product designs shifted to make production more modular and thus easier to coordinate at distance. The telecom and Internet revolutions triggered a suite of information-management innovations that made it easier, cheaper, faster, and safer to coordinate separate complex activities spatially. Email, editable files (*.xls, *.doc, etc.), and more specialized web-based coordination

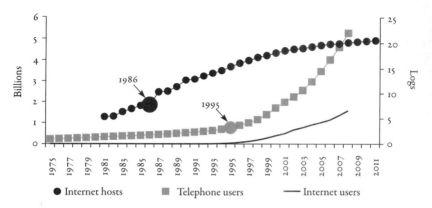

FIGURE 24: Growth of global Internet Hosts and Phone Lines, 1975 to 2011.

For an industry that is all about digitization, it is surprisingly difficult to find statistics on information and communications technology that go back to before the New Globalization started in 1990 or so. The book titled *The ICT Revolution* by Daniel Cohen, Pietro Garibaldi, and Stefano Scarpetta, for instance, presents no systematic figures back that far.

What is available are figures on Internet hosts, Internet users, and telephone users. These give a strong hint that the ICT Revolution occurred somewhere between 1985 and 1995, although the evolution of the numbers looks less like a revolution than a rapid evolution.

DATA SOURCES: International Telecommunication Union (ITU) and World Bank data; Daniel Cohen, Pietro Garibaldi and Stefano Scarpetta, *The ICT Revolution* (Oxford: Oxford University Press, 2004).

software packages revolutionized people's ability to manage multifaceted procedures across great distances.

While the steam revolution took decades to transform globalization, the ICT revolution took years. Figure 24 displays several ICT indicators, showing that there was an inflection point in the growth of Internet hosts in 1985 and in telephone subscribers in 1995.

The ICT revolution, however, was not the only big change in this time frame. The development of air cargo both stimulated and was stimulated by the development of international production networks.

Air Cargo

Air freight first became commercially viable due to the surplus of planes available after World War II, but it did not really get going until the mid-1980s with the rise of Federal Express, DHL, and UPS. Indeed the development of reliable air cargo services mirrors the rise of global value chains for rather obvious reasons. Air cargo allowed manufacturers to know that intermediate goods could flow among distant factories almost as surely as they flow among factories within a nation. In fact, as economists David Hummels and Georg Schaur show in a 2012 paper ("Time as a Trade Barrier"), fully 40 percent of the parts and components imported into the United States are imported by air.[2]

The key here is not cost. While air shipments have been getting cheaper, air cargo even today is many times more expensive than sea freight. The critical attraction of sending things by air is speed. European freight sent by sea, for example, takes an average of twenty days to reach U.S. ports and a month to reach Japan. Air shipments take a day or less.

The speed is also associated with certainty and this matters. When things go wrong in an international production network, air cargo allows the offshoring firms to fix it in days, or maybe even hours, rather than the weeks it would have taken when things were shipped by land or sea.

With the basic facts and timing of the ICT revolution and air cargo developments in hand, we can turn to the impact that these changes wrought.

Phase Four: Globalization's Second Unbundling

Evidence of the changed nature of globalization can be found in a wide range of economic statistics. According to the three-cascading-constraints view of globalization, the North to South shift in manufacturing is what really started all the big changes. The astounding impact of the New Globalization on the location of manufacturing activity is thus the first set of facts to examine.

Impact on Manufacturing

The New Globalization is associated with a sharp reversal of fortunes when it comes to manufacturing. The Old Globalization produced an industrialization of the North and a deindustrialization of the South. The New Globalization has turned this situation on its head. The North—the group of countries called "industrialized nations" twenty years ago—has seen a rapid fall in the number of jobs and value added shares in the manufacturing sector. At the same time, manufacturing output has soared in six developing nations—called the Industrializing Six (I6)—namely, China, Korea, India, Indonesia, Thailand, and Poland.

As is well known, some developing nations made it before 1990. Economies known in the 1970s as "newly industrializing"—Hong Kong, Taiwan, Singapore, and Korea—industrialized rapidly from 1970 to 1990. The real about-face, however, came much later. What had been a gentle decline in the share of manufacturing in the G7 nations accelerated from about 1990. It fell in the years between 1990 and 2010 from two-thirds to under a half. (See Figure 2 in the Introduction).

Figure 25 focuses on national shares of world manufacturing output for the G7. While the turnaround for the G7 as a whole is very sharply defined, shares of the three biggest G7 manufacturers (top panel) show a more varied pattern. During two "miracle decades," Japan's manufacturing output swelled rapidly and this in turn was associated with a tremendous overall income growth takeoff. This rapid rise eventually caused a great deal of conflict with the United States as Japanese autos, electronics, and machinery threated the postwar dominance of American goods; up to 1990 or so, Japan's rising share is the mirror image of the falling U.S. share. This changed with the second unbundling. Since 1990, Japan has joined the general G7 downward trend.

Interestingly, U.S. manufacturing output enjoyed positive growth for the first decade of Phase Four—perhaps because it gained international competition from outsourcing to Mexico and Canada. Regardless of the cause, the share growth has since vanished; U.S. manufacturing output joined the general G7 movement starting around 2000. Germany's share declined steadily through the four decades.

The deindustrialization path of the four smaller G7 nations is shown in the bottom panel of Figure 25 (note the change in scale). Italian manufacturing share declined throughout, but the decline accelerated from the early 1990s and accelerated again around 2000. The United Kingdom, by contrast, witnessed big gains up to the 1980s and has declined since, with the negative growth clearly picking up around 1990. Canada and France also steadily declined up to about the year 2000, when their declines picked up speed.

Figure 26 shows that even among the I6, share gains were very unevenly spread. China—shown in the top panel due to its very different scale—clearly took the lion's share. The pattern is nothing short of astounding. China's manufacturing sector, which was completely uncompetitive in 1970, was the second largest manufacturer in the world in 2010.

For the other I6 countries, the growth experience has been more varied. Some, like Korea, have been on an upward path since the beginning (Korea was one of the group known as the newly industrializing countries). For others, such as Indonesia and Thailand, the uptick started in the 1980s. Poland joined the rapid share growth only after the Berlin Wall fell in 1989. India, which started far ahead of Korea, has seen steady progress with some hint of an acceleration around 1990.

As one would expect, the rapid industrialization of the I6 boosted their growth. Considering that almost half of all humans live in

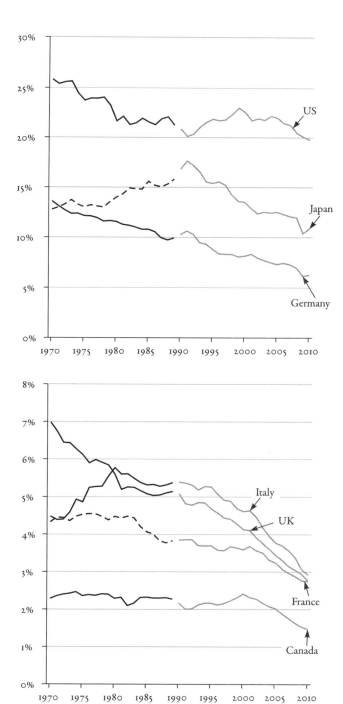

these nations, this growth explosion had momentous ripple effects. One was the shocking shift in world GDP shares.

Impact on Economic Activity: Shifting GDP Shares

The "shocking share shift" chart (Figure 23) showed how the Group of Seven's share of global GDP declined from two-thirds in 1990 to under one-half today. As shares add to a hundred, the G7's share losses must correspond to share gains for others. Who were the GDP share winners?

The answer is that the G7's share loss went to very few nations (Figure 27 top panel). Only eleven nations saw their global shares rise by more than three-tenths of one percentage point between 1990 and 2010. Together, these Rising Eleven, or R11 for short—China, India, Brazil, Indonesia, Nigeria, Korea, Australia, Mexico, Venezuela, Poland, and Turkey—accounted for fourteen of the seventeen percentage points lost by the G7. The whole rest of the world—almost 200 nations—accounted for the remaining three percentage points.

Even among the R11, the share shift was unevenly distributed. China alone accounted for about seven percentage points, as the bottom panel of Figure 27 shows. Adding in the next two largest gainers (India and Brazil) brings the gain by the top three share-gaining nations to ten percentage points of world GDP.

FIGURE 25: Trading places in manufacturing: G7 world shares of manufacturing, 1970 to 2010.

The three big manufacturing nations in the G7 had very different experiences in recent decades. Japan's share of world manufacturing output was on the rise until 1990 but then started a steady decline. Japan's rise was approximately matched by U.S. share losses; after a few years of recovery, the United States joined the downward slide from about 2000. Germany, by contrast, has been sliding down the share slope since the data begins in 1970.

The other G7 nations are now all on a path of steady, swift decline with most experiencing a steeper decline since either 1990 or 2000.

DATA SOURCE: UNSTAT.org data.

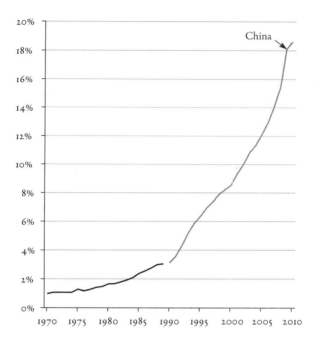

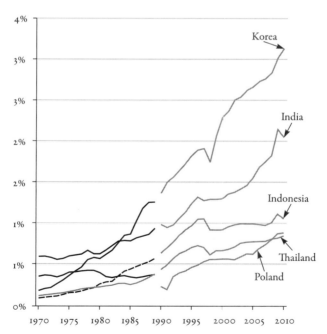

Manufacturing Winners and GDP Winners

There is a good deal of overlap between the two groups of winners—the Industrializing Six and the Rising Eleven. In fact, all of the rapid industrializers are among the R11 risers, except Thailand. Given the long-standing association between rapid industrialization and rapid growth, this overlap is hardly surprising. But how did other members of the R11 grow so much more rapidly than the world average? For most of the remaining R11 members—Brazil, Indonesia, Nigeria, Australia, Mexico, Venezuela, and Turkey—the word "commodities" springs to mind as the obvious explanation.

The Organization for Economic Cooperation and Development (OECD) has produced a new beautiful new trade dataset that allows us to follow up on this hint. The data is shown in Figure 28, but understanding the evidence requires a bit of background. The numbers in the chart show the breakdown of these nations' export growth by broad sector of the economy: primary, manufacturing, and services. For example, Chinese export growth came about 90 percent from the manufacturing sector (shown in the top bar of the top panel). But this 90 percent number is not based on the standard definition of exports—namely, the value of goods as they leave the country. Rather 90 percent reflects the composition of what is called "value-added exports."

FIGURE 26: World manufacturing shares of the Industrializing Six, 1970 to 2010.

China's fantastic, epoch-defining industrialization took off around 1990, fueled by foreign firms bringing factories and jobs to China along with everything necessary to produce world-class products. In just two decades, a sixth of the world manufacturing "pie" moved from outside China to inside China even as total world manufacturing was growing steadily.

The experience of the other 16 nations is more of a mixed bag. In Poland, the rising share is proceeding steadily, but Thailand and Indonesia have seen a deceleration of their share growth.

DATA SOURCE: UNSTAT.org data.

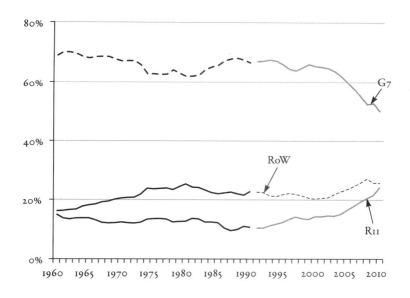

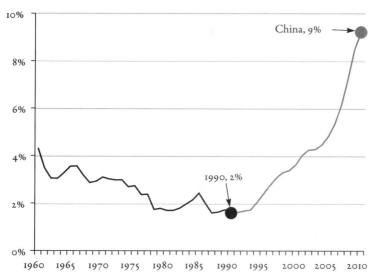

What is the difference between standard export statistics and the value-added exports numbers? To get value-added export statistics, the OECD strips out the value of imported intermediates used in making the exports. Thus one can, roughly speaking, view standard exports as "gross" exports, and value-added exports as "net" exports.

The merit of value-added statistics is that they give a much clearer idea of where exports are actually made—both by sector and by nation. In countries where global value chains are important, like China, there can be important differences between the gross and the net numbers. The iPhone example makes this distinction plain.

In standard export terms, China exported about $2 billion of iPhones to the United States in 2009, but most of this $2 billion represents value that had been added outside of China. When one nets out the value of goods and services that China imported in order to make the iPhones, it turns out that Chinese value-added exports of iPhones was only about $0.2 billion.[3] In this case, the $2 billion is the gross export; the $0.2 billion is the value-added export.

Figure 28 shows that the R11 can be grouped into three broad categories. The top five bars of Figure 28 indicate that five of the R11 "made it" due to dynamic manufacturing sectors (China, Korea,

---

FIGURE 27: The G7, R11, and China: global GDP share redistribution, 1960 to 2010. The impact of globalization in Phase Four was geographically specific. The G7's GDP share loss was won by just eleven rising economies (the R11), defined as nations that gained at least three-tenths of a percentage point of world GDP share from 1990 to 2010. The R11 are China, India, Brazil, Indonesia, Nigeria, Korea, Australia, Mexico, Venezuela, Poland, and Turkey. The share of the rest of the world (RoW) has been fairly flat since 1990.

As the bottom panel shows, China lost ground up to 1990, but made up for it rapidly from 1990 onward. In fact, about half of the total R11 gain is due to China's share gain alone.

DATA SOURCE: World Bank DataBank (GDP in U.S. dollars) with author's calculations. Since the shares measure the size of economies rather than individual welfare, the charts use figures that are not corrected for the local price of nontraded goods.

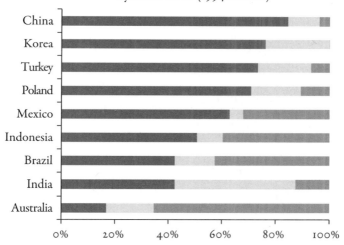

Domestic value-added in export growth,
by source sector (1994 to 2008)

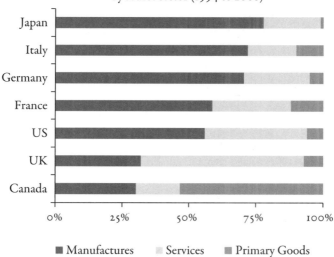

Domestic value-added in export growth,
by source sector (1994 to 2008)

■ Manufactures   ▨ Services   ■ Primary Goods

Poland, Turkey, and Mexico). The second category includes nations that made it via primary exports. Australia is the only one that is clearly in this category, as over 60 percent of the value-added in its export growth came from the primary goods sector. It is likely, however, that Venezuela and Nigeria (whose data are missing from TiVA) would also be in this club.

The final category is India. India's value-added export growth has been remarkably biased toward services, although the manufacturing sector accounts for about 40 percent of its growth. This reflects

---

FIGURE 28: How did emerging markets do it? Manufacturers versus commodity exporters

The group of rapidly growing developing countries (Rising Eleven, or R11) achieved their growth in very different ways. One group did it on the back of manufacturing, another group relied on commodities, and one nation, India, achieved export success via its service sector. Evidence for this can be gleaned from the chart (see text for an explanation of what value added exports are and how they differ from standard exports).

As the Figure shows, more than half the value added that is contained in the export growth of China, Korea, Turkey, Poland, Mexico, and Indonesia comes from their manufacturing sectors. The share for China, as might be expected, is very high—namely 85 percent. For these countries the export boom was clearly driven by rapid industrialization—much of it associated with globalization's second unbundling.

Other members of the rapid-growth group include countries whose export booms relied more on commodity exports. Australia is the clear standout with about 65 percent of the value added export growth coming from the primary goods sector. Some of this comes from the success of their "hard" commodity exports (things like iron ore) and some comes from their "soft" commodity sectors (wine, grain, meat, and the like). The success of Brazil is fairly evenly split between commodities and manufacturing, as is that of Indonesia (a big oil exporter).

India is a unique case in that its export boom was driven by its service sector rather than its manufacturing or primary goods sectors.

NOTE: The 1995 and 2008 period is chosen since 1995 is the earliest data available and 2008 is the last year before the Global Crisis started distorting the trade data.

DATA SOURCE: OECD online database on "Trade in Value Added" (known as TiVA), www.oecd.org.

the country's well-known prowess in information technology services, call centers, and the like.

Brazil and Indonesia defy simple classification. Their booming value-added exports were generated about 40 percent from the primary sector and 40 or 50 percent from the manufacturing sector.

For comparison, the bottom panel of Figure 28 shows the same decomposition for the G7. Most of these countries saw most of their (meager) value-added export growth coming from manufacturing, but services were notably dominant for Britain and the primary sector was critical for Canada.

Impact on Trade

Around the time when the G7's share of global income nosedived, North-South international commerce changed dramatically. In particular, the nature of trade between technologically advanced nations and select developing nations shifted. It began to look a lot more like the North-North trade that had dominated world flows since World War II.

Trade among rich nations has long involved a great deal of back-and-forth trade—namely lots of exports and imports of the same type of goods. For example, Germany exports machinery to France and France exports machinery to Germany. While some back-and-forth trade occurs in final goods (e.g., Fiats and Renaults in Europe) most of it is—and always has been—associated with intermediate goods. For example, trade in automobile parts has long been important between Canada and the United States. Figure 29 shows the share of trade between the listed pairs that is of the back-and-forth type (technically known as intra-industry trade, or IIT for short).

The key point to take away from Figure 29 is that after about 1985, back-and-forth trade picked up sharply between the original manufacturing giants and nearby developing countries. The focus is on the three G7 manufacturing giants—the United States, Japan, and

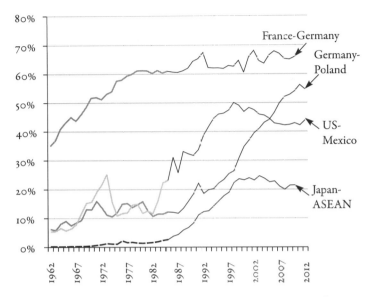

80%

70% — France-Germany

60% — Germany-Poland

50%

40% — US-Mexico

30%

20% — Japan-ASEAN

10%

0%

1962 1967 1972 1977 1982 1987 1992 1997 2002 2007 2012

FIGURE 29: North-South back-and-forth trade boomed starting around 1985.

It may seem strange that nations export a lot of the same sorts of goods that they import, but this has long been common among rich nations. The phenomenon is much easier to understand when thinking of it as indicative of factories that are spread across international borders. For example, Airbus planes are assembled in France, but the parts are made all over Europe. Some parts, for example, are made in France, exported to the Germany for further processing, and then re-exported to France for assembly into the final goods, say an A320.

Until the second unbundling got going in the late 1980s and early 1990s, most of this two-way trade happened among rich nations. The case of France and Germany, which is displayed in the chart, shows that in the 1970s over 70 percent of all French-German trade was of this intra-industry type. When factories started crossing North-South borders as part of the New Globalization (namely, globalization's second unbundling), the North-South trade flows started to resemble the North-North trade flows.

To illustrate this, the chart focuses on German, U.S., and Japanese trade with their main developing-nation offshoring partners, specifically Poland, Mexico, and members of the Association of South East Asian Nations (ASEAN). The abrupt change in trade flows clearly illustrates how the New Globalization has changed trade patterns. Many other pairs of trade flows between the G7 nations and the rapidly industrializing developing nations show a similar pattern but they are not included in the chart for the sake of clarity.

NOTE: The bilateral Intra-Industry Trade (IIT) indices shown are defined at the three-digit Standard International Trade Classification level of aggregation.

DATA SOURCE: UN Comtrade database, comtrade.un.org/db/.

Germany—since they accounted for about half of world manufacturing in 1990.

There are other ways of measuring this back-and-forth trade, but these tell a similar story. One measure that can usefully be calculated far into the past was developed by two Portuguese economists, João Amador and Sónia Cabral.[4] Their measures show that the global change in North-South trade patterns has not been observed in Africa or Latin America (apart from Mexico).[5] In short, the revolutionary changes in manufacturing enabled by ICT have, for the most part, completely bypassed South America and Africa.

The Amador-Cabral measure also shows that this new North-South trade is concentrated in relatively few sectors. Specifically, electrical machinery and electronics made up the lion's share of the level and the growth in the 1990s. What this tells us is that the off-shoring trend is actually rather narrowly focused on a handful of manufacturing sectors. The data is less clear for service sectors, but again the trend seems to be fairly focused for now. Chapter 10 suggests that this narrow concentration may widen out massively if technology produces near substitutes for physical presence (virtual presence and the like).

Impact on Developing Nation Policy

Evidence of the "revolution" comes from more than just the outcomes. We can detect it in the policy-setting behavior of nations. In fact, something rather peculiar happened at the start of Phase Four. Between the mid-1980s and the mid-1990s, governments in developing nations around the world reversed decades of opposition to freer trade and investment. They suddenly started to remove barriers to cross-border flows of goods, services, and investment that they had kept in place for decades. In short, protectionism seems to have become destructionism in the eyes of developing nations. This is odd.

Historically, all industrialization and growth takeoffs were government engineered—all except the first one (in the United Kingdom).

As economic historian Robert Allen writes in his excellent book *Global Economic History: A Very Short Introduction,* the other G7 nations caught up to the United Kingdom using the "standard set" of four policies: 1) unifying the domestic market with internal tariff elimination and building infrastructure; 2) erecting external tariff barriers to blunt the competitiveness of British manufactured goods; 3) chartering banks to finance industrial investments and stabilize the currency; and 4) establishing mass education to ease the farm-to-factory transition.[6]

The protectionist element of this industrialization formula was not based on the anthem of far-left thinkers. Promoting developing nation protectionism was the mainstream view. In 1958, for instance, one of the greatest modern free traders, Gottfried Haberler, penned the "Haberler Report" recommending that the General Agreement on Tariffs and Trade (GATT) allow developing nations to maintain high tariffs as a means of promoting their industrialization. This provided critical intellectual support for the GATT loophole (discussed in Chapter 2) that allowed developing nations to set and maintain high tariffs.

As history would have it, most developing nations implemented this standard four-pack once the yoke of colonialism was lifted in Phase Three. All this changed in Phase Four; protectionism became destructionism.

When the global value chain revolution started picking up steam, many developing nations realized that trade barriers were harming their chances of getting their share of the offshored jobs. The most obvious sign of this was the full-throated unilateral tariff cutting that began around 1990.

The top panel of Figure 30 shows the facts for broad regions. Some of this tariff liberalization, especially in Africa, was driven by International Monetary Fund (IMF) conditionality, but even nations not under such external pressure lowered rates. The bottom panel shows that the figures for Latin American nations are even

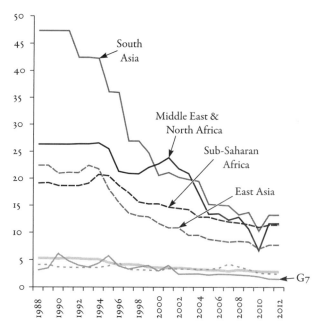

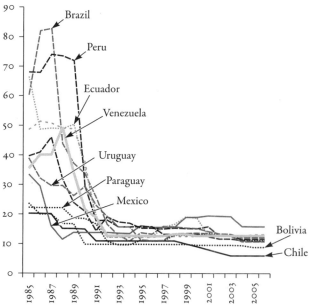

more dramatic. While most remain in the 10 percent range, the drop in the years around 1990 is nothing less than spectacular.

Why did so many developing-nation governments decide to liberalize so suddenly? And why did they all come to the decision at about the same time? The answer—according to the three-cascading-constraints view—is that tariffs that might have been pro-industry under the Old Globalization had become anti-industry under the New Globalization.

For example, when a developing nation joins an international production network, it typically imports a part and re-exports it after some processing. Any tariffs paid on the imported part add costs that directly harm the competitiveness of the importing nation. In this

---

FIGURE 30: Unilateral tariff liberalization by developing nations from 1985.

GATT talks between the 1940s and 1980s lowered developed nation tariffs to 5 percent or less on average. Developing nations, however, did not participate in this multilateral tariff cutting and so their tariffs were high into the 1980s. Indeed, for most of the post–World War II period, developing nations maintained tariffs that were five to ten times higher than those of what used to be called the "industrialized nations," shown as the G7 in the top panel.

Since about 1990, developing nations in regions around the world started to lower their tariffs. This was not a triumph of the GATT or WTO, nor was it fundamentally related to the rash of regional agreements signed among developing nations. The change was driven by conscious decisions by the nations themselves; quite simply, they decided that high tariffs were hindering their development rather than helping it.

In Latin America, especially South America, the tariff cuts look like a river falling off a cliff in the late 1980s or early 1990s (bottom panel). The official tariffs are now mostly around 9 or 10 percent, but since many of these nations have free trade agreements (which set tariffs to zero on bilateral trade) with their major trading partners, very little trade in the region is subject to these official rates.

NOTE: In the chart, the G7 is represented by the tariff averages of the United States, the European Union, and Japan.

DATA SOURCES: World Bank data for top panel; Inter-American Development Bank (IDB) for bottom panel.

way, tariffs on imported parts and components make it less likely that the developing nation will be invited to join the production network in the first place. As the rationale for the tariffs was to attract industrial jobs, the rise of North-South offshoring undermined the case for high tariffs in developing nations. Seeing this, most developing nations decided that—in the era of North-South offshoring—protectionism had become destructionism as far as industrialization was concerned.

The volte-face on openness policy, however, extended to more than just import tariffs.

For decades, developing nations had a love / hate relationship with foreign direct investment (FDI). They liked the "foreign direct" part for the extra technology it brought, and they liked the "investment" part for the way it boosted their capital accounts. What they worried about was the heavy hand of multinational corporations on their economies. For almost all developing nations, the balancing of these pros and cons produced regulation of FDI. Often the rules were explicitly anti-FDI. Mexico, for example, had a whole raft of regulations aimed at thwarting efforts of U.S. companies to buy Mexican companies or set up companies in Mexico that would compete with native firms.

This attitude changed radically in the late 1980s. The evidence comes in the form of international agreements known as bilateral investment treaties (BITs). These are, in essence, concessions to rich-nation firms seeking to invest in the developing nation that signs the BIT. The concessions come in the form of disciplines that govern interactions between private foreign investors and host governments. For the most part, the provisions in these agreements constrain the developing nation's sovereignty.

For example, most BITs limit the developing nation's ability to impose controls on capital flows so investing firms can get money in or out of the nation freely. They also give foreign investors the right to submit disputes to international arbitration rather than local courts. These are the so-called Investor State Dispute Settlement provisions that have recently become controversial in the United States and Europe in the context of the Trans-Pacific Partnership agreement and the Trans-Atlantic Trade and Investment Partnership. The main arbitrator used is the International Centre for Settlement of Investment Disputes, which is located in Washington, D.C.

The remarkable thing about the signing of BITs lies in the synchronicity and suddenness with which developing nations changed their minds. Before 1985 almost none of them found that the economics gains outweighed the sovereignty loss; afterward almost all of them did. As Figure 31 shows, the number of new BITs exploded in the late 1980s and early 1990s.

The list of nations that had signed a BIT expanded rapidly from 1985. In 1985, there were eighty-six BIT signers; by 2000 the number had doubled, almost entirely due to the increase in developing nations that joined the trend. Many of them signed BITs with all the major FDI emitters (the big EU nations, the United States, and Japan) and thus the number of new BITs rose much more sharply than the number of new signers. The flow of new agreements has slacked off since most of the BITs that could have been signed between economically significant nations have already been signed.

The exchange of sovereignty for participation in international production networks can also be seen in the marked change in the type of provisions that have been included in trade agreements since the early 1990s.

Around the late 1980s and early 1990s, the nature of North-South bilateral trade deals started to change. Before this, most such agreements signed by developing nations were "shallow" in the sense that they only addressed tariffs. After 1990 or so, many developing nations signed "deep" agreements with advanced-technology nations—especially the United States, the European Union, and Japan. These new-style agreements are not deep in the "profound" sense of the

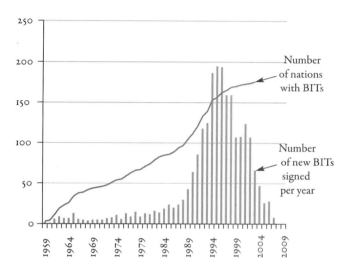

FIGURE 31: The explosion in Bilateral Investment Treaties from 1990.

At about the time that developing nations started lowering their tariffs unilaterally, they also started signing "bilateral investment treaties." These might be thought of as lopsided since they are basically a way of ensuring the property rights of foreign investors. Developing nations, however, came to see them as win-win. The investment-receiving nations—mostly developing nations—wanted to attract the jobs and factories that were being offshored as part of globalization's second unbundling. The G7 firms doing the offshoring wanted the assurances that their investments would be safe, and G7 nations were happy to sign treaties that did just this.

While BITs were known since the 1950s, they caught on like wildfire in the 1990s. There are now more than 3,000 such agreements in place covering almost all major investor-investee links globally. In principle, a BIT works in both directions but since foreign direct investment mostly flows from G7 nations to developing nations (and other G7 nations), the BITs do more to encourage North-to-South investment than South-to-North or South-to-South investment.

More recently, some of the rapidly industrializing nations who resisted signing BITs—India and China, for instance—have begun to see the merits since Indian and Chinese firms are now rapidly expanding their investments in G7 nations and some developing nations. In essence, they are moving away from being "factory" economies and toward being "headquarter" economies.

SOURCES: International Centre for Settlement of Investment Disputes (ICSID) data on BITs; chart adapted from Baldwin and Lopez-Gonzales, "Supply-Chain Trade: A Portrait of Global Patterns and Several Testable Hypotheses" (2013), Figure 3.

word. They are deep in the sense that they affect matters deep inside national borders; they go way beyond tariff cutting.

As with the BITs, these provisions typically lock in certain reforms in the developing nations but have little impact on the developed nation's laws and practices. They are basically assurances—like BITs—that make the developing nation more business friendly to firms from developed nations.

But what do these provisions touch on? Since 2011, the World Trade Organization (WTO) has gathered data on the content of RTAs, categorizing all the provisions into fifty-two different types. Examples of provisions that are plausibly linked to international production networks are given in Table 5.

The most notable, in terms of underpinning the development of global value chains, are the provisions of free movement of capital (getting investment in and out of the country), services (ensuring local availability of world-class "connective" services such as telecoms, shipping, and customs clearance), and intellectual property protection (guarding the know-how the G7 firms bring along with the jobs sent offshore).

Looking at globalization's impact on national economies hides one of the New Globalization's most positive effects—its impact on humanity's poorest members.

Impact on Poverty

One of the most disturbing aspects of the Old Globalization was its association with rising poverty. A standard measure of poverty—one of the few that is available for a wide range of nations and years—counts the number of people earning less than $2 a day. Since $2 buys much less in, say, Singapore, than it does in Dakar, the measure is corrected for local prices.

As Figure 32 shows, the number of people living under this poverty line rose from 1980 (when World Bank data begins) to 1993 by about 370 million. That is an appalling number, but globalization

TABLE 5
Examples of deep RTA provisions in the WTO database.

Provision name	Description of provision
Customs	Provision of information; publication on the Internet of new laws and regulations; training.
State trading firms	Establishment or maintenance of an independent competition authority; nondiscrimination regarding production and marketing conditions; provision of information.
State aid	Assessment of anticompetitive behavior; annual reporting on the value and distribution of state aid given; provision of information upon request.
Public procurement	Progressive opening of government purchases to foreign tenders; national treatment and / or nondiscrimination principle; publication of laws and regulations on the Internet.
TRIMs	Stands for "Trade Related Investment Measures": provisions concerning requirements for local content and export performance of foreign direct investment.
GATS	Stands for "General Agreement on Trade in Services": liberalization of trade in services.
TRIPs	Stands for "Trade Related Intellectual Property": harmonization of standards; enforcement; national treatment, most-favored nation treatment with respect to intellectual property rights.
Competition policy	Maintenance of measures to proscribe anticompetitive business conduct; harmonization of competition laws; establishment or maintenance of an independent competition authority.
International property rights	Accession to international treaties that provide stronger intellectual property rights (IPR) protection than those in the WTO.

Provision name	Description of provision
Investment	Information exchange; development of legal frameworks; harmonization and simplification of procedures; national treatment; establishment of mechanism for the settlement of disputes.
Capital movement	Liberalization of capital movement; prohibition of new restrictions.

Regional trade agreements between G7 nations and developing nations now routinely include provisions that make it easier and safer for G7 firms to move parts of their production network to the developing nation signing the agreement. In the world of trade experts, such agreements are called "deep" RTAs since they include provisions that reach deep inside national boundaries to discipline policy or, for example, regulation and intellectual property.

DATA SOURCE: World Trade Organization (WTO) data.

cannot be blamed for all or even most of the rise. Populations climbed rapidly in nations that were already poor, and many of these poor nations had governments that pursued poverty-inducing or poverty-sustaining policies. Oxford economist Paul Collier, for example, writes: "The countries at the bottom coexist with the twenty-first century, but their reality is the fourteenth century: civil war, plague, ignorance."[7] These are not nations where the global value chain revolution's magic is working. Practical, productivity-enhancing knowledge is not flowing from G7 firms to these dreadfully poor nations.

Be that as it may, one remarkable feature of Figure 32 is that the trend was overturned in sync with globalization's "changing of the guards." Since the Old Globalization turned into the New Globalization, the nations that the World Bank classifies as upper-middle-income countries witnessed a miraculous drop in poverty. Something like 650 million people in these nations rose above the $2 a day line.

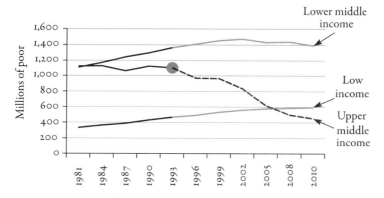

FIGURE 32: People in poverty, by income class, 1980 to 2010.

The chart shows the number of people living in abject poverty in three groups of countries. Lower-middle-income countries, upper-middle-income countries, and low-income countries.

The measure used is the World Bank poverty line, which is $3.10 per day.

The key points are that the generalized rise in poverty breaks around 1990, but only in the upper-middle-income nations. These include many of the rapidly industrializing nations that benefitted directly from offshoring and those that benefitted from the commodity super-cycle that this triggered.

DATA SOURCE: World Bank DataBank with author's calculations.

The upper-middle-income category includes most of the R11 nations—and most important, it includes China. The other standout member of the R11 is India. It falls under the lower-middle-income classification and its growth is largely responsible for the slowdown in the rise of poverty in these nations since 1993. The situation in the low-income countries, which have generally been untouched by the rise of offshoring and global value chains, continues to deteriorate.

BOX 4: SUMMARY OF PHASE FOUR

Phase Four caps a short stack of really radical transformations in the nature of globalization. In Phase One, globalization consisted of the gradual "humanization" of the planet. Globalization in Phase Two meant something quite different. The Agricultural Revolution allowed humans to settle down in villages, cities, and eventually civilizations, so globalization in this phase meant "localizing" the world economy.

Phase Three radically changed globalization yet again when the steam revolution launched a century-long sequence of developments that made humans the masters of intercontinental distances. Falling cost boosted trade, but moving goods hardly made the world flat—quite the contrary. By the late twentieth century, two-thirds of economic activity was clustered in just seven nations—the G7. Manufacturing was even more concentrated. To keep complex industrial processes working smoothly, manufacturing processes were microclustered inside industrial plants located in the G7 nations.

Phase Four has seen the economic foundation of this microclustering crumble as the ICT revolution lowered the cost of coordinating complex processes across great distances. Once it was possible to separate manufacturing processes internationally, firms pursued the option with gusto. They started moving labor-intensive stages of production from high-wage nations to low-wage nations.

Globalization was transformed by this North-South offshoring since advanced know-how accompanied the offshoring stages of production. It is these new knowledge flows that put the "New" in the New Globalization. They are what allowed a small number of developing nations to industrialize with a rapidity entirely out of line with historical experience, and this, in turn, reshaped the world economy in Phase Four.

Essential Outcomes

The key impacts of the New Globalization were:

- The G7 nations deindustrialized while a handful of developing nations industrialized.
- The effects were surprisingly concentrated geographically.
- The rapidly industrializing nations experienced spectacular growth takeoffs.
- The soaring income growth in the rapid industrializers set off a boom in commodity exports and prices known as the "commodity super-cycle."
- The combination of rapid growth in developing nation and stagnate growth in G7 produced the Great Convergence; rich nations' share of world GDP is back to where it was at the start of WWI.
- The nature of trade between the G7 and many developing nations changed dramatically.
- Almost all developing nations massively liberalized their policies on trade, investment, capital, services, and intellectual property.

At the base of all these gigantic changes was the evening out of the very uneven distribution of productive know-how that had emerged in Phase Three.

PART II

Extending the Globalization Narrative

People don't see the world around them in all its glorious and riotous detail. It is far too complex for that. They use what Nobel Prize–winning economist Douglass North calls "mental models." That is to say, people use abstractions and simplified thought-patterns to streamline reality down to something they can get their minds around.

Careful thinkers are especially reliant on mental models. As Karl Popper phrased it in *The Open Universe,* "Science may be described as the art of systematic over-simplification—the art of discerning what we may, with advantage, omit." The problem, as physicist Stephen Hawking noted, is that "when such a model is successful at explaining events, we tend to attribute to it, and to the elements and concepts that constitute it, the quality of reality or absolute truth."[1] Usually, this is all for the good. Without shared mental models, societies would find it nigh on impossible to coordinate and cooperate.

This cooperation-facilitating feature of shared mental models is why getting the model right is essential. Governments and businesses are forced to make choices without really knowing what their actions or inactions will lead to. This is not due to a lack of knowledge or understanding; it is just a reality of the human condition. Human events are too complex to forecast beyond anything but the shortest horizons, yet decisions must be made with an eye to the distant future. Shared mental models, sometimes called shared narratives, give decision makers the courage to act in the face of such uncertainty and give people the confidence to believe in these decisions.

Chapter 4 looks at the mental models commonly used to understand globalization's Phases Two and Three before describing an extension of this thinking (the "three cascading constraints" view) that makes it easy to understand how and why Phase Four's brand of globalization differs so much from that of Phase Three. Why, in other words, the "Old Globalization" created the Great Divergence while the New Globalization created the Great Convergence. Chapter 5 then proceeds to highlight what is really new about the New Globalization.

CHAPTER 4

A Three-Cascading-Constraints
View of Globalization

Economic activity is very unevenly distributed across the globe, across nations, and even within cities. But this is not the most obvious outcome. We see firms setting up in cities where rents and wages are high, traffic is horrible, and taxes are burdensome. We see people moving from low-cost rural regions with clear air to high-cost urban areas with eye-watering pollution. The explanation for such "uphill" clustering must lie in the fact that distance really matters. Yet distance matters differently for different things.

A core contention of this book is that it is essential to distinguish distance's impact on the difficulty of moving three types of things: goods, ideas, and people. And it is essential to pay attention to the order in which they fell historically. This chapter's goal is to present a mental model that accounts for the Old Globalization's impact on the world while also accounting for why the New Globalization's impact has been so different.

The cost of moving all three things were very high before globalization began. These costs were "constraints" in the sense that all three forced consumption and production to be near each other. The costs (that is, constraints) were relaxed in order. The cost of moving goods came down first, followed by the cost of moving ideas. The third constraint, the cost of moving people, has yet to be relaxed.

Following this logic, the chapter explains the three-cascading-constraints perspective by walking through, in sequence, the situation where all three constraints were binding (before 1820), the situation where only two were binding (up to 1990), and finally, today's situation where only one is binding.

Three Binding Constraints: Pre-Steam

When sailing ships, river barges, horse carts, and camels were the best means of getting from point A to point B, moving anything anywhere was challenging. Depending on the century and region, the hindrances of poor transportation technology were multiplied by banditry, high taxes, government monopolies, or outright prohibitions.

There was little difference in this era among the costs of shifting the three types of things because goods, ideas, and people all moved by the same means. Still, moving people was especially dangerous. Murder and mayhem on the high roads and high seas were constant threats. In one famous incident, Julius Caesar was captured by Cilician pirates in transit between Rome and Rhodes. Held for almost two months, he was released only after the payment of a large ransom. As an aside, readers may be cheered by this story's Hollywood ending: upon release, Caesar hunted down his captors and hanged them all.

Moving goods was not much easier, but at least goods could be passed along a chain of local traders. For example, few traders traveled the whole Silk Road; most trade passed through a succession of middlemen.

Moving ideas meant shipping writings or sending experts who could explain the ideas. This was slow. Buddhism, for example, emerged in India around 500 BCE and took two centuries to arrive in the Far East. This situation was much the same a thousand years later, as the example related by Marco Polo shows (see Box 5).

All three constraints mattered in this pre-globalization era, but the high cost of moving goods held the place of honor. The difficulty of moving goods was what really held globalization back—that is to say, poor transportation was the "binding" constraint. As we shall see, this constraint dictated the globe's economic geography.

BOX 5: MARCO POLO AND KNOWLEDGE CROSSING THIRTEENTH-CENTURY BORDERS

Marco Polo's uncles were invited by Kublai Khan to visit China in the 1200s. Intrigued by their stories, the Great Khan sent the Polos back with a letter to the pope asking for a hundred Europeans who could teach his court about Europe's leading ideas, the so-called seven arts of grammar, rhetoric, logic, geometry, arithmetic, music, and astronomy. Curious about Christianity, he also asked for some sacred oil from the lamp of Jerusalem.

After several years of delay in their home port of Venice, the Polos again set off to China, this time with the young Macro Polo and some priests in tow. The trip, which started in 1271, took three years. Many of their fellow travelers were slain or enslaved. The priests, who abandoned the voyage out of fear, never reached China; the lamp oil and the Polos did. *The Travels of Marco Polo* does not relate whether Kublai Khan ever gained the knowledge he asked for a decade earlier.

The difficulties of the return voyage bring into focus what "high transport cost" meant back then. The voyage, which was by sea, took two years. Of the hundreds of passengers who joined the convoy from South China, the Polos were among the eighteen who made it alive.

Impact: Production / Consumption Bundling and Slow Growth

The tyranny of distance in this era was so severe that the production of goods had to be spatially bundled with consumers (Figure 33). All but a slender fraction of humans were engaged in agriculture and lived in largely self-sufficient, village-size economies. To avoid having to move goods to consumers, each locale had its own butcher, baker, and candlestick maker, so to speak. Many goods were homemade.

The high cost of moving ideas and people who understood those ideas mattered in a different way. This pre-globalization world had no factories in the modern sense. Although some towns and regions

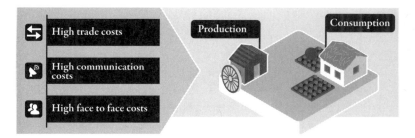

FIGURE 33: In the pre-globalized world, production and consumption were bundled geographically.

Before modern globalization, the world economy was "flat." Economic activity mainly meant agriculture, so people were poor, societies were agrarian, and economic activity was organized around innumerable villages all across the globe. Trade happened but it was for the rich.

There were exceptionally large cities that traded a lot before the nineteenth century, but they were exceptional. For instance, China's Grand Canal facilitated long-distance trade that helped supply northern Chinese cities with southern Chinese food. And Rome kept a million mouths fed with Mediterranean grain.

For most people, however, consumption meant locally made food, clothing, and shelter. Things made further than walking distance from home were prohibitively expensive given the high costs and risks of trade.

specialized in the production of some goods—like porcelain and silk cloth in China—manufacturing was what today we would call handicrafts, or at best cottage industry.

Given the high cost of moving ideas, the resulting spatial dispersion of production dampened innovation—both on the demand side and supply side. A brilliant idea meant little if only a few dozen families could exploit it, so demand for innovation was modest. Innovation flourishes when many people look at similar problems from dissimilar angles, so spatially separating problem-solvers across many villages hindered the supply of innovations.

Without innovation, living standards stagnated. Put another way, there was no agglomeration, no innovation, and thus no growth (Figure 34).

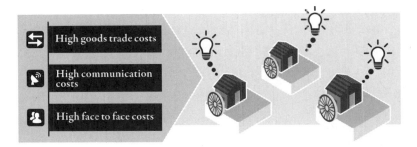

FIGURE 34: Scattered production meant isolated innovation and slow growth.

As people were tied to the land and production was bundled with people (due to high trade costs), manufacturing was small scale and widely dispersed.

Given how difficult it was to move ideas and the people who understood those ideas, the scattering of manufacturing deadened progress. Innovations remained few and they spread only slowly, if at all. The compass, for example, was invented in China and used for navigation from around 1000 AD. It took more than two centuries for this knowledge to come to European navigators.

Communication was so difficult that important ideas could be and were forgotten. Chapter 1 discussed how writing disappeared for centuries from Ancient Greece and India in the early part of the second millennium BCE. More recently, knowledge rolled backward in Europe during the centuries following the downfall of the Roman Empire in the fifth century CE. Indeed this is why the return of knowledge to Europe is called the Renaissance—French for "rebirth"—although more accurately it should be called "remembering."

As Figure 35 shows, there was virtually zero per capita income growth in the first millennium CE. In fact, West European growth was negative from the height of the Roman Empire to 1000 CE. Growth started in the first half of the second millennium—but only in Europe. And this growth is hardly what we would call growth today. European incomes grew at just 0.03 percent per year for those seventeen centuries—that converts to a rise of 3 percent income growth *per century*. Asian growth was even slower. Asian incomes rose just 25 percent during the whole seventeen centuries covered in Figure 35.

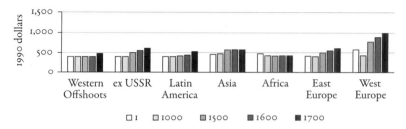

FIGURE 35: GDP per capita stagnated in most parts of the world from year 1 to 1700. Nobel Prize–winning economist Robert Solow taught us that human ingenuity is what fuels long-run growth. New ideas, new products, and new ways of arranging work directly boost output and income per worker. The inventions also lift incomes indirectly by making it worthwhile to invest in productivity-enhancing machines and skills.

This is why incomes languished in the pre-globalized world. The innovations needed to fuel growth were rare and spread slowly.

An exception was Europe after 1500 where a combination of factors encouraged clustering and trade that in turn stimulated innovation—although at a very slow pace.

DATA SOURCE: Maddison database (2009 version).

Mental Models for Pre-Globalization Trade

Despite all these difficulties, trade did happen. The earliest civilization in Sumer (Babylonia), for example, had an abundance of grain, mud, and straw, but little else. Wood, stone, and metals all came from upstream or downstream lands. Right up till the proto-globalization era (roughly 1450 to 1776, as discussed in Chapter 1), this was the typical trade pattern. As Moses Finley puts it in his book *The World of Odysseus,* "Things changed hands because each needed what the other had . . . imports alone motivated trade, never exports. There was never a need to export as such, only the necessity of having the proper goods for the countergift when an import was unavoidable." Box 6 provides an example.

The fact that trade was limited to things that were not available locally led to a conceptualization of trade that sounds quite pecu-

BOX 6: TRADING FOR MISSING ESSENTIALS IN 1000 BCE

The Egyptian "Wenamun Papyrus," which has been dated to around 1000 BCE, illustrates the motivations—and challenges—of pre-globalization trade.

The papyrus tells the tale of a priest who was sent to Lebanon by his high priest. The mission was to get "timber for the great and august barge of Amon-Re, king of gods." The priest, traveling by ship, was robbed in route but continued to Byblos to ask for the wood regardless. Since the local king wanted to be paid for the wood, the priest sent back to Egypt for more trade goods to seal the deal. The trade goods were eventually delivered almost a year later. The papyrus lists them as consisting of jars of gold and silver, royal linen, veils, 500 ox-hides, and 500 ropes.

liar from the standpoint of today's thinking. As Doug Irwin explains in his masterful book *Against the Tide: An Intellectual History of Free Trade,* the early European mental model for making sense of trade was the Doctrine of Universal Economy: "The doctrine held that Providence deliberately scattered resources and goods around the world unequally to promote commerce between different regions."

Some adherents to the doctrine condemned trade and traders on moral grounds—accusing them of what we would call rent-seeking behavior. Buying low and selling high was immoral since the trader's own labor was not engaged in the making of the goods. Others praised trade as part of the divine plan to induce economic intercourse across the universal fellowship of humanity.

As the Middle Ages progressed, the European conceptualization of trade shifted from the divine to the bottom line. The mental model that accompanied this shift was called "mercantilism."

Mercantilism—which was ascendant in Europe in the sixteenth, seventeenth, and eighteenth centuries—considered exports to be good and imports to be bad. In those days, when national treasuries really held treasure, a trade surplus was one of the few ways of adding to the pile (exporting more than importing meant that the inflow of gold and silver exceeded the outflow). According to contemporary thinking, this was a positive from the national perspective.

Land was the fundamental source of a nation's wealth in these times. The normal procedure for increasing a nation's wealth was for the king to strap on his sword, jump on a horse, and lead his armies in conquest of his neighbor's land. A large stockpile of gold facilitated this and other forms of statecraft such as paying off would-be invaders, inducing alliances, and the like. Trade, in the mercantilist mind-set, had little or nothing to do with individual economic well-being.

The second maxim of mercantilism was never import manufactured goods that you can make domestically. The motive was not so much the promotion of manufacturing per se—this was pre–Industrial Revolution, after all. Rather, contemporaneous writers stressed the positive employment effects. In England, rural laborers who had been cast out by the Enclosure Movement were of particular concern.

Two Binding Constraints: First Unbundling

The steam revolution set off a century-long chain of events that transformed the world. The books written on this subject could fill the British Library Reading Room from floor to ceiling, but when it comes to globalization, the important point is that it was a rebellion against the tyranny of distance.

Steam-powered and then diesel-powered ships had an evolutionary impact on the cost of sea travel. Eventually the evolutionary steps added up to a revolution, but in the end, ships were visiting ports as they had since the Bronze Age. The impact of railroads was more of a metamorphosis. With few exceptions, the vast interiors of the world's continents were economically isolated by the vagaries of land travel. With railroads, they were open for business.

Along with the lower cost of shipping goods, faster and safer transportation meant lower costs of moving people and ideas. People could and did migrate in massive numbers. But travel was incredibly slow, risky, and expensive. For example, most European and Asians who moved to the New World never saw their homelands again.

Most ideas moved in the old way—via books and experts—but this period did see a real change with the invention of the telegraph. By the late 1800s, most nations were connected by telegraph lines. Goods and people still had to travel by boat, rail, or road, but now ideas could travel by wire.

The telegraph had enormous effects on societies, but it did little to challenge the locality of most know-how. Long-distance communication remained extremely expensive—especially internationally. The word "telegraphic" was invented to describe the way people compacted thoughts in an effort to limit the number of words in a telegram. Telephone calls were better and cheaper per word than telegrams, but phone calls were still horribly expensive.

Given the difficulty of communicating complex know-how, the telegraph and later the telephone did almost nothing to erode the wisdom of viewing globalization as constrained exclusively by trade costs. Telecommunications remained one of those things that could—to paraphrase Karl Popper—be usefully ignored.

Impact: Booming Trade and the Great Divergence

The lower cost of moving goods relaxed the key constraint that held production and consumption closely bundled. Once this separation was feasible, the global economic differences—the starting point for the Doctrine of Universal Economy—made trade profitable. As

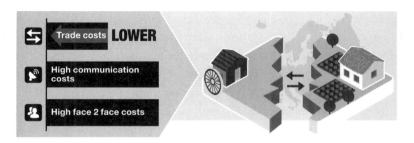

FIGURE 36: Lower trade cost allowed the unbundling of production and consumption.

The cost of moving goods over great distances fell radically in the nineteenth century due to revolutionary advances in transportation technology and the relative peace that came with Pax Britannica. This made it economical for people to buy goods that were made far away.

Once this unbundling of production and consumption was practicable, the big international price differences made it profitable, and long-distance trade took off.

The booming trade yielded new opportunities that encouraged nations to expand their most competitive sectors. It also yielded new competition that forced nations out of the sectors they were less good at. As a result, the world economy became much less "flat"; national economies tended to specialize in producing things they were relatively good at.

people started to buy goods made far away, nations increasingly specialized in their most competitive sectors and long-distance trade took off. This was globalization's first unbundling—the physical separation of production and consumption (Figure 36).

A strange thing happened when long-distance transportation became practical and affordable. The world's economic geography became lumpier, not smoother. Manufacturing shifted from villages and cottages to factories and industrial districts. Distance, it seemed, started to matter in a new way. It is instructive to look more closely at this seemingly paradoxical outcome.

The ability to sell to world markets shifted the advantage to firms operating at previously unknown scales of production. These large-scale manufacturing techniques were (and still are) highly complex.

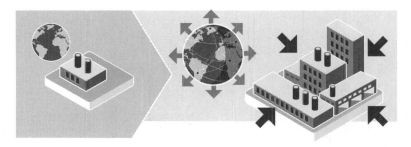

FIGURE 37: As markets expanded globally, production clustered locally.

Sales soared as trade costs fell, and this favored complicated, large-scale manufacturing techniques. Since communication was difficult and expensive, firms "microclustered" the intricate production processes into factories as a way of making the necessary coordination easier, cheaper, and more reliable.

In other words, industry clustered locally even as it dispersed internationally because trade costs fell while communications costs did not.

This complexity and the high cost of communicating over distance, had big implications for the spatial organization of production. As it turned out, managing the new industrial complexity was easier, cheaper, and surer when all stages of production were gathered in tight proximity. Factories, in other words, were created to economize on the cost of moving ideas and people, not goods (although there were other factors such as the need to be near energy sources).

To put it differently, low trade costs did not make the world flat. Rather, relaxing the transportation constraint brought the world up against a second constraint—the communication constraint (Figure 37).

As history would have it, the Group of Seven (G7) nations specialized in manufacturing, which launched them on a happy helix. Industrial agglomeration fostered innovation, which boosted competitiveness, which in turn promoted further industrial agglomeration in G7 nations. The innovation also triggered income growth as Figure 38 shows. The helix twirled upward when the resulting income boosted market size and the bigger markets led to more agglomeration, innovation, and competitiveness.

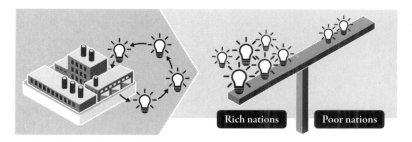

FIGURE 38: Industrial clustering boosted G7 innovation; incomes diverged as ideas stayed local.

The crowding together of large-scale manufacturing ignited the "bonfire" of cumulative innovation, and this in turn lit the fuse on modern economic growth. But since it was still expensive to move ideas and people, the accumulation of know-how in the world economy became very lopsided. Industrial innovations tended to stay local, so the North's pile of new knowledge began to tower over the South's pile. This imbalance tilted the playing field even further in the North's favor. Correspondingly, Northern incomes soared above Southern incomes.

To put it sharply, reducing the cost of moving goods while the cost of moving ideas remained high was the root cause of the "Great Divergence."

In the face of this knowledge advancement, the communication constraint started to matter hugely. Since know-how moved internationally with great difficulty, G7 productivity gains stayed national. This localization of newly created know-how yielded—in just a handful of decades—enormous gaps between incomes and wages in the North (mostly Western Europe, North America, and Japan) and the South (developing nations).

Mental Models for Globalization's First Acceleration

In the decades bracketing 1800, Victorian Britain was putting together one of history's most powerful empires. But something was different this time. For thousands of years, land was the primary source of national wealth. A nation got stronger by taking more land and diverting the surplus homeward.

Britain did its share of land-grabbing, but its power rose not by land alone. Its national wealth and military strength boomed as it shifted out of agriculture and into industry—a shift made possible by trade. This was not how Alexander the Great, Genghis Khan, or even Henry VIII did it. A changed world demanded a new set of abstractions and simplified thought-patterns to understand the new complexities. As it turned out, the new mental model was provided by a wealthy stockbroker named David Ricardo.

In his 1817 book *On the Principles of Political Economy and Taxation,* Ricardo presented a streamlined view of the world that proved so useful and so seductive that it is still at the heart of today's traditional thinking about globalization. His core simplifications were to take nations as the proper unit of analysis, to conceptualize international commerce as consisting only of trade in goods, and to view the direction of trade as driven by what he called "comparative advantage" (often referred to as competitive advantage in popular writing).[1]

In plain English, "comparative advantage" means that some nations are better at making some things than others. If no trade were allowed, smugglers would buy products in the nations that were particularly good at making them and sell them in nations that were particularly bad at making them. The smugglers would then return with their packs filled with goods for which the ranking of national competencies were reversed.

Free trade is just legalized smuggling, so the principle of comparative advantage—which could equally be called the smuggler's principle—explains why nations trade and why all nations benefit from trade.

Ricardo's thought-paradigm—"do what you do best and import the rest"—also explains the impact on national production patterns. Fresh competition from imports tends to discourage production in sectors where the nation is not particularly competent. Simultaneously, fresh export opportunities encourage production in the nation's best sectors. In this way, the "smuggling" induces nations to shift productive resources into their most competitive sectors. The result is higher productivity and incomes—and this for all the nations participating in trade.

The globalization narrative, in this line of thinking, is a story of how falling trade costs led to more trade, and this greater volume of trade improved global production efficiency since it allowed each nation to focus on producing the products that they were especially good at making.

Even in Ricardo's day, far more than goods crossed borders. There were important migrations from the Old World to the New World, multinational companies like the East India Company operated globally, and international lending was commonplace. Ricardo swept all those under the rug as things that could, with advantage, be omitted.

Good Globalization Writers Use Ricardo

Most discussions of globalization start with a list of eye-popping facts documenting heightened international flows of capital, labor, services, firms, technology, ideas, culture, and goods. When the discourse gets beyond description and turns to analysis, the prime narrative almost always switches to a focus on trade in goods. Globalization is viewed as driven by reductions in all manner of trade hindrances.

The reason for this intellectual bait-and-switch is best related with a joke told by countless economics professors:

> One evening, a well-dressed businessman comes across a disheveled economist under a streetlight searching for something on the pavement. "What did you lose? Can I help you?" the businessman asks. "I lost my keys," replies the economist, obviously a drink or

two beyond the tipping side of tipsy. In response to the business-man's next query, "Where did you lose them?" the economist says: "I lost them over there in the parking lot, but there's no light there, so I decided to look here."

And make no mistake, plenty of illumination is necessary.

Globalization is affected by driving forces that affect things (prices) that affect other things (demand and production of goods) that affect yet more things (demand for productive factors) that affect things that really matter (wages, jobs, and incomes), but these loop back to affect the first two things and the driving forces themselves.

While many popular globalization writers rely on superficial correlations to avoid deep thinking, authors who use an analytic framework end up using some elaboration of Ricardo's conceptualization, such as those worked out by Eli Heckscher, Bertil Ohlin, Paul Krugman, Elhanan Helpman, Gene Grossman, and Marc Melitz.

Adding Agglomeration to Ricardo

In Ricardo's conceptualization (as in the Doctrine of Universal Economy), the national differences in competencies are assumed rather than explained.

To account for the really broad-brush facts of globalization's first unbundling, it is necessary to adjoin a few more elements to the Ricardian picture. The formal brushstokes were added by Nobel Prize–winning economist Paul Krugman and his coauthors Oxford professor Tony Venables and Kyoto professor Masahisa Fujita. The key ideas of the "new economic geography," from their book *The Spatial Economy,* are explained in Chapter 6, but the main lines of logic can be extracted from the historical account in Chapter 2.

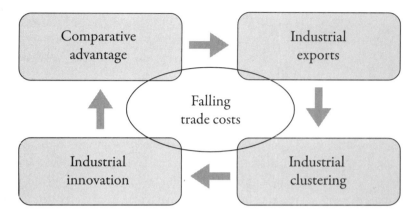

FIGURE 39: Dynamic comparative advantage: trade, comparative advantage, innovation, and growth are all entwined.

Globalization's first acceleration (that is, the first unbundling) turned the world's league tables on their head. The previously poor and backward nations in the European peninsula of the Eurasian landmass came to dominate the global economy.

The static version of Ricardo's conceptualization cannot explain this story, but it has been extended to include agglomeration and growth effects that can. The details are in the next chapter, but the basic ideas are simple to explain with the diagram—starting with the diagram's southeast box ("industrial clustering").

The clustering—that is to say, agglomeration—of industry in a nation promotes new thinking and new inventions (shown in southwest box, "Industrial innovation"). The innovation then strengthens the nation's competitiveness in the sector (shown in northwest box, "Comparative advantage"). The next step— according to the principle of comparative advantage—is that the heightened comparative advantage leads to more exports and more production. The crank comes around full circle when this extra production generates additional industrial clustering.

The basic Ricardian logic focuses on the "who exports what" question. The answer ultimately rests on its assumption of national competencies that are taken as given. The first addition is to pose a mental model where national competencies are both the outcome of and the cause of trade. It starts with a two-way link between industrial competencies and industrial agglomeration (Figure 39).

In the competencies-cause-agglomeration direction, the vehicle is comparative advantage. According to the usual Ricardian logic, the nation with the greatest relative efficiency exports the good. As trade gets freer, the nation shifts resources into this sector and production rises. The freer trade has the opposite effect on the same sector in other nations; more imports lead to less production. The result is that freer trade leads to the agglomeration of world production, sector by sector.

The logical "return trip"—from agglomeration to competencies— relies on many "vehicles." Clustering large chunks of industry in a small geographic area tends to improve efficiency and thus boost the nation's competency in industry. The reasons range from scale economies—whereby longer production runs and denser supplier networks reduce per-unit costs—to the faster innovation that comes when many people puzzle over problems together. This is how agglomeration affects industrial competencies.

An illustration of this unbeatable combination of agglomeration, innovation, and cheap transport can be seen in the Albert Bridge in Adelaide (Figure 40). Built in 1859, the entire structure was manufactured in England and shipped 22,000 kilometers—this being cheaper than manufacturing it locally.

The hyperconcentration of industrial activity in the developed economies, however, came at a cost. Most stages of production had to be done with G7 high-cost labor—at least for the two-thirds of global manufacturing that took place in G7 nations in, say, the 1980s.

Given the immense wage gaps, unbundling the factories and re-locating labor-intensive stages to developing nations would have lowered costs. However, due to high communication costs, it was uneconomic except for very modular production processes such as clothing and microelectronics. Coordinating complex activities over long distances was not yet feasible—a reality that the revolution in information and communication technology (ICT) would disrupt.

FIGURE 40: Albert Bridge in Adelaide, Australia, shipped from the United Kingdom in the 1850s.

The dynamo of scale economies, rising industrial competitiveness, and transportation improvements led to quite extreme concentrations of production. For example, the Albert Bridge was what would today be called a "prefab," having been made in England and shipped to Australia for assembly. While visiting the University of Adelaide, where this book was started, I crossed the Albert Bridge daily.

SOURCE: Photo courtesy of State Library of South Australia, Adelaide Views and Albert Bridge Collections B 4729. This image is from 1928.

One Binding Constraint: Second Unbundling

In the late 1980s, revolutionary advances in the transmission, storage, and processing of information launched a progression of changes that drastically lowered communication costs. As Chapter 3 described in detail the price of telephone calls plummeted, faxes became standard, cellular phone usage exploded, and the telecommunication network became denser, more reliable, and cheaper. In the 1990s, the Internet lowered the cost of moving ideas even further.

Two other trends interacted with cheaper communication costs—the spectacular fall in the price of computing power (Moore's Law) and the equally spectacular rise in fiber-optic transmission rates and bandwidth (Gilder's Law). Today, it is almost costless to maintain a continuous, two-way flow of words, images, and data. For digitized ideas, distance truly died, or more precisely, the ICT revolution assassinated it.

The ICT revolution did much less to lower the cost of moving goods or people. On the margin, goods trade did become faster and more coordinated. Companies like FedEx and DHL could not do what they do without today's globe-spanning telecommunications and the computer power to leverage it. Other factors further reduced trade costs—things such as technological improvements that lowered the cost of air cargo, and massive trade liberalization by developing nations. These changes, however, were gradual compared to the tectonic shifts seen in the nineteenth and early twentieth centuries.

Better communications also did not do much to lower the cost of moving people since their time-cost kept rising. Moreover, better telecommunications probably raised the need for travel, since sending hundreds of messages seems to have led to more in-person meetings, not fewer. In any case, messages and meetings are most definitely imperfect substitutes and in many ways, they are complements. It is much easier to deal with issues by email when the message sender and receiver have met in person at least once. Since we are messaging with far more people than we used to when messaging meant airmail or phone calls, we have an incentive to meet more people.

The top-line message here is that the ICT revolution relaxed the second constraint but left the third constraint in place. This uneven aspect of recent globalization had revolutionary implications for the world economy.

Impact: Production Unbundling and Emerging Market Growth

The ICT revolution boosted globalization into a new acceleration phase by relaxing the communication constraint that had generated such intense microclustering. As with the first unbundling, the key was that a new technology allowed firms to arbitrage existing international price differences.

The new communication possibilities meant that manufacturing stages that previously had to be done within walking distance could be dispersed internationally without colossal losses in efficiency or timeliness. Once the ICT revolution opened the door to offshoring, and the enormous wage gaps that arose during the Great Divergence pushed it over the threshold. This was globalization's second unbundling (Figure 41). A similar trend has also occurred in some service sectors—that is to say, offices as well as factories have been unbundled.

The New Globalization's Spatial Paradox

As with the first unbundling, the second unbundling was accompanied by a counterintuitive countercurrent. People clustered in cities even as production dispersed internationally. This rapid urbanization, which is observed all over the world, suggests that distance is getting more important, not less. Moreover, much of the offshoring of manufacturing has arisen in regional clusters rather than in global clusters.

This seeming paradox is easily resolved. Relaxing the communications constraint did not make the world flat. Rather, reducing the cost of moving ideas brought globalization up against the third constraint—the face-to-face constraint that arises from the high cost of moving people. Email and web-based coordination are fine for some things, but keeping a complex production process in harmony still requires some in-person meetings. For many sectors this means gathering people in cities. For the manufacturing sector, this means locating offshore stages in nations that managers and technicians can reach within a day's travel. Germany does most of its low-wage off-

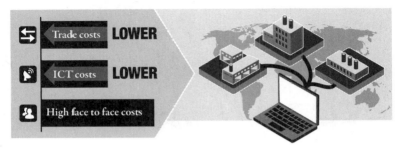

FIGURE 41: The ICT revolution triggered the second unbundling—the geographic separation of G7 factories.

For many decades, fragmentation of manufacturing would have been cost-saving for G7 firms given the very large wage differentials between, say, the United States and Mexico, or Japan and China. The problem was that it made no sense to ship production stages overseas when coordination had to be done by phone, faxes, or overnight express mail. Revolutionary advances in information and communication technology changed the cost-benefit analysis by making it much easier to coordinate different stages of production at great distance. As a result, G7 firms found it profitable to offshore some stages of production to low-wage nations.

Today, many goods are produced by international production networks that are knit together by telecommunications, email, web-based management systems, and other information structures as illustrated in the diagram.

shoring in Central and Eastern Europe, the United States does most of its in Mexico, and Japan does most of its in East and Southeast Asia. The internationalization of production thus created Factory Asia, Factory Europe, and Factory North America—not Factory World.

In short, distance started to matter in new ways since distance means very different things when it comes to moving people versus goods or ideas.

North-to-South Offshoring and Knowledge Flows

The offshoring of manufacturing had a curious impact on the distribution of global know-how. To ensure all stages worked as a coherent

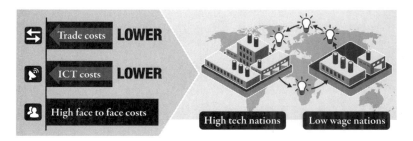

FIGURE 42: Global value chains opened a conduit for North-to-South flows of know-how.

Internationalization of production was made possible by lower communication costs. The resulting offshoring, however, didn't end the need to coordinate the various stages of production—it internationalized it. Thus to ensure the operation operated as one, the offshoring firms moved their managerial, marketing, and technical know-how along with the offshored stages.

In effect, low-wage labor was working with advanced technology. As it turned out, this combination of advanced know-how and low wages proved to be incredibly competitive—so much so that it transfigured global manufacturing. It accounts for the sudden and massive shift in manufacturing from G7 nations to a handful of nearby developing nations—especially China.

From this perspective, the offshoring of, say, Apple computer factories from Texas to China should not be thought of as "goods crossing borders" driven by China's inherent competitiveness. Rather it should be thought of as the result of American know-how moving to low-wage workers in China. Developing nations outside these new GVC-defined technology boundaries found it hard to keep up using their combinations of low tech and low wages—an outcome that has been called "premature deindustrialization."

whole, G7 also offshored some of their firm-specific knowledge (as the light bulbs in Figure 42 suggest). Dyson, the British company, is a good example.

Dyson makes products like high-end vacuum cleaners, or rather it used to. It used to design, engineer, and manufacture household appliances at Malmesbury, a town near Southampton. As a typical data point in the second unbundling, the company shifted its fabrication to Malaysia in 2003.

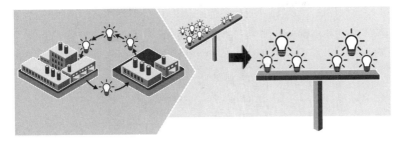

FIGURE 43: The Great Convergence was driven by know-how moving across national borders within international production networks.

The second unbundling changed technology boundaries. Technology became less defined by national borders and more defined by the contours of international production networks. The resulting gush of know-how from the North to the South has begun to re-equilibrate the knowledge imbalances that had been created during the Great Divergence. The result, as argued in the text, was rapid industrialization and growth take-offs in a handful of developing nations.

The improved competitiveness in manufacturing, however, came only to those developing nations that were on the receiving end of the offshored stages of production. Other developing nations benefited indirectly via the commodity super-cycle that was launched by rapidly industrializing developing countries, especially China.

This, in short, is why the second unbundling produced the Great Convergence while the first unbundling generated the Great Divergence. In the first, the low costs of moving goods sparked innovation in the North which stayed in the North due to the high cost of moving ideas. When it became cheap to move ideas internationally, the vast imbalances in know-how per worker led to offshoring that can be thought of as a form of arbitrage between the high knowledge-worker ratio in the North and the low ratio in the South. The Great Convergence is the fruit of this arbitrage.

Today, Dyson is what Dartmouth economist Andrew Bernard calls a "factoryless goods producer."[2] None of its workers are involved in fabrication. They are engaged in the full range of services necessary to produce the goods, but they don't actually make the goods. Now Dyson combines its technical, marketing, and management knowledge with low-wage Malaysian workers to keep its products competitive with those of other producers who are doing the same.

Because of innumerable cases like Dyson, know-how started flowing across North-South borders in vastly larger quantities than it did before the ICT revolution. Since knowledge is the key to growth, the new know-how flows transformed the world's growth map by spurring historically unprecedented growth in so-called emerging economies (Figure 43).

Mental Models for Globalization's Second Acceleration

For two centuries, trade mainly meant made-here-sold-there goods; globalization mainly meant fewer barriers to goods crossing borders. As lower trade barriers cranked up the agglomeration-innovation-competitiveness cycle, industrial nations grew rich and the Great Divergence happened.

All this flipped sometime around the year 1990. The happy helix that had shifted shares to the G7 during the first unbundling turned into the "hollowing helix." The Industrializing Six (I6) nations, discussed in the previous chapter, industrialized swiftly while G7 nations saw their share of world manufacturing nosedive. In the decades straddling the year 2000, almost a fifth of the world's manufacturing shifted from the G7 to the I6. This rapid industrialization triggered historically unprecedented income growth. Since almost half of humanity lives in the I6 nations, their growth takeoffs sparked a commodity super-cycle that "lifted the boats" of commodity-exporting nations around the world.

At first sight, this reorganization of international production might seem to be very much like that of the nineteenth century—after all, nations were focusing on what they do best. But the rapid industrializers did not industrialize as the G7 nations had done. They did not build up domestic know-how and put together domestic supply chains to become competitive. The I6 became competitive abroad by joining regional production networks.[3]

This was not how the United States, Germany, or Japan industrialized. A changed world demanded a new set of abstractions and simplified thought-patterns to understand globalization's new complexities.

Fragmentation, Trading Tasks, Offshoring, and the Next Industrial Revolution

To many observers in the 1990s, globalization seemed somehow different. In Asia, where the changes came early, academics and governments studied what was called "fragmentation." One the great postwar trade theorists, Ronald Jones, sketched an analytic framework to make sense of this fragmentation in his 1997 Ohlin Memorial Lecture. Although Jones's book *Globalization and the Theory of Input Trade* directly challenged the principle of comparative advantage and was published by MIT Press, it was widely ignored (and still is).

As globalization continued to throw up puzzles in the 2000s, the need for a new mental model grew more pressing. In 2006, the breakthrough came when three eminent Princeton economists argued that globalization had entered a new phase. In March 2006, Princeton economist Alan Blinder published a paper in *Foreign Affairs* titled "Offshoring: The Next Industrial Revolution?" His essay stirred a great deal of angst amongst the Davos crowd, but it lacked reflections on what it meant for the traditional conceptualization of globalization. The omission was filled in August 2006 by Princeton professors Gene Grossman and Esteban Rossi-Hansberg with their "new paradigm" framework—known as "trading tasks." It focused on offshoring and the increased tradability of parts and components. Presented at the famous Jackson Hole conference of the Federal Reserve Bank of Kansas City, the Grossman / Rossi-Hansberg ideas spread like wildfire. Their piece ignited my own reflections on how globalization had changed and what it meant for policy—thinking which I documented in a September 2006 paper that I wrote for the Finnish prime minister's office ("Globalization: The Great Unbundling[s]"). I spent a decade thinking, writing, and speaking on the matter before my early thoughts evolved into the three-cascading-constraints narrative.[4]

Twenty-First-Century Know-How and Nineteenth-Century Migration

Before recapping and presenting the three-cascading-constraints approach succinctly, I want to use a historical analogy to illustrate how fundamentally different the first and second unbundlings are. The analogy comes from the nineteenth century—a century that witnessed two very different forms of globalization, one involving Ricardian-like trade in goods and one involving movements of the sources of Ricardian comparative advantage.

During the first unbundling, Europe had abundant labor and little land. The Americas had the opposite, which meant—as Ricardo told us it would—that the New World shipped grain to the Old World. However, most New World land was useless for agriculture since it was just too remote for crops to be brought to market. Railroads repealed this "edict of distance" and turned vast wastelands into vast farmlands. The new farms, however, needed farmers. This is where migration comes into the story.

American policy toward European migration was, at the time, very liberal. With the sluice-gate wide open and land beckoning, hordes of Europeans moved to the Americas to exploit the massive imbalance in land-labor ratios (see Table 3 in Chapter 2). This addition of productive factors to the U.S. economy resulted in spectacular growth. It also massively boosted transatlantic trade.

Note how Ricardo's principle of comparative advantage is left speechless in the face of this sort of globalization. Or more precisely, it needs to be adapted and reinterpreted. What happened here was the movement of one nation's source of comparative advantage (labor) to another nation's source of comparative advantage (land).

If one stretches it far enough, one can think of how Ricardo's framework—which normally starts with comparative advantages fixed at the national level—could explain this outcome. After all, the migration did not reverse America's land-based comparative advantage in wheat; it exaggerated it. The resulting U.S. growth and higher exports, however, were of a very different nature than would have been expected from Ricardo's framework. First, the migration changed (strengthened) U.S. comparative advantage in the sense that wheat exports rocketed. Second, unlike lower trade costs, the impact was not global. It was geographically limited to the nations that got the mass migration (United States, Canada, Argentina, etc.).

This is how I suggest we think about the second unbundling. The ICT revolution is like the open-migration policy of the United States in that it allows the G7's source of comparative advantage (know-how) to move to the I6's source of comparative advantage (labor). But unlike the nineteenth-century case, the new knowledge flows did not merely exaggerate the comparative advantage of the receiving nations. Rather, it allowed nations like China to export a vast range of goods that they never could have produced, much less exported, using native technology.

The second unbundling is similar to the nineteenth-century case in another way—it is very geographically concentrated. The new international movement of knowledge is very carefully controlled by the firms that own it. They make great efforts to see that it stays inside the contours of their global value chains. As a consequence, the New Globalization is transforming only the developing economies that are on the receiving end of the know-how.

The next chapter goes into more depth on exactly what is new about the New Globalization.

BOX 7: SUMMARY OF THE THREE-CASCADING-CONSTRAINTS PERSPECTIVE

Since the agricultural revolution tied humans to specific plots of land, the dictates of distance forced spatial clustering of production and consumption. It was just too dangerous and expensive to move goods, ideas, and people. Trade happened, but it concerned curiosities, rarities, and luxuries.

As technology advanced, the cost of moving goods, ideas, and people fell—but not all at the same pace. In globalization's first leap, the world-shattering change was a big drop in the cost of moving goods. Rapidly falling transportation costs ended the necessity of making goods close to the point of consumption. This produced globalization's first unbundling—the spatial separation of the production and consumption of goods.

As it turned out, industry clustered in today's rich nations and this industrialization started innovation-led growth. Yet because the first unbundling left communication costs high, the industry-linked innovations mostly stayed local and this meant that the growth mostly stayed local too. In a few decades, this unequal growth produced the Great Divergence—that is to say, the historically unprecedented disparity in incomes that has marked the world for the last century and a half.

Since 1990, though, rapidly falling communication and coordination costs have ended the need to perform most manufacturing stages inside the same factory or industrial district, resulting in globalization's second unbundling—the internationalization of production processes.

Since coordinating international production requires international movements of firm-specific knowledge, North-to-South offshoring was accompanied by an absolutely massive North-to-South flow of know-how. In other words, the knowledge sluice-gate is wide open and know-how is flowing abundantly to a handful of developing nations. As a result of high technology from G7 firms fusing with low wages in developing nations, almost a fifth of world manufacturing value added has shifted from North to South.

Yet despite the relaxation of the goods and ideas constraints, "the world is spiky," as Richard Florida argued in his eponymous 2005 article in the *Atlantic*. Most international production networks and value chains are regional not global. They are inside Factory Asia, Factory Europe, or Factory North America. Moreover, as far as people-clustering is concerned, ongoing urbanization suggests distance is getting more important, not less. Both trends seem to be linked to the benefits of face-to-face interactions.

Putting it differently, the world is now up against a third constraint—the cost of face-to-face interactions. What happens when the last constraint is relaxed is the subject of conjectures in Chapter 10.

CHAPTER 5

What's Really New?

Globalization is creating a brave new world, according to the journalist Thomas Friedman. His bestselling 2005 book *The World Is Flat* opens with a description of his "Columbus-like journey of exploration." This brought him, oddly enough, to a golf game in India. Amazed that so many U.S. corporate brands could be seen from the teeing ground, he experienced a revelation: "I think the world is flat." Worldly readers may conclude that he would do well to get out more.

While this nothing-new-under-the-sun skepticism is tempting, the goal of this chapter is to argue that some things really are new about the New Globalization. In particular, the chapter seeks to identify the key ways in which globalization's first and second unbundlings differ.

The newness of the New Globalization stems from two aspects of the second unbundling—fragmentation and offshoring in manufacturing and service sectors, and the technology flows that follow the jobs sent offshore. This basic change in the international boundaries of production is thus the first topic discussed.

The Organization of Production Changed

The international organization of production changed sometime between the mid-1980s and mid-1990s; take 1990 as a convenient bookmark. While the change is simple to describe, its implications are both complex and momentous. The basic change—which I have been variously calling the New Globalization, the second unbundling, and the global value chain revolution—is illustrated schematically in Figure 44.

Traditionally, manufacturers in the Group of Seven (G7) nations sourced inputs domestically to produce what might be called made-here-sold-there-goods. A U.S. product really could be thought of as being made in America. This is the situation in the right panel of Figure 44.

Of course a few items, like the rubber for automotive tires, would have been sourced from faraway lands. Moreover, even in these glory days of G7 manufacturing, there was a lot of back-and-forth trade in parts and components among G7 nations. This was based on the advantages of hyperspecialization. In Europe, for example, the French automotive parts company Valeo specialized in air conditioners for passenger cars while the German company Webasto Bus GmbH specialized in air conditioners for buses. Yet even including these North-North exchanges, the total share of inputs sourced from abroad was fairly feeble before new information and communication technology (ICT) revolutionized production networks.[1] As a result, German exports could be thought of as the embodiment of Germany labor, capital, technology, and management. And the same was true for goods made in the United States, United Kingdom, Japan, France, and Italy.[2]

Even though it was mostly clustered locally, the manufacturing process was still complex. It typically involved multiple stages of production, as Figure 44 illustrates. This microclustering was, as discussed in Chapter 4, driven by the need to coordinate complex processes. When the ICT revolution started to melt the "coordination glue" that had forced the microclustering in factories, G7 firms increasingly internationalized their production processes to take advantage of low-cost labor in nearby developing nations—as shown in the right panel of Figure 44. The key point is that under this new international organization of production, factories crossed

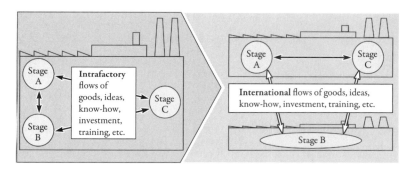

FIGURE 44: New Globalization and internationalization of production: factories crossing North-South borders.

Traditional production involved stages of production that were organized inside G7 factories and industrial districts (as illustrated in the left panel). While there were international exchanges of intermediate goods, capital, and services before the second unbundling, these were mostly among G7 nations—for example, between the United States and Canada, or within Western Europe.

The ICT revolution allowed G7 firms to separate the stages of production and reduce costs by relocating some stages to developing nations. The result was that factories started crossing North-South borders in a massive way—an outcome that had revolutionary effects for a simple reason. Since moving production to low-wage nations did not end the need to coordinate production stages, the flows of people, ideas, investment, training, and know-how that used to coordinate stages inside G7 factory now started crossing North-South borders (as illustrated in the right panel). Knowledge was the most important of the new flows. Globalization and its impact where transformed as new knowledge started surging from rich nations to poor nations.

North-South borders. This led to many changes, but the most important was the way that intrafactory flows became international flows. Indeed, the central thesis of this book is that globalization has had radically different effects on the world economy since 1990 exactly because these flows were internationalized.

The rest of this chapter looks at the surprisingly complex implications of this simple change in the organization of production. The implications are organized in four parts: 1) comparative advantage is denationalized; 2) value is shifted to services; 3) new winners and losers are created within nations; and 4) globalization gets wilder.

Comparative Advantage Is Denationalized: New-Style Competition among Nations

Traditional understanding of how nations compete economically—and what happens when this competition intensifies—is based on the principle of comparative advantage. The principle's point of departure is that nations have different competencies in different industries. As trade in goods gets freer, the market pushes nations to produce and export more of what they are relatively good at while producing less and importing more of what they are relatively bad at (see Chapter 6 for a fuller discussion).

When the second unbundling redrew the international boundaries of production as illustrated in Figure 44, comparative advantage was denationalized. That is to say, under the Old Globalization, the frontline of competition was best thought of as national borders. For example, cars made in Germany competed with cars made in Japan. Under the New Globalization, the frontline of competition is better thought of as being between cross-national production networks—call them "global value chains," or GVCs for short. When thinking about this from a national perspective, the New Globalization is much less about allowing nations to make better use of their particular competencies and much more about changing their competencies. This is well illustrated by the example of a Vietnamese firm exporting transport parts to Japan.

A case study of an anonymous Vietnamese company, "Supplier A," tells us that the state-owned firm produced agricultural machinery and parts before 1998 and had a "good labor force, but not good management."[3] It improved significantly in the 1990s after its engagement with Honda. As part of the Honda subcontracting relationship, Honda sent engineers from Japan to provide production management know-how and technology transfers that helped the company build a Japanese-like production model.

With its heightened capacities and quality, the company started receiving orders from overseas customers, especially for motorcycle parts. Although 80 percent of its sales are to Honda, it has subcontracting relationships with other Japanese motorcycle producers as well.

Think about what happened here. Before Honda's global value chain reached into the country, Vietnam's relative competitiveness in machinery and parts was based on its national traits—its labor, management, and technology. Afterward, Vietnam's competitiveness in these things depended on a denationalized blend of traits—in this example, Japanese management know-how and Vietnamese labor.

In short, the second unbundling did not help Vietnam exploit its comparative advantage—it changed Vietnam's comparative advantage. It shifted Vietnam from an importer of motorcycle parts to an exporter. This flip happened because one of Japan's sources of comparative advantage—its know-how—moved across the border and was combined with one of Vietnam's sources of comparative advantage; namely, its low-cost labor.

The outcome also improved Honda's competitiveness, including against its German rival BMW, who has started sourcing parts in India. In this sense, the offshoring of the know-how necessary to turn Vietnamese and Indian firms into reliable parts producers shifted the effective geographical boundaries of competition. It is no longer really Japan versus Germany; it is the Honda-led GVC versus the BMW-led GVC.

Changing the principle of comparative advantage in this way really matters since comparative advantage has been at the heart of all informed reasoning about globalization since the early nineteenth century. In particular, this principle helped organize thinking about three massively important questions: Which nations export what? Who gains from this trade? And what do changes in one nation's competitiveness mean for other nations? Consider the "who gains" question first.

National Gains from Globalization Put in Question

When comparative advantage is national, all nations gain from freer trade. Some citizens inside each nation win and others lose, but the winners win more than losers lose. (See Chapter 6 for a fuller discussion.) If the nation's government shares the gains and pains of globalization wisely, all can gain. That was the standard script for globalization's first unbundling.

This all-nations-win result is based on simple, ironclad logic. Trade is just allowing each nation to use its limited resources more efficiently. Indeed it is perfectly correct to think of trade as something that magically allows Switzerland, for example, to turn exported banking services (which it is very good at making) into imported bananas (which it is very bad at making). Thus with the help of trade, Swiss resources can be more efficiently employed making banking services instead of bananas.

As the soccer club analogy in the Introduction illustrated, redrawing the international boundaries of comparative advantage changes the ironclad, all-nations-win logic. In fact, when sources of comparative advantage cross international borders, it is not sure that all nations win. The basic point is simplicity itself. If the firms from a nation, say Austria, transfer technology abroad in a way that increases the international competition facing Austrian exports, then the Austrians working in Austria may well lose.

The point has been made many times by many people—most famously by Nobel Prize winner Paul Samuelson in his 2004 article "Where Ricardo and Mill Rebut and Confirm Arguments of Mainstream Economists Supporting Globalization." As Samuelson puts it in his rotund phrasing, "This invention abroad that gives to China some of the comparative advantage that had belonged to the United

States can induce for the United States permanent *lost* per capita real income." Note that Samuelson was not linking the "invention abroad" to the second unbundling—that is my assertion. He is just pointing out that if others get good at things you are really good at, the new competition is likely to harm you.[4]

A closely related logic suggests that the New Globalization has important cross-country competitive effects.

Cross-Country Competitiveness Changes

The internationalization of production across North-South borders improves the competitiveness of the Northern firms doing it. It is, after all, driven by a desire to reduce costs. The cost reduction may be used to cut prices or improve quality, or both, but the offshoring firm is clearly more competitive with the offshoring than it was without it. Consider what this means for the competitiveness of firms from other advanced-technology nations.

Suppose, for example, that Toyota can offshore labor-intensive tasks but Fiat cannot. The fact that offshoring boosts the competitiveness of Toyota means—quite directly—that it harms the competitiveness of Fiat. Toyota's offshoring clearly results in the loss of some Japanese factory jobs, but by favoring Toyota in the Toyota-Fiat competition, the offshoring can mean that certain types of manufacturing jobs are more likely to stay in Japan.

Scaling up this example to the national level, it is clear that the denationalization of production can shift the comparative advantage of third nations. Indeed it is perfectly correct to think of this as another application of Samuelson's point about what happens when one nation gets better at making things that some other nation used to be especially good at.

The policy implications are fleshed out in Chapter 8, but one implication is blindingly obvious. Attempts to resist the second unbundling while other advanced nations embrace it may be futile or even counterproductive. An advanced nation that seeks to ban the international reorganization of production may find that the resistance hastens rather than hinders its deindustrialization.

A related competiveness "spillover" affects developing nations. China, for example, has fully embraced the global value chain revolution. It is thus making, say, electric motors with a combination of Japanese know-how and Chinese labor. Brazil, by contrast, has not really participated in the new internationalization of production. It makes electric motors with Brazilian know-how and Brazilian labor. As a consequence, Brazilian electric-motor makers struggle to compete with Chinese exports. After all, high tech with low wages beats low tech with low wages. The obvious implication is that developing-nation policies that seek to resist the global value chain trend may end up hurting rather than helping its industrialization. These thoughts are developed more fully in Chapter 9.

Nature of Twenty-First-Century Trade Changes

One of the most obvious implications of the production reorganization illustrated in Figure 44 is its impact on trade, or perhaps it should be called "international commerce" seeing as it involves far more than trade in goods. In other words, when production processes straddle borders, the nature of international commerce changes fundamentally. While there are more precise terms for each element of this new cross-border commerce, it is useful to label it "twenty-first-century trade," as the name invites an immediate comparison with earlier forms of trade.

Twentieth-century trade was largely about selling goods to customers in one nation that had been made in another nation. Before the second unbundling, when production was organized as illustrated in the left panel of Figure 44, exports could usefully be conceptualized as "packages" of the exporting nation's productive factors, technology, social capital, governance capacity, and so forth. All the underlying factors of production were implicitly crossing the border since they were embedded in the factory's output but, as far as the border officials were concerned, only goods were moving past them.

This sort of twentieth-century trade is still with us. Exports of raw materials and many agricultural goods are still of the made-here-sold-there type. Indeed, even in the most unbundled sectors, like machinery, something like 90 percent of the value added in the exports of large nations like the United States and Germany is of domestic origin.

The most dynamic parts of today's trade flows, however, are radically more complex and more entangled because of the changed organization of production. Specifically, twenty-first-century trade reflects the intertwining of:

- Trade in parts and components.
- International movement of production facilities, personnel, and know-how.
- Services necessary to coordinate the dispersed production, especially infrastructure services such as telecoms, Internet, express parcel delivery, air cargo, trade-related finance, customs clearance, trade finance, and so on.

The two key points here are that international commerce became more *multifaceted*—involving flows of goods, services, intellectual property, capital, and people—and that those flows became more *entangled* in the sense that they are generated by the same cause (production unbundling). These points have big ramifications for international trade policy that will be discussed at length in Chapters 8 and 9.

South-to-North Trade Changed

There is nothing new about twenty-first-century trade from a qualitative sense. "Factories crossing borders" is old hat in North America and Western Europe. The 1957 Treaty of Rome and the 1965 U.S.-Canada Auto Pact, for example, were exactly designed to push economic integration beyond trade in made-here-sold-there goods. They were meant to facilitate the development of what would today be called global value chains.

What is really new about the New Globalization is the fact that factories are now crossing North-South borders, not just North-North borders. As a result, some North-South trade relationships are now marked by the complex, entangled flows of goods, services, people, know-how, and investments that have been going on for decades among G7 nations. But there is an important subtlety here.

These new flows are a revolution for developing-nation exporters, but an evolution for developed-nation exporters. The reduction in coordination costs that propelled the second unbundling was symmetric—after all, good telecommunications allows ideas to flow in both directions. The outcome, however, was anything but symmetric, for two very distinct reasons.

First, at the start of the second unbundling, the knowledge-labor ratio was radically higher in the North than it was in the South. Although there has been some convergence from the 1970s with what used to be called the newly industrializing economies (Singapore, Taiwan, Korea, and Hong Kong), the knowledge ratio is still much higher in G7 and other advanced-technology nations. This is important since it explains why making it easier to ship ideas across borders produced a massively asymmetric flow of know-how. Knowledge is flooding from North to South—very little is streaming from South to North.

Second, the ability to coordinate production internationally made it much easier to rely on imported parts and services, but the change was asymmetric; it was a revolutionary boost in developing nations' abilities to export parts, but only a mild stimulus for G7 parts exporters. Again, trade in parts and components is old hat. But until the second unbundling, this trade was lopsided. G7 firms sold parts and components to manufacturers in other G7 nations and to manufacturers in developing countries. What changed with the second unbundling was that the developing nations could, for the first time, export parts back to G7 manufacturers (and each other).

Customarily, developing-nation manufacturers found few foreign buyers for their parts since it was costly or even impossible for G7 firms to verify the parts' quality and reliability. All this changed when the G7 firms themselves were running or closely monitoring developing-nation factories. In the case study discussed previously, Honda could trust motorcycle parts made in Vietnam since Honda was directly involved in their production.

In this sense, the second unbundling acted like an asymmetric trade opening. It radically improved the possibilities for developing-nation exporters of parts while it only moderately improved opportunities for developed-nation parts exporters.

An example can be found in Figure 45, which contrasts the export performance of the "South" and the "North." The South is represented in the chart by the six developing nations that were dubbed the Industrializing Six, or I6 in the Introduction. The North is represented by the three dominant manufacturers among the G7, namely the United States, Germany, and Japan. The chart focuses on final vehicles and vehicle parts since the definition of parts and final goods is quite clear in this sector. Each bar in the chart shows the ratio of the export value in the two years listed, for example the 1.0 for the first bar means that the car exports by the I6 were the same in 1998 as they were in 1988.

The topline takeaway from the chart is that the I6's exports of vehicle parts absolutely exploded in both periods—much more than their exports of vehicles did. In the early days of the second unbundling, say 1988 to 1998, the I6 saw their exports of vehicle parts rise by 11.7 times, while their vehicle exports hardly budged. This stands in sharp contrast to the performance of Northern exporters. Their exports of vehicles rose by 1.3 times and their exports of parts rose by 1.6 times. The pattern is similar in the second period, 1998 to 2008,

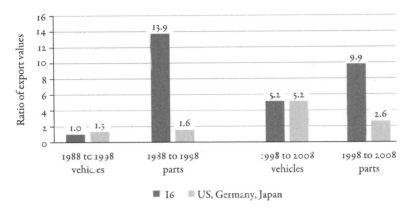

■ I6　■ US, Germany, Japan

FIGURE 45: The second unbundling especially spurred developing nation exports of parts.

Advancing globalization massively stimulated trade in vehicle and vehicle parts, but in an asymmetric way. The outcome, illustrated in the chart, makes it look like barriers to the export of vehicle parts from developing nations where especially affected.

To see this, focus first on the export-performance indicators for the developing nations (illustrated here by the data for the Industrializing Six, or I6, namely China, India, Korea, Poland, Indonesia, and Thailand). In the first period, 1988 to 1998, I6 exports of parts soared while their exports of vehicles languished. In the second period, 1998 to 2008, both categories of exports boomed, but the parts exports grew 8.7 times while their vehicle exports grew "only" 5.5 times. The pattern for the developed nations (represented by the United States, Germany, and Japan), is much more even across the two product types. In the first period, vehicle exports and parts exports grew by 1.3 and 1.6 times (respectively), while in the second period they grew 1.9 and 2.6 times (respectively).

The main take away from the chart is that the ICT revolution and associated changes in policy had an impact on trade that was asymmetric in two dimensions. It fostered exports of parts more than final goods, and it fostered Southern exports of parts much more than it fostered Northern exports of parts.

DATA SOURCE: World Integrated Trade Solution (WITS) database.

NOTE: Data are for vehicles and their parts. The bars show the ratio of the value of the group's exports in the two years (e.g., the first bar shows the value of R10 vehicle exports in 1998 over 1988).

although here the I6 exports of vehicles boomed along with their exports of parts.

Value Is Shifted to Services: The Smile Curve and Servicification

The international reorganization of production, shown schematically in Figure 44, also transformed the world of manufacturing at the product level. The main changes can be organized around a handy intellectual construct known as the "smile curve."

Introduced by Acer founder and CEO Stan Shih in the early 1990s, the smile-curve logic asserts that the distribution of value added in manufactured products is shifting. More and more of the value is being added by services that are related to manufacturing; less and less is being added by simple manufacturing itself. Put differently, much of value addition that used to happen in fabrication stages before the second unbundling has been transferred to the pre- and post-fabrication stages that are dominated by service inputs.

This general assertion, which is widely accepted among Asian policymakers and industrialists, shows up as a "deepening" of the "smile" (Figure 46). The smile-deepening has caused anxiety among rapidly industrializing developing nations. They are now worrying that they are getting the "bad" jobs—that is, jobs associated with low value added per worker—while the "good" jobs stay in the North.

Apple is a perfect example of this good versus bad job concern. In 1980, Apple started making its iconic Apple II computers in Texas and Ireland, but soon shifted the production of its circuit boards to a plant in Singapore. Apple continued to open new fabrication facilities and hire more factory workers in the United States right up until the mid-1990s. From 1996, however, Apple started to shift more of its manufacturing outside the United States. The last Apple manufacturing facility in United States was shuttered in 2004. Ultimately, Apple completely exited the fabrication stages for its products.

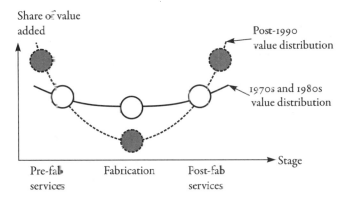

FIGURE 46: The smile curve: how the second unbundling shifted value along the value chain.

The smile curve is a handy way of illustrating some of the main changes that were produced by the New Globalization at the level of individual products. In the diagram, a typical value chain is characterized as being made up of just three stages: pre-fabrication activities (such as design, finance, and organizational services), fabrication activities (things done in factories), and post-fabrication activities (such as marketing, post-sales services, and the like).

The assertion behind the change illustrated is that the fabrication stages are losing value since they are being commoditized and shifted to lost-cost locations in developing nations. Since the shares have to add to 100 percent, the drop in the fabrication stage's value-added shows up as rises in the value in the pre-fabrication and post-fabrication stages. In particular, the pre- and post-service jobs tend to go to (or stay in) cities in G7 nations.

This smile curve is also consistent with the trend called "servicification" of manufacturing since the total value being added in what looks like the manufacturing sector (the fabrication stages) is falling while the value being added in what look like service sectors is rising.

SOURCE: Baldwin, "Global Supply Chains: Why They Emerged, Why They Matter, and Where They Are Going," Centre for Economic Policy Research, Discussion Paper No. 9103, August 2012. Figure 18.

Today, most Apple products are designed in California and Apple handles the marketing, distribution, after-sales service, and many add-on services via its App Store, iTunes, etc. The fabrication stages, by contrast, are mostly done in China and organized by unrelated companies like Foxconn. To Asian policymakers this could be thought of as the good, high value-added jobs staying in the United States while the bad, low value-added jobs move to Asia.

Second Unbundling and the Smile Curve

Before the second unbundling, the three stylized phases of value addition described in Figure 46 were performed in G7 nations. Thus, all three were done with a combination of excellent G7 know-how and excellent G7 workers who were paid high wages. Production unbundling allowed G7 firms, such as Apple, to offshore the fabrication stage. Moreover, since the offshore factories were supplied with all the necessary Apple know-how, and moving goods was cheap, it did not really matter much where the factory was located. Fabrication, in other words, was commoditized by the global value chain revolution. In any case, the offshoring directly lowered the cost of fabrication, which directly lowered the value that was added by fabrication.

To many readers, this argument seems to confuse value and costs. It may remind them of the old quip that says "an economist is someone who knows the price of everything, but the value of nothing." For better or worse, the quip is literally true. Price is how value is calculated in a market economy. The price of a thing is its value—period. Thus, when the price / cost of fabrication fell, its share of value-addition also fell.

This New-Globalization-caused-it explanation of why the smile curve deepened is not the only one. Much more research is needed before an evidence-based explanation can be firmly identified. By contrast, evidence of the economy-wide impact of these changes is readily available, but it requires us to shift from the product-level smile curve that Stan Shih had in mind to an economy-wide smile curve.

Servicification and the Economy-Wide Smile Curve

The smile curve is based mostly on anecdotes. Getting systematic evidence is hard due to the mismatch between the product-level concept of a value chain and the available economy-wide data. With few exceptions, economic statistics are gathered at the firm and sector levels, not at the product level. Thus, beyond a few illuminating case studies, it is not possible to work out at the product level where the value is added.

But this is not just a problem of data. The real challenge is that at the economy-wide level, the value chain concept is obscure. Firms' value chains intersect and overlap, so one firm's upstream process is another firm's downstream process.

To overcome the firm-level to economy-level gap, the smile-curve concept has been rejigged to focus on the sectoral origin of value added in a nation's exports rather than the stage origin as in Figure 46. The notion is simple and can be illustrated with the example of an electric fan exported by Japan. The fan uses inputs that come from primary sectors (e.g., the copper for the wire, the petroleum for the plastic casing, and the iron ore for the steel frame). It also has inputs from service sectors (e.g., design, transportation, and retail services). But most of all, it has inputs from the manufacturing sector where most of the fan's value is added.

To calculate the economy-wide smile curve—that is, to identify the sectorial source of the value added embodied in exported goods—one uses a technique similar to the OECD gross-versus-net export method described in Chapter 3. The results for each nation and sector can be summarized with three numbers: the change in the value added stemming from the primary sector, from the manufacturing sector and from the service sector.

Take as an example Japan for the period from 1995 to 2005 (when the second unbundling was rapidly progressing). As it turns out, the change in the primary-sector value added embodied in Japan's exports is basically zero. The change in the manufacturing-sector value added embodied in Japan's exports is −12 percent, indicating that the manufacturing sector's share of value added dropped by 12 percentage points between 1995 and 2005. Logically, the total-share shifting across sectors has to add up to zero across the three sectors.

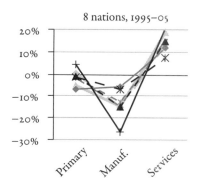

8 nations, 1995–05

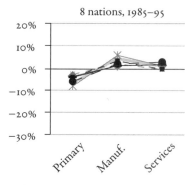

8 nations, 1985–95

FIGURE 47: Smile curve by nation, 1995 to 2005 versus 1985 to 1995.

The top panel of the chart shows that the ten years from 1995 saw a sizeable drop in the value-added coming from the manufacturing sector in many Asian nations. Since the cost of primary inputs did not change much, the value-added shares "lost" by the manufacturing sector showed up in service sectors.

There are many reasons for this shift in the source of value-added, but it is certainly consistent with the rapid rise of international production networks—also known as "global value chains," or GVCs for short. The offshoring associated with the second unbundling—or what is sometimes called the GVCs revolution—tends to reduce the cost of the fabrication stages of production for the simple reason that it is this type of stage that is often offshored. Given the way value addition is measured (it's the cost of the productive factors employed), anything that lowers the cost of inputs in the manufacturing sector directly reduces value-added stemming from the manufacturing sector. This is at least part of the reason that the manufacturing

Thus, with little happening in the primary sector, the big drop in value added from the manufacturing sector shows up as a big increase in the value added coming from service sectors.

The figures for Japan conform to the smile-curve logic. Indeed, if one plots the changes in a chart that has the primary, manufacturing, service sectors on the horizontal axis, and the change on the vertical axis, the Japanese data even looks a little bit like a smile curve (Figure 47). Or maybe it should be called a "smirk curve" since only one corner of the mouth is up. Interestingly, the same holds for the other eight East Asian nations for which this sort of calculation can be done.

Figure 47 (top panel) shows the data for Japan, Thailand, China, Korea, Philippines, Taiwan, Indonesia, and Malaysia. All of them display the basic smirk pattern in that a much smaller share of the value added is coming from the manufacturing sector and much larger share is coming from the service sector.

The botttom panel of Figure 47 shows that a very different shift happened between 1985 and 1995. In this period, there was an increase in the share of value that came from the manufacturing sector—with

---

value-added is shown to drop in the eight nations. Offshoring has had much less significant cost-saving effects on service inputs (these include everything from design and engineering services, and transportation communication services right through to wholesale and retail services). As a consequence, a greater share of the value embodied in exports is being added in service sectors.

Interestingly, the changes between 1985 and 1995 (shown in the bottom panel) are quite different. Here both manufacturing and services sectors gain at the expense of the primary sector, but the manufacturing sector gained more. This suggests that the smile curve seems to be a relatively recent phenomenon.

SOURCE: Adapted from Richard Baldwin, Tadashi Ito, and Hitoshi Sato, "Portrait of Factory Asia: Production Network in Asia and Its Implication for Growth—The 'Smile Curve,'" Joint Research Program Series 159, Institute of Developing Economies, Japan External Trade Organization, February 2014, http://www.ide.go.jp/English/Publish/Download/Jrp/pdf/159.pdf.

these shares coming out of the primary sector. This switch in the change from 1985 to 1995 versus 1995 to 2005 suggests that the big changes in value distribution can be plausibly associated with the New Globalization.

One way to think about the Figure 47 facts is to say that there has been a "servicification" of manufacturing—a trend first noticed in a 2010 publication by Sweden's National Board of Trade titled "Servicification of Swedish Manufacturing."[5] The servicification of manufacturing, which is at least in part due to the New Globalization, has transformative implications for policy—or at least should.

Governments around the world—but especially in Asia—are heavily invested in promoting development via industrialization—with a natural tendency to associate manufacturing jobs with factory jobs. The servicification point matters for such promotion efforts since it blurs the distinction between manufacturing and service sectors. For example, servicification means that the competitiveness of a nation's manufactured exports is far more dependent on availability of local or imported services now than it was before the second unbundling. Trying to promote manufactured exports without liberalizing the import of services may be self-defeating. This line of thinking is pursued in more detail in Chapters 8 and 9.

New Winners and Losers Are Created

Both central elements of the New Globalization—North-South production unbundling and the attendant asymmetric flows of know-how—changed the way that globalization affects national economies. This section flags the key changes, starting with the question of "who gains and who loses."

The story about the two soccer teams presented in the Introduction should have already alerted readers to the likelihood that the New Globalization would have new effects on the distribution of the gains and pains of globalization within nations.

Before the second unbundling, nations could be thought of as teams of productive factors that were competing with each other in product markets. When the trade became free, each nation would do more of what it was relatively good at doing and less of other things. This, in turn, had knock-on effects on the reward to productive factors in the expanding and contracting sectors.

To see the logic, it helps to work through an example that involves a developed nation trading with a developing nation. To be concrete, suppose the rich nation has an abundance of high-skill labor and technology while the poor nation has an abundance of low-skill labor. Advancing Old Globalization in this world leads the rich nation to produce more of the goods that use lots of high-skill labor and advanced technology, and the poor nation to produce less of them. This naturally drives up the reward to technology and high-skill labor in the developed nation. Likewise, free trade pushes the developing nation to make more of the goods that involve a lot of low-skill labor, and this is good for low-skill workers in developing nations. The resulting intensification of low-skill-intensive exports, however, tends to be bad for low-skill workers in rich nations.

This was basically the story of globalization in the 1980s. High-skill workers in rich nations won, while low-skill workers in rich nations lost. In both cases, the "mechanism of action" was trade—either higher exports or higher imports. The second unbundling (also known as the New Globalization) adds a new twist to the story.

Before thinking through what happens when some of the rich nation's know-how flows to the poor nation, it is imperative to understand one fact—namely, that knowledge is not like labor or most other factors of production. The knowledge of a nation—just like the knowledge of the trainer in the soccer example—can be used in both nations at once. It is what economist call a "nonrival" factor, or at least partly so.

Given this nonrival aspect of technology, the most obvious ramification of the second unbundling is that owners of the rich nation's know-how will gain. They get to leverage the value of the knowledge against both nations' labor forces. Recalling that most global value production is organized by very large G7 firms, this logic suggests that the New Globalization should be especially good for the returns of G7 firms that are able to exploit the new offshoring possibilities. In practice, this would show up as an unusually high reward to large, technology-driven firms based in rich nations, especially those engaged in offshoring. In fact, this is something that has been happening. Calculations by Stanford economist Bob Hall show that the reward to invested capital in the United States has risen significantly relative to the cost of capital since 1990.[6] It is now at an all-time high. But this is not the end of the new effects.

The new know-how makes unskilled labor in the developing nations much more productive. This directly boosts the demand for such workers in industry and, by shifting jobs from nonmarket agriculture to industry, it boosts their incomes. As a matter of fact, this has happened. As shown in Chapter 3, some 650 million developing-nation citizens have been lifted above abject poverty since the early 1990s, many of them in nations that have participated heartedly in global value chains. Note that this part of the New Globalization's impact is due to international knowledge flows as well as the trade flows thus generated; this is thus one of things that is really new about the New Globalization.

When it comes to the impact that shows up in the developed nation, the vector of transmission is heightened import competition as before. That is, the GVC-fueled rise in the output of low-skill-intensive goods tends to lead to more imports by the developed nations. This plainly harms low-skill workers in the rich nation. Again, this is something that has happened in most advanced nations. There is, however, a more nuanced result from this sort of shift.

Brilliant research by Branko Milanovic in his 2016 book *Global Inequality: A New Approach for the Age of Globalization* shows what this "new winners and losers" means from a planetary perspective. His numbers look at all humans, one by one, and ignore their nationality. He lines them line up, so to speak, from the poorest to the richest. To keep things manageable, the individuals are lumped together into twenty groups. These groups, which ignore nationality, gather people by income class. For example, the first dot in Figure 48 represents the poorest 5 percent of people in the world in 1988, and each subsequent dot shows people with progressively higher incomes (taking them 5 percentage points at a time).

The goal is to see what happened to everyone's income between 1988 and 2008—a span of time that conveniently starts before the second unbundling. The topline result from Figure 48 is that the New Globalization had very uneven effects across the global income distribution. The big hump in the middle shows that the entire middle of the global income distribution fared well. The really rich also did well (point on the far right of the chart). The groups that suffered were the people who were really poor in 1998 and those at the lower end of the income scale in rich nations (those who were in the eightieth percentile).

Although more research is needed, the outcome is certainly in line with the idea that G7 firms were "training" workers in developing nations and this created competition for low- and medium-skilled workers in G7 nations. The middle of the income distribution enjoyed good growth for one of two reasons. Either they were in one of the Industrializing Six nations highlighted in the Introduction, or they were in emerging markets that experienced commodity-led income takeoffs. The global elite won since the global value chain revolution, and the ICT revolution more broadly, allowed them to sell their know-how to a wider audience. The people who were poor and stayed poor (the leftmost dots in the chart) could be associated with the "soccer teams" who suffered since their natural competitors (the Industrializing Six) were being "trained" by the best coach while they were not.

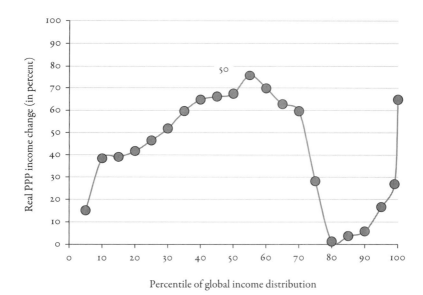

FIGURE 48: The "Elephant Curve": The second unbundling helped the global middle class and Northern elite.

The chart shows the income growth of people around the world according to how rich they were before the second unbundling (specifically in 1988). People's ranking in the global income distribution is shown on the horizontal axis. For example, those who were halfway up the income distribution in 1998 would be included in the point labeled "50" (short for the fiftieth percentile). People represented by this point did pretty well. The height of the point, about 70, shows that their incomes rose by about 70 percent between 1988 and 2008.

SOURCE: Branko Milanovic, *Global Inequality: A New Approach for the Age of Globalization* (Cambridge: Harvard University Press, 2016). Figure 1.1. Reproduced with permission of the publisher and the author.

More Polarized Workforce

Improved information technology changed the way productions tasks are organized into occupations. Specifically, it meant a regrouping of many low-skill tasks into occupations that tended to require higher skills. Although such automation tends to eliminate some jobs, the workers that stay on tend to be more productive and they tend to need more skills Thus this aspect of advancing information technology tends to be good for G7 factory workers with advanced skills and bad for low-skill workers whose job is now done by a machine.

By contrast, better communications technology allowed more stages to be moved offshore. The stages that were offshored tended to be related to simple fabrication and assembly steps that made heavy use of factory workers. Such workers were hardly members of "the one percent" in the United States, Europe, and Japan, but they were in the middle-income range for blue-collar workers. Finally, workers at the very low end of the pay and skill scale—cleaners, hamburger flippers, and the like—were not directly threatened by offshoring since their services could only be provided locally.

Adding up the impact on all three groups—workers with advanced skills, medium skills, and very low skills—produces a pattern that has been called the "hollowing out," or "polarization" of the work force. Workers at the high end of the skill spectrum are doing well and those at the low end are holding their own; those in the middle are finding offshoring to be a real problem.

The discussion so far has concentrated on the technology-transfer aspects of the New Globalization and the North-to-South flows of know-how. The next set of considerations relate to the basic nature of globalization's general impact.

Globalization Gets Wilder

The New Globalization operates with a finer degree of resolution on national economies (by stages as well as sectors), and this, as we shall see, means that the nature of globalization itself has changed in ways that are really new. But before turning to the implications, Figure 49 helps illustrate the basic "finer resolution" point.

The top panel shows a stylized version of how international competition affected a typical economy before the second unbundling.

Old Globalization

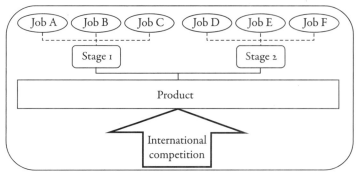

New Globalization

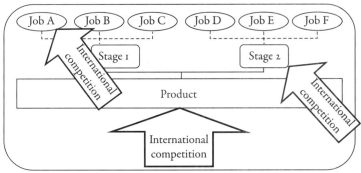

FIGURE 49: Global competition started acting with finer degree of resolution on national economies.

Before the second unbundling, firms could be viewed as "black boxes" since global competition pitted one nation's products against another's, as shown schematically in the top panel. More open trade spurred the fortunes of some firms while spiking the fortunes of others, but the firm was the finest level of disaggregation worth looking at. Since most firms in a sector stood or fell together, globalization analysts tended to focus on sectoral impacts—for example, globalization hurt low-tech, labor-intensive sectors in G7 nations while helping their high-tech, high-skill sectors. The fortunes of sectors tended to be shared with the productive factors used most intensively in the sectors, so labor skill groups were also a useful aggregate for analytic purposes (not shown in diagram).

In the diagram, "international competition" is depicted as a broad arrow that touches the economy at the product level since globalization meant goods crossing borders. Competition in the market for goods was correspondingly the only way international competition could get into an economy. Of course there were international movements of capital, intellectual property rights, and services, but these took a backseat to trade in goods. Since trade in goods was the main vector for international competition, freer trade affected economies at the sector level. The U.S. car industry, for example, was clobbered by Japanese competition in the 1980s, but the U.S. wheat sector flourished.

The second unbundling allowed globalization to reach much deeper into national economies. Now the competition arrows—as shown in the bottom panel—are touching individual stages of production and jobs. This is what is meant by "finer degree of resolution."

As drawn, Figure 49 makes it look like international competition is always a threat. But international competition works both ways. Some stages and jobs are hurt by foreign competition but, for a nation's most competitive stages and jobs, freer international competition means more opportunities to outcompete foreigners. In this way, people working in such stages and jobs gain from advancing globalization.

The second unbundling allowed international competitive pressures to operate with a finer resolution (bottom panel). Now it could reach right into the factory and help or harm one particular production stage, or even one particular job. The type of job that is harmed by extra-international competition may well be a job that exists in a wide range of sectors. For example, data-entry tasks may be offshored by a nation's competitive and uncompetitive sectors alike. One implication is that it is less useful to classify the winners and losers according to the sector in which they work or the skill group to which they belong.

SOURCE: Adapted from Richard Baldwin, "Globalization: the Great Unbundling(s)," paper prepared for the Finnish Prime Minister's office, September 20, 2006.

The change illustrated in Figure 49 has a number of important implications for the "what's new about the New Globalization" question. The first concerns what might be called the individuality of globalization's impact.

Globalization: More Individual

The sector-level impact of the Old Globalization had direct implications for workers. As discussed, expanding production and exports in a particular sector tended to boost the fortunes of the productive factors used most intensively in the expanding sectors. In most G7 nations, for example, globalization spiked the fortunes of unskilled-labor-intensive industries, so unskilled labor found the first-round impacts of globalization to be highly negative. Greater openness spurred the fortunes of skill-intensive sectors, so skilled workers tended to be favored by advancing globalization.

The North-South offshoring that has been booming since the late 1980s changed the level at which globalization affects developed-nation economies. By fragmenting the production processes, the New Globalization shifted competition from a sector-by-sector type of competition to a stage-by-stage type of competition. In a sense, competition from low-wage workers in developing nations came directly into Northern factories and offices.

This made globalization's impact more individual in the sense that the effect was more selective. In other words, globalization could help a particular type of worker in one sector if the offshoring boosted the competitiveness of the stage in which the worker found herself. But the same type of worker with the same skill set in the same company could be hurt if she happened to be working in a stage that was offshored.

To stress the point, consider the example of a French hospital. Because of advanced ICT, certain medical tasks that used to be done locally can now be done remotely. For example, arthroscopy ("keyhole surgery") is done by a doctor manipulating controls while looking at a computer screen. When the ICT got good enough, the patient and surgeon could be in different countries. The first instance came in 2001 when a New York surgeon operated on a patient in Strasbourg. It is not yet routine, but as telecommunications gets better and more reliable, remote surgery could become as routine as remote call centers are today.

If this happened, the best French surgeons would become very busy; anyone with a torn meniscus would want it repaired by one of the world's leading experts, some of whom are in France. The mediocre knee surgeons would have to find something else to do. But the individuality of the New Globalization's impact is not limited to highly skilled workers. Following trends in the corporate world, the same hospital might well offshore its billing and record-keeping and thus harm some low-skill workers. At the same time, however, the hospital's increased efficiency and the fact that it can export medical services over the Internet might very well boost the demand for other unskilled workers—say, those involved in cleaning and security.

This example of winning and losing surgeons and winning and losing unskilled workers illustrates how the first unbundling's correlation between winners and skill levels need not hold as the second unbundling proceeds. In the second unbundling, international competition is more individual. This is globalization with a finer degree of resolution.

Two corollaries of individuality are worth spotlighting. First, the increased individuality of globalization's impact tends to undermined unions' bargaining power. In most nations, labor unions are organized by sector and / or skill groups. The trouble is that individuality muddies the water. How should such a union react to globalization when it is helping some of their members while harming others? The second corollary could be called "breaking up the national team."

In the 1950s, Charles Erwin Wilson, head of General Motors, could say, "What was good for our country was good for General

Motors, and vice versa." While labor and corporations have always wrestled with each other, they were, deep down, on the same team since production stages were bundled. Production was a national thing.

The second unbundling, however, split up the G7 labor-knowledge team. This outcome implies that a nation's interests and the interests of its firms are less well aligned. The ability of firms to take their know-how elsewhere means that what is good for GM may not be good for America. In a sense, the second unbundling broke up Team America by eroding American labor's quasi-monopoly on using American firms' know-how.

A second new aspect of the New Globalization concerns the pace of change.

Globalization: More Sudden

The first unbundling had massive effects on national economies. Even starting from 1945, globalization transmuted the G7 almost beyond recognition. But the clock on Old Globalization ticked by in years, not months or weeks. Globalization's impact since the second unbundling is often much more sudden.

There are many reasons, but one is the fact that the offshoring company can overcome any bottlenecks that would have delayed a shift of manufacturing before the ICT revolution. An example helps illustrate this point.

Border Assembly Incorporated is a San Diego company that helps firms move manufacturing activities to Tijuana, Mexico (just across the border from San Diego). Its website presents an anonymized case study of a California-based furniture and wrought iron fabricator with approximately thirty employees that struggled with U.S. labor laws and wages, despite having products that were selling well.

The furniture maker contacted the offshore-facilitating company, set up a meeting, and within a week decided to move production to Mexico. Border Assembly showed its managers three buildings that same day and the furniture company selected a 10,000-square-foot factory. The necessary legal, tax, and accounting paperwork was filed, and payroll and employee benefits programs were set up. Within ten days, the furniture maker was ready to start producing across the border.

The big delay was the rewiring of the Mexican building that was necessary to accommodate the company's equipment. This was overcome in the short run by bringing in generators. As the website puts it: "Established and running in ten days. Fully operational in thirty. The furniture maker saves over half of its previous labor costs, has regained profitability, and has a staff of some of the finest metal fabricators in the world. . . . [It] is planning to expand to 100 employees."[7]

During the first unbundling, competition from a Mexican furniture maker might well have forced the closing of the U.S.-based producer as trade costs and tariffs came down. But this would have been slow. The Mexican producer would have had to develop the right products, line up a distribution network, refine the production process to match American tastes, and so on. In this hypothetical case, the U.S.-based firm might have taken years to exit. In the actual case, it exited U.S. manufacturing in a month. Or more precisely, it moved some of the marketing, managerial, and technical know-how to Mexico; production moved, but only because the knowledge flows changed Mexico's comparative advantage in this specific type of furniture. In this world, globalization's impact can be very sudden.

The next "what's new" point can also be thought of as an extension of the individuality point.

Globalization: Less Predictable

Old Globalization was primarily driven by reductions in the cost of moving goods. By their very nature, lower trade costs for goods tend to affect traded goods in roughly similar ways over time. Of course, exporting gravel is different from exporting cut flowers, but in both sectors, a one percent drop in trade costs in 1985 had an impact qualitatively similar to a one percent drop in 1980. This made globalization's impact on national economies rather predictable.

If lower shipping costs helped a nation's cut-flower sector in 1980, a further reduction in 1985 was likely to also help the sector. In short, because competition was at the sector level and globalization meant lower trade costs, the likely losers and winner from future globalization resembled those sectors that had lost or won in the recent past. This "past as a guide to the future" logic led governments to talk about "sunrise" and "sunset" sectors. Or put in Ricardian terms, deeper globalization meant a nation would shift more resources from its comparative disadvantage sectors to its comparative advantage sectors.

When international competition shifted from the level of sectors to the level of stages, the past became less reliable as a guide to the future. Or more precisely, the traditional mental model employed to do the forecasting missed the essential change—that globalization was unbundling factories and offices. In both sunrise and sunset sectors, some production stages moved, others didn't. As a consequence, the winners and losers from globalization are much harder to predict.

The real difficulty is in working out which stages will go next. It is hard since economists do not really understand in any detail the "glue" that was responsible for the microclustering in the first place. Knowing the direct cost of telecommunications is not enough since it interacts in complex and poorly understood ways with the nature of stages and their interconnectedness with other stages.

Indeed the issue is so complex that whole flocks of firms have been created to advise companies on offshoring. A snippet from the website of one of these firms, QS Advisory, gives an idea of the complexity of the offshoring decision. After noting that lots of firms offshore but few "have been able to tap its potential to deliver continuous, long-term results," the company explains the difficulty: "Exploring sourcing options and choosing the optimum one for a business requires sourcing experience and expertise in multiple business contexts. The ability to bring in diverse perspectives, understand emerging trends and a detailed insight into the potential business impact, are all critical."[8]

The unpredictability issue can also be seen in the example of apparel marketer Uniqlo. Its story shows that in a world of mix-and-match comparative advantage, good jobs can be created in losing sectors.

Low-end clothing is a classic sunset sector for nations like Japan, according to the traditional thinking. When sectors are viewed as engaging in made-here-sold-there goods and production is viewed as a national thing, then a sector like apparel (whose production is unskilled-labor-intensive) should be struggling to survive in a high-wage nation like Japan. After all, Japan's comparative advantage is in high-tech sectors, *n'est-ce pas*? More open markets should lead Japanese firms to move out of apparel and into high tech.

Uniqlo, now Asia's largest clothing company, shows that the traditional mental model is working less well as a predictive tool. More precisely, the fact that making men's undershirts is unskilled-labor-intensive work is beside the point in the second unbundling world. Uniqlo is not a success of Japan's manufacturing sector in the factory sense of the word "manufacturing." It is a success of Japan's service sector.

First and foremost, Uniqlo's success is a triumph of market research services. Uniqlo has research and development (R&D) centers in Tokyo and New York that gather information on trends and lifestyles from the streets, from their stores, and from business clients. For example, one of its biggest hits—undershirts using its "HEATTECH" fabric—combined Uniqlo's market knowledge with the technical skills of an established Japanese manufacturer, Toray Industries. Combining Uniqlo's insights about what its consumers wanted with Toray's technical knowledge about what was possible resulted in a unique fabric that people seem to love, judging from how much they buy of it.

Uniqlo is also a triumph of coordination services, quality control, and logistics. The company produces nothing directly. It gets high-quality products at low cost by directly negotiating bulk purchases from manufacturers in China and elsewhere. It has a team of technical specialists, known as the Takumi Team, working with partner factories in China. They provide technical instruction, share experiences, and check on the quality and timeliness of production.

The last implication of the New Globalization turns on the nature of ICT.

Globalization: Less Controllable

The pace of globalization has become much less controllable due to the nature of its driving forces: advanced information technology and better telecommunications. The crux of the new impact is the simple fact that reductions in the cost of moving goods and reductions in the cost of moving ideas happen in dissimilar ways.

Trade costs come down with tariff cutting and better transportation technology. All of the tariff cutting and most of the transportation infrastructure decisions were in the hands of governments. They could—and usually did—decide to go slowly to allow domestic firms and workers time to adjust. For example, after each round of negotiation by members of the General Agreement on Tariffs and Trade, the agreed-to tariff cuts were phased in over five to ten years.

Likewise, transportation technology, with a few exceptions, advanced steadily and often required large fixed investments that were naturally spread over many years. Supersize container ships are transforming shipping today, but new ships are introduced gradually. The ICT revolution in the twenty-first century is quick and chaotic by comparison.

Importantly, very little of this technology development is controlled by governments. This was not tariff cutting, whose pace was set by diplomats in Geneva. Most of the technical advances derived from private, profit-motivated R&D. And while governments could have stifled expansion of the Internet and telecoms, almost none did. To put it differently, governments controlled the sluicegates for the Old Globalization. By contrast, no one in particular controls the New Globalization's sluicegates.

BOX 8: SUMMARY OF WHAT'S NEW ABOUT THE NEW GLOBALIZATION

Firms in G7 nations are fragmenting the production process and sending some stages of production to nearby low-wage nations. To keep these international production networks running smoothly, the firms send their know-how along with the jobs. These two changes—international fragmentation of production and the transfer of know-how abroad—have had massive repercussions on the world economy. These can be grouped into two types. The first type is related to the way the New Globalization changed the nature of international competition.

The second unbundling denationalized comparative advantage by redrawing the international boundaries of competitiveness.

In other words, sources of G7 competitiveness—say, excellent management and marketing know-how—are being mixed and matched with developing-nation sources of comparative advantage—say, low-cost labor. As this recombination is happening inside the contours of global value chains, national boundaries are no longer the only relevant frontiers when thinking about international competition. Consider the implications.

To begin with, changing technology boundaries changes the answer to the "who gains from globalization" question. In particular, the ironclad logic that says that all nations gain from trade is no longer ironclad. It also shifts the implications for nations not involved in such global value chains. Quite simply, nations that try to compete on the basis of purely national competencies find it increasingly difficult to compete with those who are mixing and matching national competencies.

The New Globalization has also broken up the labor-technology team in G7 nations. German workers, to take an example, no longer have a quasi-monopoly on German technology since German firms can now apply the technology abroad quite easily.

Another implication stems from the new "factories crossing borders" aspect of the New Globalization. This change means that the complex flows of goods, services, investment, and technology that used to move only within G7 factories are now part of international commerce. This new type of trade—call it twenty-first-century trade—is more multifaceted and the facets are more interconnected.

The second set of effects are related to the fact that the New Globalization operates with a finer degree of resolution than the Old Globalization.

The production fragmentation arising from the new international organization of production means that international competition can affect national economies stage by stage, or even job by job, rather than sector by sector (as was true under the Old Globalization). One way to express this is to say that globalization is operating at a finer degree of resolution on national economies. As a consequence, globalization's impact on national economies is less predictable and more individual. The fact that it is driven by information and communication technology means the impact is also more sudden and less controllable.

PART III

Understanding Globalization's Changes

One of Lewis Carroll's wonderful, reductio-ad-absurdum characters, Mein Herr, brags of how he raised the art of map-making to its zenith. "We actually made a map of the country, on the scale of a mile to the mile!"

When questioned about how much it is used, Mein Herr admits that it "has never been spread out, yet." He explains that "the farmers objected: they said it would cover the whole country, and shut out the sunlight! So we now use the country itself, as its own map, and I assure you it does nearly as well."

The point, of course, is that taking account of everything lets you understand nothing. That's why humans use "mental models." Economics is no exception. Economic theory does vast violence to reality but the ends justify the means—it is all in the good cause of allowing a careful and complete examination of the main economic logic that links principal factors.

The shockingly different behavior of the world economy under the first and second unbundlings is one example where understanding requires abstraction on a truly epic scale. Part III takes a deeper dive into the economics necessary to comprehend the economic impact of the first and second unbundlings and why they are so different.

Chapter 6 introduces the "boot camp" economics of globalization—the minimum necessary to understand globalization's world-shaping impacts since 1820. Chapter 7 uses the economics to make sense of the facts highlighted in the history chapters.

Quintessential Globalization Economics

The economics of globalization is an expansive subject, yet the really grand features of globalization—the history-changing outcomes—can be understood with just four sets of economic logic.

The first set, and the baseline for all the rest, is David Ricardo's notion of comparative advantage. The next two logical toolkits stem from theoretical advances made in the 1990s. One of these was pioneered by Paul Krugman with Tony Venables, Masahisa Fujita, and others. It is called the "new economic geography"—even though some people are inclined to dispute whether it is really new and others whether it is really geography. The other 1990s logic set is the so-called endogenous growth theory, which is indisputably new and definitely about growth. The pathbreaker here is, among others, New York University economist Paul Romer. The last analytic framework helps organize thinking about the impact of information and communication technology (ICT) on offshoring. We begin with the logic of comparative advantage.

Ricardo and the Gains and Pains of Trade

Ricardo helps one think clearly about how even very uncompetitive nations can be competitive in something. Yet the real interest lies in how Ricardo's logic links the impact of lower trade costs to things that really matter: wages, jobs, national living standards, internal income distribution, and so on. Explaining this part of trade theory is the goal of the next few pages.

Comparative advantage simply means that it is cheaper for some nations to make some goods than others. This is the fundamental reason that nations trade, and it explains why nations export what they do. It is also the root reason why trade can be win-win for all nations regardless of their overall level of competitiveness. Put simply, all nations can gain since trade is what could be called a "two-way, buy-low-sell-high deal." This can be illustrated with the case of Swiss-Italian smuggling in the 1950s.

Just after World War II, few European currencies were "convertible"—that is, they were basically worthless outside their own nation. A French or U.S. bank, for instance, would not exchange Italian lira into dollars or French francs. As a result, smuggling involved the exchange of one type of good for another type (also called "barter" trade). An example of this was the smuggling trade that occurred between Switzerland and Italy—much of which involved Italian rice being exchanged for Swiss cigarettes. The Italian rice part is easy to understand—northern Italy is ideal for rice farms—but a tropical product like tobacco from alpine Switzerland?

The Swiss franc was one of Europe's few convertible currencies, so Swiss traders could easily get U.S. dollars to buy tobacco from Latin America and have it shipped to Basel up the Rhine River and from there overland to the Italian border. In fact, many Swiss cigarette factories were located near the Italian border to facilitate the trade. The Italian government, by contrast, made it very difficult to import cigarettes since it had the national monopoly on tobacco and was trying to spare its scarce dollars to buy essential goods like medicine and fuel.

The natural outcome of this situation was that the price of cigarettes was high relative to rice in Italy, but it was low in Switzerland. Some illustrative (that is, made up) relative prices are shown in Table 6. The prices shown are in the local currency, but since lira were worthless outside Italy, the price that mattered was the relative price of cigarettes and rice. This, after all, was barter trade. The table shows that a kilogram (kg) of cigarettes is worth a half kilo of rice in

TABLE 6

Swiss-Italian smuggling: illustrative prices.

| | Domestic market prices | |
	Italy	Switzerland
Cigarette (per kg)	100,000 liras	20 CHF
Rice (per kg)	100,000 liras	40 CHF

The numbers in this table are chosen for the sake of clarity, not historical accuracy, but you can read about the long history of Swiss-Italian smuggling in Adrian Knöpfel, "The Swiss-Italian Border-space" (thesis, École Polytechnique Fédérale de Lausanne, 2014), http://archivesma .epfl.ch/2014/045/knoepfel_enonce/knoepfel_adrian_enonce.pdf, and sources listed there. See also http://www.swissinfo.ch/ita/la—tratta-delle -bionde—degli-spalloni-d-un-tempo/7405286.

NOTE: CHF is the international abbreviation for Swiss francs.

Switzerland but a whole kilo in Italy. This relative price difference opened up an opportunity for smuggling.

A Swiss-based smuggler could buy 100 kilos of cigarettes locally for 2,000 Swiss francs (CHF), hire some strong young men to bring them over the Albrun Pass to Italy, and exchange them for rice. What would the smugglers get for their efforts? The Italian participants would surely refuse to pay the full Italian price of 100 kilos of rice for the 100 kilos of smuggled cigarettes since they could get that price legally. The Swiss smugglers would refuse anything less than 50 kilos. Just to be concrete, suppose the deal is struck at 75 kilos of rice for the 100 kilos of cigarettes.

To finish the cycle, the Swiss load up their mules with the rice, return to Switzerland, and sell the 75 kilos for 40 francs per kilo. Or perhaps somewhat less since the Swiss purchasers would need an incentive to buy from smugglers instead of the local store. To be concrete, suppose the Swiss smuggler gets 30 CHF per kilo of rice.

Who won from this smuggling? Clearly the Swiss side won, since they turned their original investment of 2,000 CHF into 2,250 CHF. But oddly enough, the Italians also won. The Italians got 100 kilos of cigarettes for the price of 75 kilos of rice, which means they effectively paid just 7.5 million lira for the 100 kilos of cigarettes instead of the full local price of 10 million liras. It is in this sense that the smuggling can be thought of as a buy-low-sell-high opportunity for both the Swiss and the Italians.

The logic is absolutely bulletproof as curious readers can verify for themselves by changing around the numbers in Table 6. The same conclusion holds for any situation where the relative price of cigarettes and rice differ in the two nations—even if Switzerland ends up as the importer of cigarettes.

Trade is just legalized smuggling, so the basic two-way gain from smuggling is also the basic reason that all nations gain from trade. That is to say, any time relative prices differ across nations, trade creates a two-way, buy-low-sell-high opportunity. Backing this up one stage—using costs of production to explain national prices—this logic means that all nations can gain whenever their production-cost profiles differ.

Impact on National Production Patterns

From this smuggling example it is clear that trade is a type of arbitrage and that it tends to narrow the preexisting differences in relative prices. What is the impact of such price changes on local production?

Plainly, it will be more worthwhile to produce the good whose relative price has risen and less worthwhile to produce the good whose price has fallen. Since being good at making the good meant that its pre-trade price was lower, this implies that each nation will make more of the good it is particularly good at making, since the internal price of such goods will rise. In the jargon, each nation tends to specialize in its comparative-advantage sector.

This sort of reallocation of productive resources is a second source of the gains from trade (the first source was the two-way, buy-low-sell-high deal). The reallocation of productive resources from each nation's least productive sector to its most productive sector boosts every nation's average productivity.

Comparative Advantage in Action: The Meiji Japan Example

Comparative advantage in action can be seen in a fascinating pair of studies by Daniel Bernhofen and John Brown. They look at the economic impact of Japan's shift from a stance of basically no trade to much more open trade in the decades between 1850 and 1870.[1]

When trade opened up, some Japanese goods had relatively low prices and some had relatively high prices compared to international prices. According to Ricardo's logic of comparative advantage, the natural products for the Japanese to export were those whose prices were relatively low inside Japan before the opening. The exporting, however, would tend to drive up the Japanese price to the international level. On the other side of the trade balance, the goods that were most naturally imported were those that were cheaper abroad than in Japan. And here the import competition should push down the Japanese price. The net result should be a pattern where prices in Japan rise in the export sectors and fall in the import sectors.

Looking at net exports—where negative net exports mean imports—and the change of prices from 1851 to 1869 shows that the predictions of Ricardo's oversimplification are roughly what happened (Figure 50). In a follow-on study, the authors estimated that Japanese incomes rose by something like 9 percent due to the opening. The gains discussed so far are called the "static" gains from trade since they take each nation's competitiveness as frozen in time. If nations have the right policies, these static gains can be amplified by what are known as "dynamic" gains—that is, extra gains that take time to develop. One important source of these gain-boosters is an increase in the scale of production that lowers average costs.

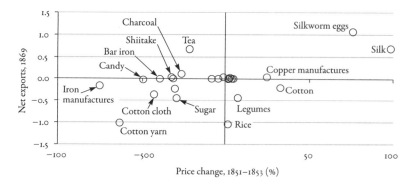

FIGURE 50: Japanese exports expanded most for those goods whose prices rose the most.

The principle of comparative advantage predicts that a nation will export the goods that are relatively cheap domestically since these are the goods the nation is particularly good at making compared to foreigners. The sudden opening of Japan shows the theory works pretty well: the biggest export sectors, like silk and silkworm eggs, are those where Japanese pre-trade prices rose the most toward the higher international prices. The sectors with the biggest imports (called negative net exports in the chart), like cotton yarn and cloth, are those where the prices fell the most when cheaper imports pushed Japanese prices down toward international levels.

DATA SOURCE: Daniel Bernhofen and John C. Brown, "A Direct Test of the Theory of Comparative Advantage: The Case of Japan," *Journal of Political Economy* 112, no. 1 (2004): 48–67.

Gains from Greater Scale Economies

Even in today's globalized world, local market size matters. For a whole host of reasons ranging from standards and regulations to consumer preferences, firms are frequently dominant in their home market while being marginal players in foreign markets. This very common situation is known as market fragmentation.

As it turns out, market fragmentation reduces competition, raises prices, and keeps too many firms in business. As a result, nations with small markets tend to have too many firms that are too small to be globally competitive. This is especially a problem in developing nations.

Having lots of firms is not the problem, of course. The problem is that the lack of competition allows domestic firms to get away with charging high prices—high enough to cover the high costs that come from their small size. Consider how trade liberalization can help in such situations.

When trade opens up, the extra competition from foreign firms creates a pro-competitive effect that can, in turn, compel big changes in a nation's industrial structure. In particular, in reaction to heightened competition and falling profits, firms tend to merge in a search for greater scale and thus lower costs. The least efficient firms are eliminated or integrated into larger, more efficient firms. The combined firms have larger market shares and thus they can realize greater economies of scale. When things go right, the end result can be a more efficient industrial structure with fewer, bigger, more efficient firms. Moreover, the trade openness means that they are competing more directly with big foreign firms, so despite the lower numbers of competitors inside each nation, firms in the industry face more effective competition.

The Pains from Globalization

Every change in price, every new technology, and every shift in demand creates winners and losers. There are two obvious cleavages when it comes to the gains and pains of globalization: consumers versus producers, and skilled versus unskilled workers. Any time deeper globalization lowers a price, the consumers of those goods win and the producers lose. Likewise, when globalization causes expansion of one sector and contraction of another, the factors of production used most intensively in the expanding sector tend to win, while those in the contracting sector tend to lose.

It is important to recognize two things about the pains of globalization. First, there is no gain from globalization without pain. Second, the solution to this dilemma is to establish a "social contract" that gives all citizens a stake in the gains and a share of the pains.

The New Economic Geography

The second package of economic logic, the New Economic Geography—known affectionately as NEG by aficionados—explains the riddle of uneven spatial development, which, simply put, is: How can lower trade cost—which should make distance matter less—produce such dramatically unbalanced distributions of economic activity such as cities, and the G7's outsize share of world gross domestic product (GDP)?

The NEG cracks the riddle by focusing on firms' location decisions. According to what might be called "NEG-ative reasoning," these decisions rest on the balance of two collections of opposing forces:

- Dispersion forces that favor geographic dispersion of economic activity
- Agglomeration forces that favor geographic clustering of economic activity

The balance between them determines why, for instance, a very large fraction of British firms locate in Greater London, but not all of them do. Or why the share of global economic activity in the G7 rose to two-thirds in 1990, but no higher.

Dispersion and Agglomeration Forces

There are many dispersion forces, but most operate on only a very local scale (like urban congestion or high rents). These are not relevant to the global facts. NEG concentrates on two dispersion forces that operate through goods prices and thus can operate at the global spatial level via trade in goods. These dispersion forces are wage gaps and local competition.

More specifically, the location of manufacturing is affected by wage gaps for high-skill workers and wage gaps for low-skill workers. For instance, high-education labor is relatively more abundant than low-education labor in rich nations, while the reverse is true in many developing nations. The result is a tendency toward a spatial sorting of skill-intensive industries to high-wage nations and labor-intensive industries to low-wage nations.

The second global-level dispersion force is local competition—the force that makes firms want to put trade costs between themselves and the bulk of their competitors. This was the force, for example, that fostered U.S. industrialization when the United States put up high barriers against British manufacturers in the nineteenth century. Firms found it profitable to set up in the United States not because it was so cheap to operate there, but rather because the trade barriers protected them from their low-cost, British-based competitors.

Agglomeration forces are the opposite of dispersion forces—they encourage geographical clustering. Technically, when the spatial concentration of economic activity creates forces that encourage further spatial concentration, we call these agglomeration forces.

As with dispersion forces, a multitude of agglomeration forces have been identified, but most operate on a scale that is too local to help explain, for example, how the U.K.'s industrialization could deindustrialized China. The two main agglomeration forces used in the new economic geography are supply-side and demand-side circular causality. These are what the twentieth-century development thinker Albert Hirschman somewhat confusingly called "backward and forward linkages."

If an economy already enjoys the presence of a great deal of economic activity (as measured, for example, by GDP), then doing business in the economy will—all else equal—be attractive to firms seeking to be near their customers. Regions with people and firms who are producing a lot are almost always also regions where people and firms are spending a lot. As this attraction draws more firms and more economic activity, the causality is circular. Customers attract producers whose workers become new customers who then attract more firms.

Were it not for dispersion forces, extreme location outcomes would be observed. This is one key reason why the G7 nations can still attract industry despite their high wages.

No firm is an island. Firms buy intermediate inputs from other firms. Because distance from suppliers increases costs, the presence of many firms in a given location tends to make that location attractive on a cost-of-production basis. This is especially relevant in sectors that use lots of intermediate goods and services.

Because of this agglomeration force, a nation that already has a broad industrial base can attract additional industry since the base makes the nation an attractive place to produce. As suppliers attract more suppliers, the causality is self-reinforcing, or circular. This is a key reason why cars made in Germany, for example, can be competitive with cars made in low-wage nations like Thailand.

Generally speaking, demand links operate on an economy-wide basis (say, France versus Uruguay) while supply links operate more on a sectoral basis (say, the car sector or software sector). In many cases, they operate together.

Locational Equilibrium: Balancing the Forces

In the NEG framework, the location of industry shifts to balance agglomeration and dispersion forces. To see how this works it is useful to conduct a small thought experiment. Consider a two-region world where initially the two regions are identical in size and each region has half the world's industry. To start the experiment, suppose some migration occurs for reasons outside the vacuum chamber of our theory. This means that one region (call it the North) becomes bigger than the other region (call it the South) in terms of market size.

If there were no change in the location of industry, firms in the now-big North would be especially profitable since they get to serve a larger fraction of their customers without incurring trade costs while the degree of local competition is unchanged. By the same

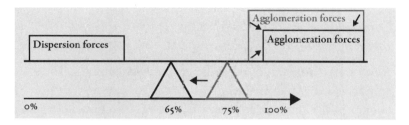

FIGURE 51: Equilibrium location balances agglomeration and dispersion forces. In this example, the initial situation has 75 percent of industry located in the big region. If something lowers the strength of the agglomeration forces, some industry moves from the big region to the small region. As this relocation is happening, the impact of the dispersion force diminishes. The departing firms tend to weaken the local competition in the big region while strengthening it in the small region. Relative wages also adjust in ways that prevent all firms from moving to the small region. In this example, the new equilibrium is, say, 65 percent of industry in the big region.

SOURCE: Adapted from concepts in Richard Baldwin, "Integration of the North American Economy and New-paradigm Globalization," Working Paper WP049, Policy Horizons Canada, September 2009, http://www.international.gc.ca/economist -economiste/assets/pdfs/research/TPR_2011_GVC/04_Baldwin_e_FINAL.pdf.

token, or more precisely the flip side of the token, firms based in the South would earn below-normal returns.

Quite naturally, some firms would move from the South to the North and this movement would tend to equilibrate the profitability of the two locations. Specifically, the firms moving would make competition less intense in the South and more intense in the North. Likewise, the clustering of firms in the North would tend to bid up Northern wages while the out-movement of firms from the South would tend to push down Southern wages.

Observe how both the local-competition effects and the wage effects act in a scissor-like manner. As more firms move North, competition and wages in the North rise while at the same time they fall in the South. This scissor effect is why initial migration shocks lead some firms, but not all firms, to move to the North. An example of this rebalancing is illustrated in Figure 51.

Firms Get More Footloose as Trade Gets Freer: The "Home Market Magnification Effect"

All this reasoning was done holding trade costs constant. The main upshot was that industry tends to concentrate more than proportionally in the big market. But the reasoning so far does not explain what happens to the location of industry when trade costs fall. Falling trade costs are the "Hamlet" of the first unbundling's drama, so it is important to extend the reasoning to cover this situation. The key effect is the so-called home-market magnification effect.

One might expect that since location matters less when trade costs are lower, a given shock would result in less relocation. This is wrong. Somewhat paradoxically, it turns out the firms tend to be more footloose—not less footloose—when trade costs fall. In a nutshell, the reason is that more relocation is needed to re-equilibrate dispersion and agglomeration forces—exactly because location matters less.

Consider the impact of a firm in our thought-experiment that moves from the South to the North in response to a shift in profitability. The firm now sells its wares in the big North without incurring trade costs, but at the same time, it is no longer exporting to the North. Thus. on the one hand, the firm's relocation raises the degree of *local* competition in the Northern market directly, but on the other hand it reduces the extent of *import* competition in the North. The total impact on the degree of competition in the North is the net of the two conflicting effects (more local competition but less import competition). As long as trade costs are positive, the South-to-North relocation will raise the degree of competition in the North, but the net impact is *higher* when trade costs are *high*. This means that it takes more migrating firms to re-equilibrate profitability when trade costs are low.

Extending the logic, it is straightforward to see that the number of firms that must move from the South to the North in order to equilibrate profitability after the initial change in market size must be *larger* when trade costs are *lower*. Intuitively, competition is more localized when trade costs are high, so the competitive effect of a single firm's South-to-North relocation is greater when trade costs are higher. To get the same amount of re-equilibration, more firms have to move to the North when trade costs are low. This is counterintuitive, but the logic is nonetheless airtight. Firms become more (not less) footloose when trade costs are low.

Endogenous Growth Takeoffs and Economic Geography

The static NEG reasoning discussed hereto is a useful indicator as to the direction things may move, but globalization's headline events involved growth rates—not just one-off shifts. Fortunately, connecting location and growth is quite simple.

The big breakthrough Paul Romer made when he launched the endogenous growth theory in the 1980s was conceptual and mathematical. The mathematical part is of no interest here and the conceptual part is so simple it is hard to believe no one had thought of it before Romer. In fact, it is related to Isaac Newton's well-known phrase, "If I have seen a little further it is by standing on the shoulders of giants."[2] Or in today's more prosaic phraseology, knowledge creation generates "spillovers" that make future innovation easier.

Think of each innovation as creating two types of knowledge. The first bit is quite specific and directly remunerated—call it a "patent." The second bit is more diffuse in the sense that it advances the general state of knowledge and thus makes it easier to innovate, but no one can patent this knowledge—it is a public good. Because of the second type of knowledge, each innovation lowers the marginal cost of future innovations. Technically, this means that innovation is subject to a learning curve—the marginal cost falls as innovation experience rises.[3]

As it turns out, the falling cost of innovation is the key to avoiding diminishing returns as the stock of "knowledge capital" rises. First note that productivity-enhancing knowledge is capital. Unlike consumption goods, knowledge does not disappear after its first use. It lingers to provide a continuous flow of productive service into the future. But it is a very special form of capital. To see this, contrast physical and knowledge capital.

Physical capital is useful since it raises the productivity of other factors, such as labor, but the incremental benefit diminishes as the amount of capital per worker rises. For example, big output gains can come by adding tools worth a hundred euros per worker when workers have few tools to start with. The extra output from adding an extra hundred euros of tools per worker is much less when workers already have a great set of tools. For this reason, the capital-to-labor ratio rises but eventually stalls when the marginal cost of more tools per worker just balances the marginal benefit. That's when physical capital accumulation stops. The only thing that can keep it going is an external change, like an expanding workforce or technical advances that increase the benefit of raising the capital-to-labor ratio.

Know-how is not similarly fated. It does not suffer diminishing returns. Indeed, knowledge has been accumulating steadily since the Industrial Revolution and yet new increments of knowledge seem to be as productive as ever. Putting the non-diminishing-returns of knowledge together with some mathematical conditions, innovation can drive growth forever. The marginal benefit of innovation declines as the knowledge stock expands, but the marginal cost also declines, so new product and process innovations continue to be worthwhile.

It is important to note that while the stock of knowledge does not face diminishing returns, the *growth rate* of knowledge does. If something raises the reward to innovation a little bit, the growth rate will rise only a little bit. Or to phrase the point using the jargon, the diminishing returns happen for the growth rate of knowledge, not the stock of knowledge.

The next step is to get distance into the story line so that we can think about the growth implication of falling trade costs (in the first unbundling) and falling communications cost (in the second unbundling). Romer's framework had no distance lever for globalization to pull, but more recent work has bolted on a few such levers.

Growth in a Global Economy

Distance matters for innovation and growth; Isaac Newton's innovators can't get up onto the shoulders of giants if the giants are too far away. Putting this sort of consideration into the framework was done when Gene Grossman and Elhanan Helpman took endogenous growth theory to an international setting in their 1991 book *Innovation and Growth in the Global Economy.*[ ] Again, the key insight is simplicity itself. They allowed the growth-promoting knowledge spillovers to cross borders, but only imperfectly.

The mechanics can be seen with another small thought experiment. Start from two closed economies, each of which is on a self-sustaining growth path that is entirely independent of the other's growth. Moving from no trade in ideas (that is, the knowledge spillovers are only within nations) to costless movement of ideas would increase the growth rate of both nations. The mechanism of action is the way spillovers from foreign innovations lower the cost of innovation domestically. That is, the shift to perfectly free cross-border spillovers means that innovators instantly benefit from twice as many spillovers. This instantly lowers the marginal cost of innovation, so the growth rate in both nations would rise. In a way, the new spillovers that we linked to the foreign-created knowledge provide a subsidy to domestic innovators.

Knowledge Spillovers, the Great Divergence, and the Great Convergence

Tying together the endogenous growth and the New Economic Geography frameworks explains how the steam revolution could have encouraged agglomeration that produced the Great Divergence while the ICT revolution encouraged dispersion that resulted in the Great Convergence. A diagram (Figure 52) helps illustrate the logic.

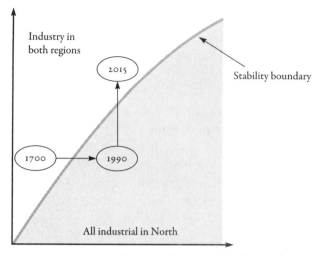

Freeness of international knowledge spillovers

Industry in both regions

2015

Stability boundary

1700 → 1990

All industrial in North

Freeness of international trade in goods

FIGURE 52: Stabilizing and destabilizing integration: first and second unbundlings.

The diagram shows how the freeness of trade and the freeness of knowledge spillovers combine to determine whether industry is clustered all in one region—either the North region or in the South region—or, by contrast, dispersed evenly across the two regions.

Making trade freer encourages the full agglomeration of industry in one region. This is called the "spatial paradox" since it seems paradoxical that activity should cluster more as distance matters less, but this is what happens. The logic of this was discussed in the text, but it is obvious in everyday life. For instance, when transportation gets easier inside a nation, economic activity tends to clusters in cities. Changes that free up trade without freeing up knowledge spillovers correspond to moves in the diagram like the one shown by the arrow connecting the illustrative dates, 1700 and 1990.

Making knowledge spillovers freer works on clustering in the opposite direction. If all the industry is in the North (as it is at point 1990 in the diagram), most of the knowledge is also in the North. Consequently, making knowledge spillovers freer—shown by the vertical arrow connecting 1990 and 2015—encourages industry to disperse. Such dispersion can be thought of as a form of arbitrage between the North that has lots of knowledge and high wages, and the South that has little knowledge and low wages. If the arbitrage gets easy enough, that is to say the freeness of knowledge spillovers rises sufficiently, the situation will flip from all industry in the North to industry being evenly distributed between North and South.

The thinking behind Figure 52 builds on the Krugman-Venable abstraction in that there are just two nations and they are initially perfectly symmetric, so industry is divided fifty-fifty. To begin with, two economic aspects of distance are marked in the diagram. The ease of moving goods is marked on the horizontal axis. It is illustrated with the "freeness of trade" whose scale ranges from zero (when there is no trade) to one (when there is perfectly free trade). The ease of moving ideas is shown on the vertical axis and it is measured with the "freeness of knowledge spillovers" whose scale ranges from zero (when spillovers are fully localized) to one (when spillovers are perfectly internationalized).

As it turns out, there is a tradeoff between the freeness of trade and spillovers when it comes to agglomeration. This tradeoff is put into the diagram with the curve labeled as the "stability boundary," which shows the combinations of the two forms of freeness where a symmetric division of industry is the equilibrium outcome (in the New Economic Geography sense of the word).

To illustrate the workings of this framework, start with the point marked 1700. This is where trade is very costly, so industry is dispersed equally between the two regions (called North and South). When trade gets freer, but nothing happens to the freeness of spillovers, the freeness combination moves horizontally in the diagram. If it goes

---

The upward sloping stability curve is one way of summarizing the opposing effects of the two forms of freeness. Freer knowledge spillovers favor dispersion of industry while freer trade favors its concentration, so if the two freenesses rose in just the right combination, industry would stay dispersed. The exact-right combination is what defines the stability boundary. As such, combinations to the right of the stability boundary (the shaded area) correspond to outcomes where all industry is in the North and happy to stay there. The unshaded area in the northwest part of the diagram has industry dispersed half-half between the North and the South.

SOURCE: Adapted from concepts in Richard Baldwin and Rikard Forslid, "The Core-Periphery Model and Endogenous Growth: Stabilising and Destabilising Integration," *Economica* 67, no. 267 (August 2000): 307–324.

far enough, it crosses the stability boundary and, as explained in the NEG discussion, all industry clusters in one region (in the North to be concrete).

The diagram, however, is not just about industrial clustering. It also has a growth takeoff in the background. At a point like 1700, the dispersion of industry conspires with the high cost of moving ideas and the result is that neither region is growing. Innovations are scarce and spillovers are difficult so the furnace of modern growth—innovation and innovation-spurring knowledge spillovers—it not yet lighted. When industry clusters, as it is at the point 1990, the furnace ignites and growth takes off in the North.

What happens when knowledge spillovers get freer internationally? Keeping trade freeness unchanged, but raising the freeness of spillovers, shows up as a vertical move in the diagram. If spillovers get free enough, the world economy crosses the stability boundary again and industry gets dispersed half-half. The big difference, however, is that Southern growth booms as it industrializes. Moreover, since the spillovers are internationalized at point 2015, growth in the South is also good for growth in the North.

Economics of Supply Chain Unbundling

As mentioned, globalization's second unbundling shifted the locus of globalization from sectors of the economy to stages of production. To understand this shift, new thinking is needed. Traditional thinking about the economic effects of globalization are based on Ricardo's intellectual infrastructure and its modern extension. These concepts willfully ignored production unbundling since it was not important for the facts that the theory was developed to explain.

The economics of offshoring is best looked at by decomposing it into two phenomena: fractionalization and dispersion. Fractionalization concerns the unbundling of production processes into finer stages of production. Dispersion concerns the geographic unbundling of stages. The two are linked insofar as the organization of stages may be crafted with dispersion (offshoring) in mind. Consider the two in turn.

The Fractionalization Dimension (Slicing up the Value Chain)

The offshoring of G7 production stages to developing nations boomed in the 1990s and 2000s. Understanding the "whys" and "hows" is important for comprehending what happened, but it is even more important for thinking about what will happen as ICT gets even better, cheaper, and more pervasive. This requires an analytic framework for thinking about firm-level organization of production.

Think of a firm's production process at four levels of aggregation. Tasks make up the lowest level; tasks are the full list of what must get done to make the product and sell it to consumers. The list of tasks includes all prefabrication services like research and development, product design, marketing research, project financing, accountancy, and more. It also includes postfabrication services such as shipping, warehousing, retail, after-sale services, advertising, and the like.

The second level, occupations, is the most obvious. This is the level of aggregation defined by the list of tasks performed by an individual worker. Next come "stages." Stages are the group of occupations located in close proximity. Finally there is the "product"—that is, the thing that creates value for the firm. TOSP is the acronym for this framework of tasks, occupations, stages, and product. The TOSP framework is schematically presented in Figure 53.

Given the TOSP framework (Figure 53), decisions about how to "slice up the value chain" can be classed into two choices: 1) which tasks should be allocated to which occupations and 2) which occupations should be allocated to which stages.

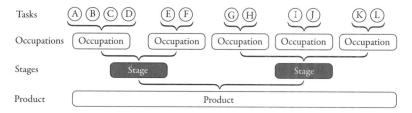

FIGURE 53: Tasks, occupations, stages, and product—the TOSP framework.

Production processes can be usefully thought of as having three natural groupings underneath each product that the firm produces. The finest level consists of all the required tasks. Someone has to be in charge of getting each task done, so the next level is "occupations," defined as the individual workers performing the task (often with the help of machinery). In most production processes, workers are placed close to other workers, which defines the third natural grouping: stages. In most cases, the second unbundling (which is to say offshoring) concerns stages of production, not occupations or tasks.

SOURCE: Richard Baldwin, "Global Supply Chains: Why They Emerged, Why They Matter, and Where They Are Going," in *Global Value Chains in a Changing World,* ed. Deborah K. Elms and Patrick Low (Geneva: World Trade Organization, 2013). Figure 11.

The Specialization versus Coordination Trade-off

Deciding how to organize production is impossibly complex in the real world—that is, in the world of Mein Herr's one-mile-to-the-mile-map world. The choices that real firms make fill days and years of middle-manager time, but allowing for all that detail would obscure the main trade-offs. Abstraction is in order.

Fortunately, Adam Smith laid out a useful approach to the matter. The key trade-off is between *specialization* and *coordination*. In his 1776 book *The Wealth of Nations,* Smith discusses the gains from specialization in the context of an eighteenth-century pin factory. As Smith writes: "One man draws out the wire, another straights it, a third cuts it, a fourth points it, a fifth grinds it at the top for receiving the head; to make the head requires two or three distinct operations; to put it on, is a peculiar business, to whiten the pins is another; it is even a trade by itself to put them into the paper."

Fractionalizing the process in this manner allowed workers to get really good at their assigned tasks. As Smith puts it in his circulatory eighteenth-century English, "I have seen a small manufactory of this kind where ten men only were employed. . . . But though they were very poor, and therefore but indifferently accommodated with the necessary machinery, they could, when they exerted themselves, make among them . . . upwards of forty-eight thousand pins in a day." That is forty-eight hundred pins per worker.

Smith contrasts this productivity with a situation where each worker does all the tasks: "But if they had all wrought separately and independently, and without any of them having been educated to this peculiar business, they certainly could not each of them have made twenty, perhaps not one pin in a day." Productivity is thus radically improved, "in consequence of a proper division and combination of their different operations." Curious readers can see an illustration of Smith's pin factory on the back of the British twenty-pound note.

The downside of splitting up tasks is the difficulty of coordinating the whole process. This is the fundamental trade-off—the benefit of specialization versus the cost of coordination.

Applying this to the TOSP framework, the idea is that fewer tasks per occupation and fewer occupations per stage tend to improve efficiency, as workers can get further down their learning curves and the workplace can be single-mindedly optimized. But specialization raises coordination costs since someone has to make sure that the specialists are not working at cross-purposes.

Better ICT: A Double-Edged Sword for Fractionalization

When thinking about the history and future of the second unbundling, a critical factor is how ICT developments will alter the fundamental efficiency-coordination trade-off. Curiously, the impact of better ICT cuts both ways. On one hand, some types of ICT reduce the benefits of specialization, in the sense that they make it easier for one worker to do more tasks without sacrificing efficiency. On the other hand, other ICT improvements reduce the cost of coordination and thus make it easier to deal with more specialized occupations and stages. The key insight was provided by economists at the London School of Economics and Stanford University, namely Nick Bloom, Luis Garicano, Raffaella Sadun, and John Van Reenen, in a 2009 paper "The Distinct Effects of Information Technology and Communication Technology on Firm Organization."

Some aspects of ICT affect communication and organizational technologies—call them *coordination technologies* (CT). These facilitate the transmission of ideas, instructions, and information.[5] Coordination technologies favor specialization by reducing the cost of coordination. Better coordination technologies will thus tend to foster more fractionalization—that is, more slicing up of the value chain, more offshoring, more foreign direct investment (FDI), and more trade in parts and components.

Other aspects of ICT, by contrast, make it easier for individual workers to master more tasks—call them *information technologies* (IT). Since IT basically means automation, better IT disfavors specialization by reducing the cost of grouping many tasks into a single occupation. This happens in several ways. Today, many factories can be thought of as computer systems where the peripherals are industrial robots, computerized machine tools, and guided vehicles. Additive manufacturing (also known as 3D printing) is the extreme where IT allows a single worker to perform all tasks simply by operating one machine. Perhaps this type of advanced manufacturing should be called "compufacturing" since rather than machines helping workers make things, the workers are helping machines make things.

To sum up, coordination technologies and information technologies cut in opposite directions when it comes to fractionalization. Better CT favor fractionalization by making it cheaper; better IT discourages fractionalization by making it less necessary. In terms of the TOSP framework, improving ICT may lead to either more or fewer tasks per occupation, and either more or fewer occupations per stage.

The Spatial Dimension (Offshoring)

If it were not for offshoring, fractionalization would be purely a matter of domestic industrial organization and thus of little concern to students of globalization. But offshoring is very much a part of twenty-first-century globalization, so the next piece of the puzzle concerns the spatial dispersion of production stages—especially to low-wage nations.

The approach works off the principle that firms seek to put each stage in the lowest-cost location—where all manner of costs are considered. In reality, places differ along many dimensions that matter. The World Economic Forum's competitiveness index, for example, has 110 different measures. The goal here is to follow Karl Popper's dictum and focus only on the things that cannot usefully be ignored. A natural focus is on the cost of productive factors with a special emphasis on wages adjusted for things like productivity, quality, availability, and reliability.

The cost of offshoring stems from "separation" costs while the gain stems from lower production costs. The production costs include wages, capital costs, raw material costs, and implicit or explicit subsidies. The separation costs should be broadly interpreted to include both transmission and transportation costs, increased risk, and managerial time.

The location decision may also be influenced by local spillovers of various types. In some sectors and stages—say, fashion clothing—proximity between designers and consumers may be critical. In others, product development stages may be made cheaper, faster, and more effective by colocation with certain fabrication stages.

There are few mysteries when it comes to offshoring's impact on firms' factor costs. If a low-skill-intensive stage is moved to a developing nation with low wages, the firm will save money. Clearly, at least two wage gaps must be distinguished: low-skill and high-skill.

If low-skill labor is cheap in one country while high-skill labor is cheap in another, firms will tend to move unskilled-intensive stages to the former and skill-intensive stages to the latter. "Headquarters economies," like Germany, have sent labor-intensive stages to nearby low-wage "factory economies" like Poland. High-skill labor, however, remains relatively abundant and thus relatively cheap in headquarters economies, so stages that are intensive in the use of highly skilled labor tend to stay at home.

Wage gaps are not the only motive for supply chain internationalization. Supply chains existed among high-wage economies long before the second unbundling. But the North-North dispersion of production stages is driven by much more micro gains from specialization. For example, when it comes to automobile air conditioners, the French company Valeo competes in the European market through excellence, not low wages. While each European carmaker could make its own air conditioners, scale economies mean that it is cheaper for Italian and German automakers to source them from France. Given the systemic importance of learning-by-doing and the growing role of scale economies in an ever more fractionalized supply chain, it is natural that regional champions emerge in particular parts and components. This explains much of the North-North production sharing that has been prevalent since the 1960s (as discussed in Chapter 3).

Tipping Points and Coordination Costs

While factor costs are simple to take into account, consideration of the separation costs poses some intricacies. Table 7 helps illustrate the point. It presents a simplified example of a manufacturing process—one with six stages, each of which must be coordinated with all the others.

TABLE 7

Coordination-cost matrix.

		Number of offshore stages						
		0	1	2	3	4	5	6
	6	0						
	5		5					
	4			8				
Number of	3				9			
onshore stages	2					8		
	1						5	
	0							0

The table shows how the difficulty of coordination varies as a given production process is broken up and dispersed internationally. In this simple example, suppose that some coordination is necessary between every pair of stages. The costs, however, are different depending on where the stages are. The coordination is assumed to be very cheap when both stages are in the same nation; say the costs are zero to be concrete. However, the cost of coordination in this example is not negligible when the two stages are in separate nations. The key to understanding the coordination costs of various offshoring configurations is thus to count the number of international coordinations that are necessary when a given number of stages are offshored.

When one stage is placed abroad, five cross-border coordinations are necessary since Stage 1 has to coordinate internationally with Stages 2 to 6. When two stages are offshored, eight coordinations will be necessary (Stage 1 with Stages 3 to 6 and the same for Stage 2). As the table shows, the maximum number of coordinations is nine and this is when half the stages are offshored. The number declines when more than half are offshored.

If only one stage is offshored—say, Stage 1—then there will be five bilateral, cross-border relationships to maintain. Specifically, the offshored, Stage 1, has to coordinate with Stages 2 to 6, which are still onshore. This is shown in the box corresponding to one offshore stage and five onshore stages in Table 7. If two stages are offshored, say, Stages 1 and 2, there are eight cross-border relationships—namely, Stages 1 and 2 with each of the four onshore stages. If the offshoring now spreads to three sectors, we get the maximum amount of cross-border coordination—Stages 1 to 3 must coordinate internationally with Stages 4 to 6, making nine, bilateral communications necessary.

In terms of communication costs, offshoring half the stages is plainly the most costly configuration. If even more stages are offshored, the cross-border coordination costs start to fall. They are clustering offshore rather than onshore, but clustering anywhere reduces the need for international coordination. Specifically, it is easy to see that as Stages 1 to 6 are progressively offshored, the need for international coordination first rises, from five to eight to nine, and then falls back down to eight, then five.

This is what is called "tipping point economics." Three stages offshored is the tipping point. Once it is worth sending at least three stages abroad, it will probably be worthwhile to send more than three. The technical name for this rather common situation is called "convex coordination costs."

It is important to note that this convexity means that coordination costs act as an agglomeration force. That is to say, the solution to minimizing coordination costs is to keep all stages bundled together.

An unusual feature of the convexity of coordination costs is that offshoring will tend to be delayed in the sense that a stage that would be cheaper to do abroad will stay at home to economize on coordination costs. But when offshoring does occur, "too many" stages will go since clustering stages saves on coordination costs. This is called offshore "overshooting." Thinking this through, it also means that as coordination costs fall further, some stages will be "reshored"—a phenomenon that seems to have started in the 2010s.

Fractionalization and Offshoring Interactions: The Nature of Jobs

Fractionalization and offshoring have, so far, been considered separately, yet they can and do interact in important ways—ways that might involve firms changing the mix of tasks per occupation, or occupations per stage, to take advantage of offshoring possibilities. It is perhaps easiest to illustrate this point with an example.

An *Atlantic* magazine article by Adam Davidson contrasts the lives of two workers at a Greenville, South Carolina factory that makes fuel injectors.[6] One worker does manual labor that requires little training or education and she earns $13 an hour. She just puts a partly processed fuel injector into a machine and pushes a button; the machine then welds a cap on. For her job, judgment, skill, and experience are not job requirements. Indeed, her bit of the supply chain could conceivably be automated.

The second worker that Davidson follows has a quite different set of tasks and a quite different skill set. He gets paid $30 an hour and got his job after three years of schooling and five years of experience in another factory. He works a $500,000 machine that mills engine valves to within a quarter of a millionth of a meter. This involves frequent testing and readjustments since the drill bits erode with use.

There are several lessons from this example when it comes to how fractionalization and offshoring are related. For example, the IT part of ICT is bifurcating the skill range. The high-tech turning machine requires far more skill and training than was formerly needed by factory workers, but the woman's place-and-push job probably requires even less skill. Better IT makes it easier to wrap labor-intensive tasks into occupations that involve higher degrees of skill and more expensive machines. In this way, IT tends to have two important effects: it makes the stages that remain in G7 nations more skill-intensive and it reduces the overall number of workers needed. This situation also allows firms to group many unskilled tasks into stages that can be offshored. Advancing ICT is thus helping G7 nations hold on to some manufacturing jobs, but these jobs tend to require high-skill workers.

Another lesson is that globalization is not always the main cause of deindustrialization. The woman's real competitors in this story are not Chinese workers, but American-based robots. Earning $13 an hour, she was more economical than a robot in 2012, but many of her coworkers had already been replaced.

Finally, even in an era of cheap transport, the dictates of distance force the bundling of high-skill and low-skill occupations. The woman's job is not offshored since it is just too expensive in dollars, time, and coordination costs to have the caps welded on in nations where $13 is a monthly, not hourly wage.

With this economics in hand, we turn to explaining the big facts.

CHAPTER 7

Accounting for Globalization's Changed Impact

"It is quite true what philosophy says," remarked Soren Kierkegaard, "that life must be understood backwards. But then one forgets the other principle: that it must be lived forwards."

To understand history backwards, this chapter proffers a guided tour of nineteenth-, twentieth-, and twenty-first-century globalization using the map provided by the three-cascading-constraints perspective and the basic economics presented in the previous chapter. The tour is organized around the key facts highlighted in Chapters 2 and 3.

Understanding the First Unbundling's Stylized Facts

Chapter 2 identified five top-line facts that marked globalization's first unbundling:

- The North industrialized while the South deindustrialized
- Trade boomed
- Growth took off worldwide but sooner and faster in the North than in the South
- The Great Divergence happened
- Urbanization accelerated, especially in the North.

All these stylize facts can be easily understood as implications of globalization's first unbundling. The explanation starts with the first two facts since they are tightly linked.

Northern Industrialization, Southern Deindustrialization, and Trade

In a deservedly famous paper on "Globalization and the Inequality of Nations," Paul Krugman and Tony Venables explain the first two facts with the new economic geography (NEG) framework. The paper—known among cognoscenti by its working title, "History of the World: Part I"—shows that the NEG logic very neatly accounts for the way that falling trade costs produced industrialization in the North and deindustrialization in the South.[1]

The Krugman-Venables explanation—which probably has Immanuel Wallerstein smiling with its World-System–like story line— starts with an enormously unrealistic, but enormously illuminating, abstraction. Namely, they view the world as made up of only two regions—North and South. The North is shorthand for today's rich nations (represented, for convenience, by the Group of Seven, G7, nations), and the South is shorthand for today's developing nations (represented, for convenience, by the Ancient Seven, A7 civilizations in today's China, India, Egypt, Iraq, Iran, Turkey, and Greece / Italy). The Greek / Italian case is special in the sense that these nations switched from the A7 to the G7 in this account before the first unbundling really gets going in the early nineteenth century.

The curtain goes up on the Krugman-Venables story with industry equally dispersed between the North and South since people everywhere were tied to the land and horrible transportation tied industry to people. When trade costs fell in the nineteenth century, competitive pressures pushed each region to specialize. As history would have it, the G7 started specializing in industry and this specialization triggered a process of circular causality. That is, Northern industrialization boosted Northern incomes and expanded the size of the Northern market. The market expansion completed the circle by making the North a more attractive place for industry. Southern industry never really had a chance once the circular causality got going. In short, Northern industrialization and free trade deindustrialized the South. See Chapter 2 for the facts and Chapter 6 for details of the Krugman-Venables logic.

The big problem with interpreting history through the lens of the Krugman-Venables abstraction is the initial size of Asia. Before 1820, China alone had 33 percent of world gross domestic product (GDP)—six times more than Britain and indeed twice the size of the North Atlantic economies taken together. India's economy was as large as all the North Atlantic economies combined. Thus it was the small region that won, not the big region. The G7 became the core while the A7 became the periphery. The unvarnished Krugman-Venables logic suggests that the opposite should have happened.

The historical evolution is illustrated in Figure 54. This plots the A7's and G7's shares of world population on the horizontal axis and their respective shares of world income on the vertical axis. If the static Krugman-Venables model were applied literally, the first unbundling should have created the Great Divergence, but Asia should have won. The A7 dots should all have been above the 45-degree line and rising. All the G7 dots should have been below it and falling. History chronicles exactly the opposite ending.

One way of explaining this outcome is to turn to political history and blame colonialism and imperialism. While gunpowder was invented in China, its military use was developed in Europe—honed by centuries of intra-European war. When the Age of Discovery arrived, European military technology was far ahead and the gap continued to grow in subsequent centuries. According to this explanation, Europeans used guns to colonize the A7 and suppress their industry. There is something to this reasoning. For example, the American colonies—which eventually became the United States— were explicitly forbidden from exporting manufactured goods, but exports of raw materials like cotton and wood were encouraged. Colonies were supposed to supply England with raw materials and buy British manufactured goods. Likewise, the emigration of British

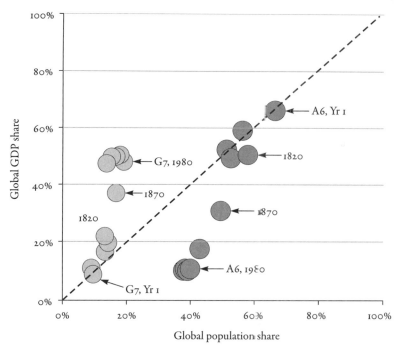

FIGURE 54: North and South shares of global population and GDP, year 1 to 1990.
The shifts in GDP during the first unbundling seemed to go the wrong way, according to new economic geography (NEG) models. In the NEG thinking, the initially big region (i.e., China and India) should have got the industry and takeoffs but in fact it was the small region—Europe—that won. The chart shows that in year 1 the "ancient six" (A6)—that is, the seven ancient civilizations minus Italy—was far, far larger than the G7. Nonetheless, the world share of GDP rose in the small region and fell in the big region.

DATA SOURCE: Maddison database (2009 version).

skilled manufacturing workers and the export of British textile machinery were forbidden by Acts of Parliament.

There are also economic arguments. For one, the South was not as innovation-friendly an environment as the North, so its size advantage was squandered. It is also surely important that per capita incomes in the North were much higher than those in the South. In 1820, Chinese average incomes were only a third of those in the United Kingdom. Since spending on manufactured goods tends to be low for people near subsistence levels of income, overall GDP may be a poor indicator of the market size that matters—namely, the market for manufactured goods.

Physical geography must also have been important. The notion of "market access" stresses the benefits to a nation of being near other large, high-income nations. China and India are quite distant from each other and from the Atlantic economies. Land transport has always been hindered by the Southeast Asian jungles and the Himalayas, and the sea route is not particularly direct and must pass through the choke point of the Strait of Malacca. The North Atlantic economy, by contrast, is comparatively proximate. Europe and the Americas are connected by the Atlantic, and both sides have reasonably good river access to their interiors. Surely the full answer lies in a combination of the political, economic, and geographic factors.

The next two facts to be explained are the differential growth takeoffs in the North and the South, and the Great Divergence.

Growth Takeoffs and the Great Divergence

The Krugman-Venables reasoning focuses on industry and GDP shares but ignores growth. To account for the G7's growth takeoff and the resulting massive divergence of incomes, growth has to be added to the equation. This is done using the growth logic developed by Gene Grossman and Elhanan Helpman. As explained in the previous chapter, the basic mechanism turns on the way that knowledge creation makes it easier to create knowledge.

Although modern agriculture has been subject to important technical advances since the 1960s, innovation in globalization's first century was dominated by industrial innovation. As the G7 economies were gaining industry and the A7 economies losing industry, G7 innovation became easier while A7 innovation became harder.

Northern industrialization, in other words, advanced Northern growth, while the Southern deindustrialization held back Southern growth. More specifically, the clustering of industry in the G7 nations implied a spatial clustering of innovation in the G7 nations. Given how continuous growth is driven by knowledge spillovers, and how knowledge spillovers were localized by the high cost of moving ideas, the region that got the industry also saw its growth takeoff sooner.

The causality, however, went both ways. The industrialization-induced innovation gave Northern industry a powerful cost advantage over industry in the South. This favored the North as a location for industry, thus further advancing Northern innovation and hindering Southern innovation. In this way, lower internal and international transport costs produced industrial agglomeration that generated industrialization and a growth takeoff in the North. The same forces produced deindustrialization and a delayed growth takeoff in the South.[2]

Having explained why the first unbundling produced faster income growth in the North, accounting for the Great Divergence is straightforward. As numerically minded readers will have already understood, it was exactly this growth gap—plus the inescapable implication of growth compounding—that put the "great" into the Great Divergence after just a few decades.

Urbanization

The only fact of the first unbundling that is left unaccounted for concerns urbanization. Urban economics has many explanations for the close association between globalization's first unbundling and rising city size. Among the most compelling is Ed Glaeser's simple assertion that cities are a way of economizing on communication costs. Cities are where people meet and exchange ideas.

As Glaeser put it in a 2009 Economix blog post: "Globalization and technological change have increased the returns to being smart;

human beings are a social species that get smart by hanging around smart people. A programmer could work in the foothills of the Himalayas, but that programmer wouldn't learn much. If she came to Bangalore, then she would figure out what skills were more valuable, and what companies were growing, and which venture capitalists were open to new ideas in her field. The information flows that come from proximity might also help to build the relationships that would enable her to create her own start-up. A remarkable number of information-technology start-ups in India were formed by partners who connected in Bangalore."[3]

This account of rising city size finds an almost perfect analogy in the logic behind the formation of factories. As discussed in Chapter 4, easier trade expanded the market for industrial firms and the extra scale led them to adopt more complex processes. To save on coordination costs, the production was clustered into factories.

Understanding the Second Unbundling's Stylized Facts

Chapter 3 identified seven essential outcomes from Phase Four.

- The North deindustrialized while a small number of developing nations industrialized
- The rapid industrializers saw their growth soar
- Commodity prices experienced a super-cycle that initiated growth takeoffs in commodity exporting nations
- The Great Convergence occurred
- The nature of North-South trade changed to involve much more back-and-forth trade
- Most developing nations embraced trade liberalization
- The impacts were very geographically specific.

The first four essential outcomes are closely entwined with the South's industrialization, so they provide a good starting point.

Southern Industrialization, Northern Deindustrialization, and Offshoring

Phase Four was witness to a partial reversal of the reversal of fortune that occurred in Phase Three—at least for some of the ancient civilizations. For example, Chapter 3 showed that the G7's share of world manufacturing fell from about two-thirds to under a half, while that of six developing nations rose almost as much.

From the perspective of the New Economic Geography, such colossal changes in the location of economic activity must have been driven by a great weakening of the agglomeration forces that had arisen during the first unbundling, or a great strengthening of dispersion forces. The defining features of the second unbundling—the new North-to-South knowledge flows—tells us that it was a bit of both.

The central point turns on the realization that knowledge spillovers—which acted as an agglomeration force in the nineteenth century—started acting as a powerful dispersion force in the twenty-first century. When Northern innovations stayed in the North due to the high cost of moving ideas, the rising pile of know-how made the North a very attractive place to produce. Now that G7 firms can leverage their firm-specific know-how by combining it with low wages in nearby developing nations, the knowledge spillovers are making the South a very attractive place to produce. The result is that industry is running from the "core" to the "periphery."

Turning from agglomeration forces to dispersion forces, the argument gets subtle and focuses on wages as a dispersion force. During the first unbundling, rapid industrialization pushed up wages in a way that slowed down the agglomeration. During the second unbundling, the wage-industrialization link was muted by particular features of global value chains. More exactly, G7 firms moved, and are still moving, specific pieces of know-how to specific production facilities in China and other emerging markets. They try very hard to prevent this knowledge from becoming generalized to other firms in the offshore destination.

The motives for this guarding of technology had little to do with wages, but the consequence was a much weaker wage-industry link in the second unbundling as compared to the first. The point is that workers in the offshored factories got paid something that was tied to what might be called their "next best option" wage, that is, what they would have earned if they stayed in rural regions and used local know-how. Because the advanced know-how in the factories stayed in the factories, the next-best-option wage did not rise quickly despite the rapid industrialization.

In a nutshell, the dispersion forces that might have slowed down the shifting of industry from North to South were neutralized by the fact that know-how transfers were happening mostly inside global value chains.

Growth Takeoffs, the Super-Cycle, the Great Convergence

Having explained how the second unbundling generated the industrialization of a handful of developing nations, it is simple to account for three more of the essential outcomes. Since 1990, globalization has been dominated by reductions in the cost of moving ideas. According to the growth theory discussed in the previous chapter, such freeing up of international knowledge spillovers provides an extra growth boost to the industrializing South. This sort of growth takeoff linked to rapid industrialization is exactly what happened in China and the other I6.

The growth acceleration in the I6, however, produced outcome number three—the commodity super-cycle and attendant growth takeoffs in commodity exporting nations. The connection is quite direct. By stimulating the demand for commodities, the I6's rapid income expansion pushed up the prices of the full range of commodities— everything from wheat to powered milk to iron ore and oil. As most of the commodity exporting nations were developing nations, the super-cycle stimulated Southern incomes more than Northern incomes.

The fourth outcome, the Great Convergence, stemmed directly from the booming growth in the South. The large growth gaps between the G7 and the developing nations during the 1990s and 2000s compounded into the "shocking share shift" that was discussed in the Introduction.

Why the Impact Was Very Geographically Specific

The second unbundling transformed the realities of twenty-first-century manufacturing. Manufacturing boomed in developing nations that switched the basis of their competitiveness from a low-tech / low-wage bundle to a high-tech / low-wage bundle. Manufacturing slumped in locations that stayed with a combination of either high-tech and high-wage or low-tech and low-wage. Developing nations that were too far from the high-tech manufacturing giants (the United States, Japan, and Germany) or unwilling to do what it took to join international production networks saw little change.

According to the three-cascading-constraint narrative, the changes are so geographically specific since the third constraint on globalization—the high cost of moving people—is still binding. The manufacturing revolution only happened in developing nations that high-tech firms decided to invite into their production networks. To economize on face-to-face costs, these firms concentrated offshoring in a few nearby nations.

India is a special case; it has joined global value chains via services that are much less subject to the face-to-face constraint.

The third outcome is a direct and rather obvious implication of North-South production sharing. Goods that move inside international production networks can cross borders multiple times.

Why Developing Nations Changed Their Behavior

For developing nations that could attract G7 production networks, the second unbundling was a true revolution. It opened a new pathway to industrialization and growth. The technology transfer that everyone had hoped for in the 1970s, 1980s, and 1990s was finally happening—but not the way twentieth-century development theory said it would. Instead of building the whole supply chain domestically to become competitive internationally (the twentieth-century way), developing nations were joining global value chains to become competitive and then industrializing by densifying their participation.

This new industrialization pathway was more than an opportunity; it was also a threat. With China industrializing the new way, other developing nations could no longer do it the old way—the way that had previously worked for the United States, Germany, France, Japan, and most recently, Korea. Simply put, low-tech / low-wage cannot compete with high-tech / low-wage.

More practically, developing nations that wanted a chance to join the second unbundling—also known as the global value chain revolution—had to embrace certain policies. The key insight to thinking clearly about such policies comes from the view of global value chains as "factories crossing borders." According to this view, fostering global value chain participation involves two categories of assurances: supply chain assurances and offshoring assurances.

Supply chain assurances address the necessity of connecting factories that cross borders. Twenty-first-century supply chains involve the whole trade-investment-service-intellectual-property "nexus," since bringing high-quality, competitively priced goods to customers in a timely manner requires international coordination of production facilities via the continuous two-way flow of goods, people, ideas, and investments. Threats to any of these flows became barriers to global value chain participation and industrial development. This is why industrial protectionism became destructionism in the twenty-first century.

With these points in mind, it is easy to understand the radical change in the attitudes of developing nations toward trade liberalization and pro-investment, pro-services, pro-intellectual property rights (IPR) reforms. It is also easy to understand why the policy changes were synchronous with the changes in manufacturing and trade. The second unbundling drove all of them. More specifically, bilateral investment treaties (BITs) and deep bilateral regional trade agreements (RTAs) were signed with advanced-technology nations to provide the assurances.

Interestingly, many developing nations embraced these disciplines but few saw a takeoff in their global value chain participation. This is a classic outcome of misthinking globalization—in particular it is misthinking the role of distance when it comes to face-to-face costs (that is, today's binding constraint). For people, there is a very large difference between flying somewhere and back in the same day and taking longer trips.

This may explain why the global value chain revolution has yet to come to South America and Africa, but is spreading like wildfire in Asia, Central America, and Central Europe. Put simply, most parts of Africa and all of South America are just too far from Northern know-how.

BOX 9: SUMMARY OF ACCOUNTING FOR THE IMPACTS OF THE OLD AND NEW GLOBALIZATION

When trade costs fell, industry clustered in the G7 economies and triggered growth-enhancing innovation. Since the cost of moving ideas fell much less, the innovations stayed in the North. The North industrialized and the South deindustrialized. Because of this uneven experience with industry, the Northern growth takeoff was earlier and faster than the South's takeoff—and the result was the Great Divergence and rapid growth in international trade flows.

When the ICT revolution lowered the cost of moving ideas inside the boundaries of international production chains, G7 firms started to arbitrage the gigantic imbalance in the planetary distribution of know-how by moving Northern knowledge to the South. The result was a rapid industrialization of the nations involved in these global value chains and a rapid deindustrialization of the G7 firms' home nations. As before, rapid industrialization triggered rapid income growth, but this time the growth affected about half of humanity rather than just a fifth as it had done in the nineteenth and twentieth centuries. The resulting hike in commodity demand yielded a two-decade-long boom in commodity prices and exports, which subsequently triggered growth takeoffs in commodity exporting nations ranging from Australia to Nigeria.

This chapter showed how these history-bending outcomes can all be explained by applications of the economics discussed in Chapter 6.

PART IV

Why It Matters

Globalization has been a transformational force for almost 200 years. Some countries reacted with a head-in-sand response—North Korea today and Albania up until the 1990s come to mind. But most nations decided to accept globalization and make the best of whatever cards history had dealt them. For rich nations, this mostly meant embracing policies that shared globalization's gains and pains among all citizens while preparing workers for the jobs of tomorrow. For developing nations, it mostly meant adopting policies that would help them industrialize.

In most cases, the thinking behind the response was based on the traditional conceptualization of the Old Globalization. This was fine for globalization's first 170 years, but no longer. One of this book's central assertions is that applying the conventional view to today's challenges is wrong; it is a misthinking of globalization.

Harvard economist Greg Mankiw provides a clear example in his April 24, 2015, opinion piece in the *New York Times*. His essay urges the U.S. Congress to grant President Obama the authority necessary to get twenty-first-century trade agreements passed—agreements like the Trans-Pacific Partnership (TTP) and the Transatlantic Trade and Investment Partnership (TTIP). Laying out the case, he writes:

> The economic argument for free trade dates back to Adam Smith, the 18th-century author of The Wealth of Nations and the grandfather of modern economics. ... Americans should work in those industries in which we have an advantage compared with other nations, and we should import from abroad those goods that can be produced more cheaply there.

And Mankiw is in good company. He was one of thirteen leading U.S. economists to sign an open letter to the U.S. Congress that makes the same points. These are not marginal characters; they are all leading professors of economics and each served as the chief economist to a U.S. president.

Regardless of their pedigrees, these economists are misthinking trade policy. They are applying the Old Globalization's logic to a New Globalization trade agreement. To harken back to the soccer team analogy from the Introduction, they are characterizing the TPP as if it were encouraging an exchange of players. Taking this as given, the rest of their argument is rock solid. Freer trade does allow all nations to gain by "doing what they do best and importing the rest." But the fact is that TPP is much more like the soccer coach training the other team. TPP will make it easier to move advance know-how to low-wage nations—an outcome that is not covered by Adam Smith's reasoning.

Since so much globalization policy was crafted with the Old Globalization in mind, much of the policy response is misshapen or at least suboptimal. To take a couple of obvious examples, economic institutions like labor unions tend to be organized by sectors and skill groups since that was the level at which the Old Globalization affected economies. And national education strategies typically seek to train children for promising jobs in promising sectors since the Old Globalization cut a predictable path that defined sunrise and sunset sectors. Likewise, governments around the world seek to dampen the pain of structural adjustment with policies linked to declines in particular sectors or particular geographic areas (often those that had specialized in sunset sectors). Most of these policies are inappropriate for today's globalization, which is more sudden in its impact, more individual in its effects, more uncontrollable for governments, and more unpredictable overall (as argued in Chapter 5).

Ultimately, there can be no magic solutions to the changed nature of globalization. The New Globalization makes life harder for governments. But the intrinsic difficulty is multiplied by the fact that many governments and analysts are using the Old Globalization's mental model to understand the New Globalization's effects.

Part IV runs through a broad range of policies that need to be rethought in the light of the fundamental changes in globalization. Chapter 8 focuses on how one might rethink globalization policies in advanced nations; Chapter 9 does the same for developing nations.

Rethinking G7 Globalization Policies

"The art of progress is to preserve order amid change and to preserve change amid order." This maxim, by the philosopher Alfred Whitehead, sums up the challenges that globalization poses for governments around the world, but especially in advanced countries.

The crux of the matter, from a political perspective, is that progress requires change, but change involves pain as well as gain. If governments want support for continual progress, the citizens must have a faith that both the gains and pains will be shared. In rich nations at least, such faith is in short supply. According a 2014 Pew Research Center poll, 60 percent of Italians, 50 percent of Americans and French, and 40 percent of Japanese believe that trade destroys jobs.[1]

This chapter considers some of the rethinking that may be useful in the light of the changes in globalization discussed in the previous chapters. The focus is, in turn, on competitiveness policy, industrial policy, trade policy, and social policy.

Rethinking Competitiveness Policy

Competitiveness is not what it used to be. When popularized in the 1990s, the notion was unhelpful at best and possibly harmful.[2] Intoxicating audiences with powerful metaphors and provocative buzzwords, the purveyors of the "competitiveness problem" won head-of-state attention. A little knowledge can be a dangerous thing, but in this case it was joined by smashing good rhetoric and became, as Paul Krugman put it, a "dangerous obsession."[3]

The damage stemmed from the solutions that seemed to flow naturally from the way competitiveness gurus posed the problem. Competition of the everyday type compares what I'm doing to what others are doing—whether it is in business, love, or sports. The very word "competition" evokes a win-lose mind-set; what is good for you is bad for me—after all, we are competing. Policymakers, in other words, started viewing national problems like a footrace when in fact the problems were more like losing weight. Someone wins a footrace and all the others lose; the outcome depends on relative performance. When it comes to weight loss, all can win and the outcome depends on one's own effort, not relative performance.

Fortunately, lessons have been learned. Nowadays, competitiveness policy is just growth policy in sexy underwear. The emphasis has shifted back to what nations must do themselves to raise living standards. Comparison to other nations is a matter of national benchmarking, not national competition.

New Considerations for Competitiveness Policy

The traditional globalization paradigm thinks of production as a national thing. This thinking, plus the ineluctable logic of growth (see Box 10), directs policy in a very clear direction. Competitiveness policies that are pro-growth must foster investment in human, physical, social, and knowledge capital and ensure the new capital is deployed wisely.

Inducing heightened investment in any of these forms of capital would be pro-growth when production stages were bundled within factories, or at least within nations. This led governments to put the type-of-capital question to one side. Instead, they focused on the market-failure question, that is to say, on why the market wasn't investing enough. Spillovers or market failures were usually part of the answer. With this simplification in mind, good policy was clear. The government should focus on forms of investment characterized by market failures. The policies chosen usually involved:

BOX 10: THE INELUCTABLE LOGIC OF GROWTH

Raising living standards means raising output, for the very simple reason that a nation's income depends on its output. Gross domestic product (GDP) is a measure of both output and income since, if someone makes it, someone owns it.

Raising output year after year requires workers, farmers, technicians, and managers to produce higher value year after year. This in turn requires more and better tools year after year—where "tools" broadly means physical capital (machines, infrastructure, and so forth), human capital (skills, training, experience), social capital (trust, rule of law, sense of social justice), and knowledge capital (technology, product development, and the like).

- Promoting investment in knowledge capital with government-sponsored research, private-sector R&D subsidies, tax breaks, and support for research-oriented universities
- Promoting investment in human capital with policies linked to education, training, and retraining
- Promoting investment in infrastructure and social capital.

The thinking focused mainly on which policies would foster the greatest spillovers (the answer was usually R&D) or correct the biggest market failures (the answer was often infrastructure).

Competitiveness Policy for a Fragmented, Footloose World

Things are more complicated in the fragmented, footloose world of the second unbundling, as economist Simon Evenett of the University of St. Gallen and I pointed out in our 2012 paper for the British government on value creation and trade in manufacturing.[4]

The main point is that wise governments should distinguish carefully between factors of production that are internationally mobile and those that are internationally immobile. Both matter. Both contribute to national income. But, as Enrico Moretti points out in his must-read book *The New Geography of Jobs,* good jobs created in G7 nations have a local multiplier effect, which good jobs created by G7 firms abroad do not.[5]

A Two-Dimensional Evaluation

The point that some forms of capital may escape abroad suggests that an important consideration for policy should be the "stickiness" of the various productive factors. As usual, government intervention is only a good idea when the market is missing something, so spillovers also matter. Combining these two observations leads naturally to a two-dimensional ranking of factors of production—namely, their mobility and their potential for spillovers—when evaluating government policy aimed at enhancing the supply of such factors. Figure 55 schematically presents a general conceptualization of potential targets for pro-growth policies.

Trying to promote G7 manufacturing through policies aimed at highly mobile factors, like financial capital and basic science, is likely to have little local effect on industrial production. The newly created capital tends to flow to the nation where its reward is highest. The nation implementing the policy has to pay for the policy but gets a mere fraction of the benefit. The clear implication is that such support should be accompanied by international coordination. Moving back down the mobility scale, physical capital is somewhat less mobile internationally (after it is sunk) and it has intermediate spillovers.

Highly skilled labor presents an attractive combination of low mobility and high spillovers. This combination is one of the reasons that almost all governments believe that subsidizing technical education is one of the best ways to promote their nation's industrial competitiveness.

A good way to think about this situation is to turn the problem around and look at how foreign countries could exploit other na-

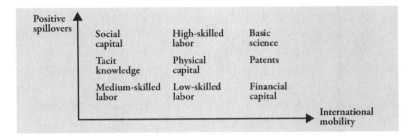

FIGURE 55: Targets of policy: stickiness and spillover potential.

A standard feature of rich nations' competitiveness policy is the promotion of certain productive factors such as human capital, knowledge capital, and physical capital. The traditional justification is that the social reward to increasing the nation's stock of such factors exceeds the private reward (so the free market—left to its own devices—will produce too little of the factor). "Positive spillovers" is the jargon for situations where the social reward exceeds the private reward In the world before the second unbundling, the extent of spillovers was perhaps the major economic factor considered by economic policy analysis.

In a world where the sources of comparative advantage can cross borders, the analysis should also think about the "stickiness" of productive factors when deciding which to promote. For example, if the United States gives a big tax break to foster new products and then most of the resulting value added ends up happening abroad, the spillovers that justified the subsidy may not benefit the U.S. tax payers who subsidized the knowledge creation.

SOURCE: Modified from Baldwin and Everett (2012). Figure 1c.

tions' growth-promoting policies. Policies that attract foreign-educated, high-skill workers, for instance, make a lot of sense in this framework. It is also a policy pursued by many nations. The H-1B visa program of the United States is one well-known example. In Switzerland, it's the doctors.

Something like a quarter of all doctors practicing in Switzerland have foreign medical degrees—most of them from Germany, France, Italy, and Austria. The doctors flock to Switzerland because of the good pay and attractive working conditions. As the sending nations charge no tuition for medical school, it is clear that the Swiss health sector enjoys a heathy subsidy from its neighbors.

This unintended consequence of education policies is rather obvious. What is less obvious is how the same thing is now happening within international production networks. When Carrier announced in 2016 that it would close its facility in Indianapolis and move production to Mexico, it was implicitly saying that it was going to use some of its tax-break-subsidized R&D to create jobs abroad. That does not mean that the offshoring is wrong. And it does not mean that the R&D subsidy is wrong. What it illustrates is the fact that the nature of and justification for R&D subsidies should be refined to encompass the nature of the New Globalization.

Tacit knowledge is the next in the schematic diagram. It is defined as knowledge that seems to encourage spatial clustering of production. Such knowledge is difficult to promote directly, but it has the great advantage of being unlikely to leave the nation once it is created. This unique combination explains why so many nations are trying to create industrial clusters or hubs. The position of medium- and low-skill laborers requires little comment; they are marked by a close connection between the public and private benefits.

Finally, each nation, and indeed each location in each nation, has "social capital" that affects the attractiveness of the location for workers and firms. Social capital means human interaction that depends on trust and reliability. As well-traveled readers will know, the extent to which societies are marked by these intangible factors varies enormously. Since economic interactions require trust, the presence of a sense of social justice and trust can be an important magnet for economic activity. In terms of spillovers, social capital is localized, but it provides benefits across many stages and sectors.

The stickiness versus spillover thinking can be augmented by considerations of risk. The point is that considerations concerning the vulnerability of jobs and activities to the vicissitudes of the New Globalization depend in part on their position in global value chains.

When value creation happened mostly inside a single factory or at least within a single nation, there was little reason for policymakers to worry about where the nation's workers were located within the economy's value network. When production processes are fractionalized and easily dispersed internationally, centrality in the value network can matter.

If a particular activity serves only one type of customer, the offshoring of the client can lead to offshoring of the supplier. Economic activity, after all, likes to be near its customers. By contrast, a worker engaged in producing a good or service that is demanded by a wide range of sectors will have an easier time adjusting to the caprices of future globalization. The logical bedrock of this point is nothing more than the old "all eggs in one basket" point in a world where changes are more sudden and more unpredictable.

A similar line of thinking applies to the types of skills that governments might want to promote with competitiveness policies. Here again centrality of demand matters and should be an additional consideration. For similar reasons, flexibility of skills is also a good thing.

Human Capital Is Key

This checklist of targets suggests that of the many factors of production, people and skills are perhaps the most important when thinking about a new paradigm for competitiveness policy. Most workers are not internationally mobile for personal reasons, so domestic investment in human capital tends to stay domestic. Another source of stickiness arises from agglomeration forces. Skilled service workers are often subject to agglomeration economies. As discussed in Chapter 6, this means that a skills-cluster is more than the sum of its parts, which in turn means that the cluster can pay over-the-odds wages.

Human capital has the extra attraction of being flexible. Skills that produce excellence are often transferable across sectors and stages, which allows workers to adapt to changing demands. Human capital is also central in the input-output structure. Skill-intensive services are inputs into many different stages and products, so demand for such tasks is more stable.

Rethinking Industrial Policy

G7 governments have long paid a huge amount of attention to manufacturing jobs, with an emphasis on factory jobs. And they still do. While there may be many political reasons for this, there is also a solid economic argument for it that rested on productivity growth.

For more than a century, manufacturing has been the leading sector when it comes to productivity growth. Of course, shop-floor workers were only part of the story. Much of the progress came from product and process innovations in the manufacturing sector, but the factory was viewed as the spatial anchor. In any case, as long as all stages were bundled nationally, production was a national thing and factories were as good a marker as any for the productivity gains.

The fractionalization and offshoring of production stages that took off in the 1990s changed matters. The manufacturing value chain was fractionalized, with labor-intensive fabrication stages separated out and offshored along with the G7 know-how necessary to bring the offshore fabrication up to G7 standards. This high-tech / low-wage combination radically lowered the cost of fabrication. While this commoditized fabrication, it did not commoditize the pre- and post-fabrication service stages. The result was the smile curve discussed in Chapter 3.

Whether governments are looking for more good jobs or trying to boost the competitiveness of their exports, the shift in value to services means that there should be much less industry in twenty-first-century industrial policy.

Good Manufacturing Jobs without the Manufacturing

When companies like Uniqlo combine their advanced knowledge with low wages, the value added in fabrication plummets. This makes it nigh on impossible for Japanese workers using Japanese technology to compete with Chinese workers using Japanese technology. It would be a fool's game to try to promote such jobs in Japan. There still are good manufacturing-related jobs in Japan, but many of them are, and increasingly will be, service jobs. Policymakers should correspondingly embrace a broader view of "good jobs."

The agglomeration economies mentioned previously create another important fact: "sticky" jobs tend to be good jobs, and vice versa. As Moretti writes: "In innovation, a company's success depends on the entire ecosystem that surrounds it. . . . It is harder to delocalize innovation than traditional manufacturing. . . . You would have to move not just one company but an entire ecosystem." The same applies to many kinds of services.

As the servicification of manufacturing advances, the competitiveness of a nation's manufactured exports will increasingly depend on the local availability of a broad range of excellent, reasonably priced services. In a sense, excellent and diverse service sectors should be thought of as twenty-first-century industrial bases. Consequently, G7 industrial policy should not just be about industry, or at least not just about industry in the factory sense of the word. It should be about fostering manufacturing-linked services as well.

Lose Some Jobs or Lose Them All?

More lessons can be learned from another example of a company that lived the second unbundling in real time. When Dyson moved its production to Malaysia in 2003, the move was derided in the British press at the time. In a *Daily Mail* story covering the move, trade union official Roger Lyons said: "Dyson has betrayed the 800 people whose jobs are being shipped out and hundreds more jobs from supply chain companies. He has betrayed British manufacturing and British consumers who have put him and his product where it is today."

Founder and owner James Dyson defended the move as saving jobs. In a *Guardian* interview, he said:

> We are a much more flourishing company now because of what we did and it's doubtful if we could have survived in the long term if we had not done so. . . . We employ 1,300 at Malmesbury [the U.K. site]—engineers, scientists, and people running the business. The decision to shift production to Malaysia was not good for Britain in one sense because we don't employ manual labor any more. But we are taking on more at higher pay rates and more value-added levels.

Dyson seems to have been right.

According to a 2014 report in the *Financial Times,* Dyson announced plans to create 3,000 science and engineering jobs in the United Kingdom by 2020. The main problem was a shortage of skills. Dyson said: "We hope to create the space for them here in Malmesbury, but with a shortfall of 61,000 engineers every year in the U.K., finding them is difficult." Nevertheless he remarked that the United Kingdom as a "great place to invent," despite the shortfall of engineers.

The focus on services naturally leads to questions about infrastructure for such workers. Or to put it differently, where will the industrial zones for this type of "industrial" activity be?

Cities as Twenty-First-Century "Factories"

According to Harvard economist Ed Glaeser, talented people gather in cities because this makes them more productive. What this means for rich-nation competitiveness policy is straightforward. Human capital and cities are likely to be the foundations of the twenty-first-century landscape of work. Cities are where people meet and form local networks for face-to-face connections and exchanges. They are where people exchange ideas and where competition among ideas plays out. Cities are where most new technologies develop and start-ups flourish.

Cities also optimize the matching between workers and firms and between suppliers and customers. In this sense, cities become skill-clusters—or "brain hubs" as Enrico Moretti calls them. The link between the success of a city and human capital is a close one. One of the most persistent predictors of urban growth over the last century is the skill level of a city.

The reason people gather even as manufacturing scatters is that high-skill jobs in the tradable sector tend to be subject to more face-to-face demands as well as agglomeration economies (discussed in Chapter 6). In writing about the United States, Enrico Moretti explains the agglomeration forces as follows: "More than traditional industries, the knowledge economy has an inherent tendency towards geographical agglomeration. . . . The success of a city fosters more success as communities that can attract skilled workers and goods jobs tend to attract even more. Communities that fail to attract skilled workers lose further ground."

The Netherlands is one government that has seized on this line of thinking. The result, written up by the Netherlands Bureau for Economic Policy Analysis in its report, *The Netherlands of 2040,* suggests that ICT advances are leading to a spikier work landscape. As the 2010 report puts it, in the twenty-first century, "Cities are the places where high-educated people cluster, where start-ups flourish and face-to-face interactions increase productivity. As a result, cities are the places where productivity grows."

The policy implications are absolutely clear for the authors of the Dutch report: "Cities should not be thought of as mere collections of people, but rather as complex work spaces that generate new ideas and new ways of doing things."

Good jobs may still be associated with manufacturing, but they will be in the pre- and post-fabrication stages rather than in fabrication. Many of these jobs will be located in cities.

Collecting the various points together suggests that G7 policy-makers should:

- Stop thinking manufacturing exports and start thinking service inputs into manufactured exports
- Stop thinking good sectors and start thinking about good (service) jobs
- Stop thinking of domestic factories as the industrial base and start thinking of the service sector as the twenty-first-century industrial base
- Start thinking of cities as production hubs that nurture rapid recombination of diverse, world-class services.

To be a bit callous, well-functioning cities are one way G7 governments can "China-proof" their good jobs.

Rebuilding the Team: Social Policy

The New Globalization broke the unwritten social contract linking a nation's labor and a nation's technology. Under the Old Globalization, a rising technology tide would lift all the boats—even if some people were riding in much bigger boats than others. Under the New Globalization, a rising technology tide may lift the boats of foreign workers as much as domestic workers. An example can be used to illustrate this point.

The state of South Carolina used to have textile-mill jobs aplenty. That's over. The local witticism quips: "A modern textile mill employs only a man and a dog. The man is there to feed the dog, and the dog is there to keep the man away from the machines." This story, related by Adam Davidson in his *Atlantic* article (mentioned in Chapter 6), captures how competition from China and Mexico shut down most mills and digitally assisted manufacturing transformed the rest into "nearly autonomous, computer-run machines." Low-skill American industrial workers are competing with robots at home and Mexicans abroad. Neither game is going well.

But this is not quite correct. Under the Old Globalization, South Carolina workers could be competitive with high wages since they had a quasi-monopoly on U.S. high technology. The New Globalization has split up this team. South Carolina workers today are not competing with Mexican labor, Mexican capital, and Mexican technology as they did in the 1970s. They are competing with a nearly unbeatable combination of U.S. know-how and Mexican wages. The ill-defined sense that globalization is no longer a sport for national teams is one reason voters fear globalization.

What does this mean for social policy? Since progress comes from change, and change causes pain, governments that want to sustain progress must, as stressed before, figure out ways to share the gains and pains of progress among citizens. While this was always true, the New Globalization means that governments in G7 nations need—more than ever—to protect workers, not jobs. Moreover, as today's globalization demands more flexibility from workers, it is even more important to ensure that labor flexibility does not lead to precarious living standards. Governments need to provide economic security and help workers adapt to changing circumstances.

Rethinking Trade Policy

Before the second unbundling, trade policy was mostly about trade. Exports were "packages" of a single nation's productive factors. From a political perspective, trade policy was mostly about helping national firms sell more abroad.

Trade policy after the second unbundling is not just about trade. Exports and imports are "packages" of multiple nations' productive factors. Maximizing the value that is added by a nation's productive resources now involves deploying some of the resources abroad in global value chains. In the Dyson example, for instance, offshoring helped create new jobs and higher pay for engineers in Malmesbury. Trade policy must therefore aim at making global value chains (GVCs) work better.

For G7 nations, this means writing trade rules that help their firms maximize the value of the tangible and intangible assets. To understand the point, it helps to rethink goods. One can think of a Toyota Land Cruiser not as a vehicle but rather as a bundle of Japanese labor, capital, innovation, and managerial, marketing, engineering, and production know-how. In 1982, the Land Cruiser could be exported to any nation without regard to the destination's property rights because it was basically impossible to unbundle the inputs. Toyota's intangible property rights were protected by law in Japan and by physics abroad. Now, things are quite different.[6]

Today, Toyota assembles Land Cruisers in several nations and sources the parts and components from factories around the world, including many developing nations. Since the parts all have to fit together seamlessly, Toyota does not rely only on local know-how. It combines Japanese capital, Japanese innovation, and Japanese know-how with local labor when producing parts for its international supply chain. The result is that physics provides much less protection for Toyota's intangible property.

Production unbundling, in other words, creates new vulnerabilities to intangible property. Deeper disciplines are necessary to ensure Toyota's property rights are respected in the developing nations that get the Toyota factories. This is more or less the main goal of deep regional trade agreements (RTAs) like the Trans-Pacific Partnership (TPP).

But what sort of discipline is needed? Chapter 3 discussed the "deep" disciplines that are now routinely included in RTAs and gave some concrete examples. Here an organizing framework is provided for thinking about the type and nature of the necessary disciplines.

When it comes to rules and disciplines, the critical difference for trade policy is the increased complexity and interconnectedness of things crossing borders—what could be called the trade-investment-services-intellectual-property nexus. This nexus, which was dubbed "twenty-first-century trade" in Chapter 5, entails two categories of disciplines.

The first category encompasses measures that make it easier to do business abroad. When firms set up production facilities abroad—or form long-term ties with foreign suppliers—they typically expose their capital as well as their technical, managerial, and marketing know-how to new international risks. Threats to these tangible and intangible property rights became twenty-first-century trade barriers since global value chains tend not to be established in nations that fail to provide such assurances. For example:

- The sharing of tacit and explicit technology and intellectual property is facilitated by assurances that foreign knowledge-capital owners will be treated fairly and their property rights will be respected.
- Foreign investments in the training of workers and managers, physical plants, and the development of long-term business relationships are facilitated by assurances on property rights, rights of establishment, and anticompetitive practices.
- Assurances on business-related capital flows—ranging from new foreign direct investment (FDI) to profit repatriation—also help foster the investment part of the trade-investment-services nexus.

The second category consists of all the various policies that ensure international production facilities can remain connected. Bringing high-quality, competitively priced goods to customers in a timely manner requires international coordination of production facilities via the continuous two-way flow of goods, people, ideas, and investments. For example:

- Connecting factories often involves time-sensitive shipping, world-class telecoms, and short-term movement of managers and technicians, so assurances on infrastructure services and visas are also important.

- Tariffs and other border measures also matter, just as they mattered in the twentieth century, but more so since the ratio of value added to value on individual shipments falls as the production chain fragments.

This list suggests four types of twenty-first-century trade barriers that were not barriers to twentieth-century trade: competition policy (known as antitrust in the United States), movement of capital, intellectual property rights, and investment assurances. To this we can add business mobility—that is, assured short-term visas for technicians and managers.

Global value chains enjoy little or no global regulation. This twenty-first-century international commerce is currently underpinned by an ad hoc combination of regional trade agreements, bilateral investment treaties, and unilateral reforms by developing nations. But supply chain governance is evolving rapidly. G7 nations, especially the United States, are leading efforts to knit together the ad hoc governance into "mega-regionals"—like the Trans-Pacific Partnership and the Transatlantic Trade and Investment Partnership—and mega-bilaterals such as those between the EU and Canada or Japan and the EU. This is an important development; a network of rules is needed since global value chains cover a network of nations.

BOX 11: SUMMARY OF ADVANCED ECONOMY POLICY IMPLICATIONS

This chapter showed that understanding the deep cause of the changed impact of globalization—specifically the fact that globalization now involves massive amounts of Northern know-how moving to a handful of developing nations inside the confines of global value chains—suggests a reformulation of rich-nation policies that touch on competitiveness and growth policy, industrial policy, trade policy, and social policy.

Specifically, competitiveness policy in a world marked by fragmented, footloose production should consider the "stickiness" of production factors that are promoted by government policies as well as the extent to which the promotion yields spillovers that the private sector ignores. Industrial policy should focus less on industry and more on service-sector jobs related to industry. Moreover, since many of these jobs are and will continue to be in Northern cities, governments should think about cities as twenty-first-century factories. Urban policy should be crafted with an eye on international competitiveness. Finally, the rupture that the New Globalization caused between G7 labor and G7 knowledge owners should be redressed by enhanced social policy measures that focus on workers, not jobs, and on helping sectors and workers adjust to the vicissitudes of globalization rather than trying to resist the changes.

CHAPTER 9

Rethinking Development Policy

In 2012, just over two billion people—that is, about one in every three people on the planet—lived below the World Bank's poverty line of $3.10 a day. At a stretch, the $3.10 provides food, clothing, and shelter, but if anything goes wrong, people at this income level die. A bad infection, a flood, a robbery, or a difficult childbirth can all be fatal. Depressing as this statistic is, the truly miraculous thing is the way that the number has fallen since the Old Globalization flipped over into the New Globalization. In 1990, two out of three people lived below the $3.10 line.

Most of the global progress on poverty came in the handful of developing nations that were most affected by the New Globalization—China above all. Plainly something important and new is going on with development and it seems clear that the changes are associated with the second unbundling. To my way of thinking, the change is driven by the international reorganization of production that is sometimes called the "global value chain" (GVC) revolution.

Before 1990 or so, successful industrialization meant building a supply chain at home since that was really the only way to become globally competitive. All of today's rich nations did it this way; Korea was the last. Today, however, there is a different path. Developing nations join international supply chains to gain competitiveness and then grow rapidly because offshore production brings capabilities that would otherwise take decades to develop domestically.

While the revolutionary implications of the New Globalization are being incorporated into thinking about development, twentieth-century mental models linger. The chapter thus starts with a quick overview of that thinking. If nothing else, it provides an excellent springboard for organizing reflections on the new thinking.

Note that this chapter builds on my paper, "Trade and Industrialization after Globalization's Second Unbundling," but it also draws on the World Bank's new project, which studies ways of making global value chains work for development.[1]

Traditional Thinking about Industrial Development

Mainline thinking about development has seen three waves—or really two waves and a surrender, according to leading development economists David Lindauer and Lant Pritchett. In their 2002 paper, "What's the Big Idea? The Third Generation of Policies for Economic Growth," Lindauer and Pritchett relate how the first-generation "big idea" was unbelievably influential.[2] Its intellectual elegance and implicit optimism seduced most post–World War II policymakers. And it still holds sway in many parts of Latin America and Africa.

Paul Krugman bestows the name "high development theory" on this first generation in a famous online essay "The Fall and Rise of Development Economics." He writes: "high development theory can be described as the view, that development is a virtuous circle driven by external economies." Underdeveloped countries have simply failed to get the virtuous circle going. He continues: "In most versions of high development theory, the self-reinforcement came from an interaction between economies of scale at the level of the individual producer and the size of the market."[3] The job of policymakers was to get the virtuous circle spinning.

In the first wave of thinking, the standard way of implementing this "big push" was to reserve the local market to local productions by raising import tariffs sky-high. This was called the "import substitution industrialization" strategy. Its widespread failure was brought home by the 1980s debt crises.

A second wave of theories, called the "Washington Consensus," embraced the same virtuous cycle groundwork but relied more on free markets as the cycle starter. By the time Lindauer and Pritchett penned their piece, enthusiasm for the second wave had gone flat. Many tried it but few succeeded. Worse yet, the success stories seemed to defy the thinking. The roaring success of Asia, especially China, was something Lindauer and Pritchett called "puzzling."

Surrender is what came next. As Harvard economist Dani Rodrik wrote in his book *One Economics, Many Recipes,* "Maybe the right approach is to give up looking for 'big ideas' altogether."[4] There is one economics, but many ways to apply it. But this is not really a third-generation big idea. As Lindauer and Pritchett point out: "The current nostrum of one size doesn't fit all is not itself a big idea, but a way of expressing the absence of any big ideas." This chapter suggests that the puzzling success of China and other rapid industrializers is only puzzling if one tries to use the Old Globalization thinking to understand the New Globalization's impact on developing nations.

To bring the reasoning down to a very tangible level, we turn next to a sequence of case studies. These focus on how some nations succeeded while others failed in developing world-class auto sectors.

A Suggestive Case Study: Autos

On paper, automobiles seem like an ideal subject for an import substitution strategy of the type favored by the first wave of development thinking. A country can start with the rather simple process of assembly and then use the demand for parts arising from assembly to start producing some of the previously imported parts. And indeed, getting started was easy.

The first step involved what the industry calls "complete knockdown" kits (CKDs). The CKD arrives in a container from the "mother" factory with all the parts necessary to make a single car. With the help of managers and technicians from the mother factory, the developing nation that buys the kit can assemble it into a car in a process that is not too dissimilar to what hobbyists do when they assemble model airplanes from a box of plastic parts.

The upside of CKDs was that the local minister of industry could claim that his or her country was on the way to getting a car industry. The downside was that the next step—replacing imported parts with locally produced parts—almost never worked. A very wide range of nations tried to develop an internationally competitive car industry using an import substitution strategy and almost all failed. Two chief difficulties explain the failure: small markets and technical difficulties.

Given all the expenses involved in forming the kits at the mother factory and locally assembling them in inefficiently small factories, such cars were completely uncompetitive on the world market. Sales were thus limited to the local market and local sales were limited by various combinations of small populations, low incomes, and high prices.

As it turned out, the whole kit-assembling business was only viable if the developing nation had a high tariff on final automobiles and a low tariff on CKD kits. In 1997, for example, the Malaysia tariff on imported small cars was 140 percent while its tariff of CKDs was 42 percent. That 100 percent margin was enough to subsidize inefficient Malaysian assembly, but it meant that the local price of cars was very high. A 140 percent tariff on cars guaranteed that the price of locally assembled cars was about 140 percent higher than the international price. This severely restricted the number of local sales.

The second problem, the technical problem, has three aspects: 1) Much of the tricky technology in autos is actually embodied in the parts (e.g., engines, exhaust systems, cooling systems, electronics); 2) these parts are often very specifically linked to a particular model of auto; and 3) the parts tend to be intimately interconnected with other parts. For example, if a local firm decided to replace the imported exhaust system in the CKD with a locally made system, it would have to somehow ensure that the system worked well with the engine. This almost inevitably meant that the want-to-be local producer of parts needed the help of the foreign maker of the CKD kits. Such help was not always forthcoming.

A successful import substitution strategy would mean the emergence of a new rival—something the foreign CKD maker would not be happy to see. For example, Malaysia's first foray into building an automotive supply chain started with the Proton Saga, which was basically a Mitsubishi Lancer Fiore assembled in Malaysia. Mitsubishi, naturally, had little interest in the Proton Saga becoming an export success and thus a competitor with its Lancer Fiore.

Despite this, one developing nation, Korea, did play and win this game. Over a period of a decade or two, it built a domestic supply chain for automobiles that made everything from engines and brakes to wind screens and hubcaps. It is a great story.

Korean Success

Starting from 1962, Korea's Ministry of Trade and Industry adopted explicit industrial policies that targeted various segments of the auto supply chain. Initially, Korea assembled kits, but as control of the domestic industry was handed to large conglomerates known as *chaebols,* the Korean counterparties were on a more equal bargaining footing than was the case in many developing nations.

The first "big push" was to get Korean firms into the business of car assembly. The assembly operations helped build local competencies ranging from simple skills for industrial workers to operational experience for managers.

A second push was part of Korea's 1973 Heavy and Chemical Industries Project. Korean assemblers had to put in plans for building a low-cost car that met government-crafted specifications. This produced Korea's local cars; namely, the Hyundai Pony and a Mazda-designed car called the Brisa. The local value-added content of these cars reached as high as 85 percent. Some key components, however, were still imported.

As it turned out, Hyundai's new car proved a hit with Korean consumers. Almost 300,000 cars were sold by 1982. While exports were limited, the domestic market drove healthy growth; output had risen tenfold by 1990.

The third big push by the government, instituted in 1978, had mixed results. The government pushed the firms to make large investments, but these turned out to be loss-making given the downturn of the early 1980s.

In response, the Ministry of Trade and Industry restructured the firms and reoriented the whole industry. The idea was to focus on export markets—the United States in particular—in order to achieve the large scales of production that were necessary to be competitive. An important component of the realignment involved quality upgrading and investing in new factories. Critically, Hyundai also set up its own dealer network in the United States and Canada to ensure it could get to consumers.

As in most things that work well, luck played a role. The booming export success of Japanese cars in the 1980s had triggered a protectionist backlash in the United States, at about the same time that Korea sought to enter the North American market. The U.S. government imposed quotas on Japanese auto imports. With its natural competitors thus hobbled, Korean exports of low-end cars to the United States boomed. Just as the theory said it should, the massive scale economies that could be realized on the back of exports to the United States created booming demand for Korean-made parts, and this allowed them to be made locally at efficient scales of production. The Korean car industry by this point included almost the entire supply chain.

The Korean success can be seen in Figure 56. Korean exports of final autos soared (top panel) just as German exports soared (bottom panel).

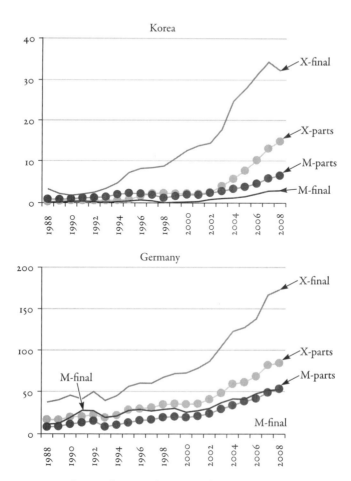

FIGURE 56: Korea's car and parts trade compared to Germany's.

Korea's trade pattern in parts and final vehicles now resembles that of Germany—lots of car exports (marked X-final in the chart) and lots of imports of parts (M-parts) and exports of parts (X-parts). Before the Asian crisis, the Korean pattern was much more an import substitution pattern. It had big exports of final cars, but quite low imports of parts and almost no exports of parts.

DATA SOURCE: Standard International Trade Classification (SITC) data from WITS online.

Storm Clouds and Volte Face

While Korea's industrial strategy in this sector was a smashing success in terms of exported cars, the victory was built on sand. The companies were very highly leveraged, carrying debt-to-equity ratios over 500 percent in the mid-1990s. The auto parts industry, following the standard import substitution logic, had limited foreign involvement and stressed domestic know-how. The native parts and component suppliers were small and had problems with quality and innovation. This fed into the development of a reputation in the United States of low reliability and lack of advanced features.

When the 1997 Asian crisis struck, three of the four car companies went broke and were bought out. Kia was bought by the sole survivor, Hyundai. Samsung Motors was bought by Renault. Daewoo Motors (formerly called Shinjin) was bought by GM.

The domestic supply chain also experienced a transformation via a surge in foreign investment into the industry. With foreign direct investment (FDI) policy liberalized during the financial crisis, dozens of world-class component producers set up majority-owned facilities in Korea.

In this way, the strategy of building the whole supply chain at home to become competitive abroad was reversed. Korea switched from the twentieth-century import substitution strategy to the twenty-first-century global value chain strategy. The 1997 financial crisis was the catalyst, but the realities of global competition were the basis. The world auto sector had become so scale-intensive, and the costs of R&D had mounted so high, that no company could survive by relying on a fully national supply chain.

By the 2000s, Korea's car sector was a full-on member of the global value chain club. Yet because it built a supply chain *before* the second unbundling, Korea is now a headquarters economy rather than a factory economy. This can be seen in the evolution of the imports and exports of parts in Figure 56.

Thai Success and Malaysian Failure

The Korean case shows what happened when a nation switched from building the whole supply chain at home to setting up a supply chain internationally. The next two cases look at one nation that adopted the "join strategy" (Thailand) and one nation that embraced the "build strategy" (Malaysia).

Like most ambitious developing nations in the 1960s, Thailand's auto industry relied on imported kits that were assembled for local sales. The country moved beyond this business model by pursuing a subtle industrial policy. Specifically, Thailand raised local content requirements. In reaction, U.S. and European makers exited, but Japanese companies decided that Thailand would be a good export platform for Southeast Asia and beyond. To fulfill the requirements, Japanese assemblers asked their Japanese suppliers to set up production in Thailand. The assemblers also nurtured Thai suppliers, helping them with quality, management, and technical matters. The strategy was also helped by the booming growth that Thailand was experiencing at the time—growth that was certainly linked to the global value chain revolution in autos and other sectors.

Note that while Thailand embraced international supply chains, it did not follow a laissez-faire strategy. Trade and FDI policies were quite liberal but local content rules were used strategically. One such policy, the Engine Production Promotion Scheme, set out demands that engine assemblers use only engine parts that had undergone specific local processing.

This would not normally have been feasible given the low scale of production, but the various Japanese companies collaborated among themselves. They set up unified plants to make the necessary parts inside the country. Another innovation was to raise scale economies by focusing on a particular market segment rather than trying to produce a whole range of models. Most of the output is of light pickup trucks and vans.

Why did the Japanese companies not fear new competition from Thailand? The answer is that Thailand convinced them that it was not trying to set up a fully independent competitor. It was happy being a key link in the value chain. This gave Japanese firms the confidence to bring great technology to the country. Thailand is now known as the "Detroit of the East."

The Malaysia story has the same beginning but a very different ending. To start with, its kit-assembly step was marred by an absence of scale economies. Each foreign carmaker was eager to sell a few units to Malaysia and so readily engaged in local assembly activities despite the derisory levels of production. Needless to say, the small scale of local production per model made it impossible to develop local components. The average local content was under 10 percent.

When Malaysia's strongman premier Mahathir Mohamad took power in 1981, he sought to emulate Korea's success in the 1960s and 1970s by launching a state-guided big push. His big-push policy was called the Heavy Industries Corporation of Malaysia (HICOM). The focal point was a "national car project" called Proton. It was launched as a joint venture with Mitsubishi but HICOM held 70 percent of the shares. The main model, the Proton Saga, bore a striking resemblance to Mitsubishi's Lancer.

In terms of local sales, high tariffs meant that the Saga was much cheaper than directly imported cars. It thus dominated the local market, but this was a Pyrrhic victory because HICOM's plans came to fruition just as the second unbundling torpedoed the build-your-own industrialization strategy. The world's major carmakers were offshoring certain stages of production together with their know-how to low-wage nations. The resulting surge in cost-competitiveness destroyed the economic logic of single-nation automobile production.

The point, however, was not yet well understood at the time. With government help, Proton started manufacturing more parts inside the country. This production benefited from few scale economies since

Proton's output was very small by global standards, despite its dominance of the local market.

Another big push came in the 1990s as the Proton introduced new models and produced them with varying engine sizes. This doubled Malaysian production from 1990 to 1997. The government's grand plan, however, went much further. It announced a new project, "Proton City," which would be an integrated automobile manufacturing plant with a production capacity rising to 250,000 units in 2003. During this Proton expansion, a second national car company called Perodua was set up. Perodua was a joint venture with the Japanese carmaker Daihatsu, and it produced the Kancil, which was a modified version of Daihatsu's Mira.

The 1997 Asian crisis struck Malaysia almost has hard as it did Thailand, but this did nothing to revise Mahathir's dream of building an automobile supply chain entirely at home. Due to grave financial difficulties, Perodua was sold to its Japanese partner, but Proton was bailed out by the state and Proton City, near Tanjung Malim, was completed.

Proton launched a domestically designed car using know-how it got by buying the British car company Lotus. The car, however, has been chronically caught in a scale-competitiveness conundrum. Its low production volumes result in high costs per car that keep Proton from pricing its cars competitively—an outcome that guarantees low production volumes.

The company is now struggling. It sells only 150,000 cars—far below its production capacity of 350,000. While the domestic auto market has boomed, Proton lost market share to cars that are produced locally by Perodua and direct imports. Its export sales, which peaked two decades ago, are negligible.

Differences in the Thai and Malay experiences show up in a dramatic fashion after the 1997 financial crisis in Asia (see Figure 57). The top panel shows how Thai production raced beyond Malaysian produc-

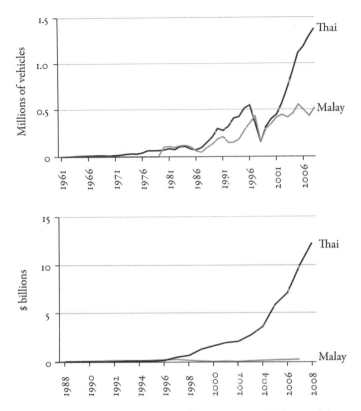

FIGURE 57: Auto production and exports, Thai success, and Malaysian failure.

The success of Thailand's join strategy and the failure of Malaysia's build strategy are clear in these two charts. Thai production (top panel) and exports (bottom panel) have boomed as it has become the export platform of choice for Japanese auto companies. Malaysia's production numbers have staggered upward, but its cars are not competitive abroad.

The results in terms of employment are equally stark. By the mid-2000s, there were over 180,000 workers in the Thai auto industry compared to 47,000 in Malaysia (not shown in the diagram).

SOURCE: Adapted from Wanrawee Fuangkajonsak, "Industrial Policy Options for Developing Countries: The Case of the Automotive Sector in Thailand and Malaysia," Master of Arts in Law and Diplomacy Thesis, The Fletcher School, Tufts University (2006, table 9, figure 1), Malaysia Automotive Association, and Thailand Automotive Institute.

tion from about 2000. The bottom panel shows how Thai autos have been an export hit, while Malaysia auto exports have been a flop.

Rethinking Industrialization

Walter Heller, the chief economic adviser to U.S. president John Kennedy, is reputed to have quipped: "An economist is someone who says, when an idea works in practice, 'let's see if it works in theory.'" Having seen how the distinction between building and joining a supply chain worked in practice, it is time to look to the theory. This is a core duty since it forces one to be clear about what has really changed.

The bedrock of industrialization is the notion that a country could be good at industry, if only it had more industry. It is a classic chicken-and-egg problem; no eggs without chickens and no chickens without eggs. But here, rather than eggs and chickens, the nub is the sales-and-scale conundrum we saw in the Malaysian case.

To put it in a positive way, the conundrum is that a nation that has a deep and wide industrial base can be globally competitive in a wide range of final goods and this competitiveness, in turn, provides the sales necessary to justify an industrial base operating at an efficient scale. What Malaysia's auto sector experienced was the negative side of things. Low scale meant low sales and vice versa.

In the jargon of economics, this is a "multiple equilibrium" situation. It is worth looking at in a bit more detail.

Multiple Equilibria Economics

As we shall see, the heart of the global value chain revolution's impact on industrial development turns on the way it affected multiple equilibrium economics. To illustrate how and why this happened, I like to use the simple analogy of a child's playground seesaw, which perfectly captures the issues (Figure 58).

In a line-sketch view of industrial development there are two stable outcomes—that is, two equilibriums.

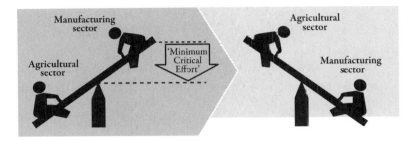

FIGURE 58: Multiple equilibriums, seesaws, and industrialization's "minimum critical effort."

The seesaw on the left illustrates a system with multiple equilibriums. One state of the world is where the left child (agricultural sector) is down because most people work the land. Forcibly, the right child (industry) is up. The other equilibrium (in the right-hand panel) is where the right child is down, because many workers are in industry, and the child on the left is up.

To move the system from one equilibrium to the other requires a "big push." The child has to be pushed down below the dotted line. Any lesser push and the system returns to the initial situation. On a playground, the size of the push varies with the height of the seesaw. In an economy, it depends on the lumpiness of production.

The nonindustrial equilibrium is where most of the nation's produc-tive resources are in agriculture rather than industry. The same holds for seesaws. In the left panel of Figure 58, one child is down, indi-cating that the preponderance of labor is in the agricultural sector. This necessarily means that employment in manufacturing is low (the other child is up). But this is an equilibrium since without an industrial base, the manufacturing sector is uncompetitive, so there are few jobs in industry. Labor is, consequently, more productive in agriculture, so people are content to work the land.

The industrial equilibrium is where everything is reversed. This sit-uation, shown in the right panel of Figure 58, is where the nation is competitive in industrial goods since industry attains a scale that is sufficient to make it competitive (the child on the right is down). The manufacturing efficiency that comes with this large-scale production makes creating and accepting jobs in industry an attractive proposition. Workers and firms are thus happy to stay in the industrial sector.

The seesaw analogy immediately raises the next question: How does an economy get from the agrarian equilibrium to the industrial equilibrium?

The "Minimum Critical Effort"

In the 1950s, development economist Harvey Leibenstein discussed ways of getting from the bad equilibrium to the good one. What was needed, he argued, was a sufficiently large jolt. His term, "minimum critical effort," referred to a specific mechanism but it captures the basic problem with multiple equilibrium situations.[5]

In Figure 58 (left panel), the minimum critical effort is exemplified with the arrow and the dotted lines. If employment in industry does not get beyond a certain level (that is, if the right child is not pushed below the lower dotted line), the industrial equilibrium cannot be attained. The agrarian equilibrium will reassert itself as soon as the artificial stimulus to industry is removed.

If instead the industrial employment level gets pushed beyond the tipping point, the industrial equilibrium is the one that will prevail because a self-enforcing logic takes over. A sufficiently wide industrial base makes the nation's industry competitive, which in turn increases sales in a way that allows the industrial base to expand.

Stage-Level Industrialization Is Easier

This traditional sector-level thinking—agriculture versus manufacturing in the example—was transformed by information and communication technology (ICT). The ICT revolution allowed firms from the Group of Seven (G7) nations to unbundle certain production stages and offshore them to nearby developing nations. Mexico, for example, could be competitive in certain stages of car production without having to produce a globally competitive car.

This fundamentally changed the bedrock of industrialization—not in terms of how it worked, but in terms of how difficult it was to do. After the second unbundling, industrialization became easier for nations joining global value chains for at least four distinct reasons:

- The "big push" could be made in small steps.
- The heightened coordination possibilities that came with the ICT revolution made it easier for developing nations to export parts.
- When globalization operates on an economy with finer resolution, national competitive advantages are magnified.
- The know-how necessary to set up single stages is much easier for developing nations to absorb than the know-how that is necessary to set up a whole sector.

There is also a fifth reason that is so simple it requires little elaboration: global value chains make the sales-scale conundrum evaporate since the multinational firms setting up the offshore facilities have already attained global competitiveness. For firms inside a global value chain, demand and market size are no longer a factor.

Let's consider the four points in sequence.

The Second Unbundling Made Industry Less Lumpy

When a developing nation joins an international supply chain, it can free-ride on other nations' industrial bases. The developing nation can thus become competitive in a single stage without having to be competitive in all of them. The multiple equilibrium logic still applies. Factories must still meet minimum efficient scales of production and the local workforce must still possess a minimum range of competencies. But the scale and range for a single stage are much smaller.

The direct implication is that industrialization becomes more accessible. The point is illustrated schematically in Figure 59. Instead

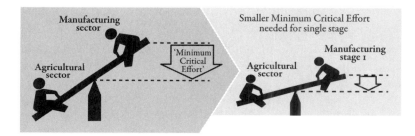

FIGURE 59: Global value chains make it possible to accomplish a "big push" in many "small nudges," by reducing the size of the necessary minimum critical effort.

Switching from one equilibrium to the other requires a concerted effort. When it comes to seesaws, the strength and duration of the push depends on height. High seesaws require a much bigger effort than do shorter ones. The same is true of economies marked by multiple equilibrium. When sustaining industry requires a very large industrial base, the size and duration of the "big push" may exceed the capacities of most nations. With global value chains (GVCs), developing nations can piggyback on other nations' industrial bases, so the big push can be done in small steps—one offshored facility at a time.

of having to get the whole car industry competitive—as Korea did and Malaysia failed to do—a developing nation can gain competitiveness in a single stage of production. This changes the challenge from the big problem of how to engineer a multiyear, multiphase "big push" to a bunch of smaller problems. Schematically, the sector-level big push is shown by the seesaw on the left while the one on the right shows the stage-level small nudge.

To put it differently, the second unbundling reduced the lumpiness of industry and thus reduced the size of the "minimum critical effort." This made industrialization easier and faster for developing nations joining international supply chains.

An Asymmetric Opening for Developing-Nation Parts Exports

The whole big-push-to-small-nudges shift was made possible by the fact that the ICT revolution was especially favorable to developing-nation exports of parts and components—a point that was clarified in Chapter 5.

Developed nations have exported parts to developing nations since time immemorial, as the auto case studies illustrate. What the second unbundling did was to allow developing nations to return the favor. The ICT revolution made it possible for G7 firms with advanced technology to monitor and control manufacturing processes in developing nations to an extent that was previously unconceivable. This control meant that parts made in low-wage nations could reliably be slotted into a global production process (Figure 60).

The next point is logically more subtle as it concerns the way that slicing up the value chain exaggerates nations' competitive advantages.

Finer Resolution Means Stronger Comparative Advantage

As the tasks, occupations, stages, and product (TOSP) framework from Chapter 6 pointed out, each product or service is the fruit of several stages of production. When all of these stages are done by a single nation, the competitiveness of the final good is some sort of average of the nation's competitiveness in each stage.

The point, which is illustrated in the left panel of Figure 60, means that even if a developing nation had a roaring competitive advantage in, say, mufflers, this advantage was submerged since the nation could not export just mufflers. The developing nation could only exploit its advantage in mufflers if it could also produce the engine and the gearbox—that is, if it was competitive in the final product.

With the second unbundling, the developing nation can exploit its specific edge in mufflers. With advanced ICT, foreign motorcycle companies, for instance, can monitor and coordinate with the developing-nation muffler factory in real time and at very low costs. This liberates the developing nation's comparative advantage in mufflers from the shackles of its competitive disadvantage in other manufacturing stages.

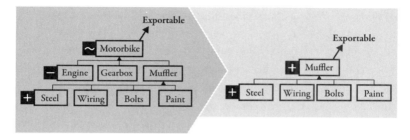

FIGURE 60: Less lumpiness means stronger comparative advantage.

The second unbundling exaggerates comparative advantage since the competiveness of various stages are not diluted by having to be averaged with uncompetitive stages. Here the developing nation's competitiveness in making, say, mufflers was never allowed to shine when muffler production was forced together with gearbox and engine production. With the second unbundling, nations can focus on the precise production stages where their competitiveness is strongest. This is a very general point that holds for both rich and poor nations. The cost competitiveness of bundled stages is the average of all the stages, which, logically, is less competitive than the most competitive stage in the bundle.

Know-How Movements by Stages instead of Sectors

The same point can be seen in the example of wire harnesses (Box 12), where Vietnam was able to exploit a stage-level comparative advantage. Transfers of know-how from Japan to Vietnam were not an important part of the story. In many cases, however, the transfer of know-how is essential in making the offshoring production competitive. But a limiting factor often is the developing nation's ability to absorb the necessary technology transfer. After all, technology transfer usually means training teams of people and getting them to work in harmony.

This was in fact one of the main sources of industry's lumpiness before the second unbundling. That is to say, one of the most important sources of the chicken-and-egg problem facing industrializing nations was the difficulty of managing the acquisition of the necessary knowledge and developing the necessary local competencies. When production was bundled, little bits of know-how were not much use

BOX 12: WIRE HARNESSES: VIETNAM EXPORTING AUTO PARTS

Sumitomo Electric Industrial Ltd is Japan's largest supplier of wires, cables, and optical fibers. In 1996 it moved production of wire harnesses to Vietnam by setting up the company Sumi-Hanel Wiring Systems.

Wire harnesses are assemblies of wires used in automobiles and other machinery. The harness secures the wires against damage and reduces the space it takes up in the final good. Using premade harnesses also makes assembly of the final good faster and more standardized.

The fabrication of a wire harness involves cutting wires to the right length, stripping the insulation, and fitting connectors to the ends. The wires are assembled and clamped together on workbenches and protective sleeves are put on. The process is becoming more automated, but much is still done by hand due to the many different processes and wide range of designs. Harnesses are not generic; they are designed specifically for each final product.

Creation of wire harnesses can be thought of as a single stage in the production of final goods. This stage is ideal for offshoring since most of the raw material is imported (thus its quality is controlled), little advanced machinery is required, and it is labor-intensive.

Before the second unbundling, it would have been very difficult for Vietnam to exploit its comparative advantage in this particular stage of production. The wire-harness stage would have had to have been done in concert with many other stages to ensure the system as a whole worked seamlessly. The second unbundling, however, allows developing nations to better exploit such comparative advantages, stage by stage, without first having to construct the whole supply chain at home.

BOX 13: KNOWLEDGE TRANSFER: TABASCO IN COLOMBIA

Transfers of single-stage know-how were critical in the case of the international supply chain for the U.S. hot sauce brand Tabasco. Tabasco's owner, the American company McIlhenny, wanted to source hot chili peppers at lower cost and thus turned to a Colombian firm, Hugo Restrepo y Cía. Ongoing, two-way exchange of information was required to ensure the raw chilies and chili paste were up to Tabasco standards. McIlhenny provided expertise to Hugo Restrepo in exchange for a promise to sell only to McIlhenny. The U.S. firm sent experienced agronomists to Columbia twice a year to work on quality and reliability. The result was an important transfer of know-how concerning crop and production management.

on their own. The nation needed very large segments of know-how to be competitive in a sector, but this lumpiness of know-how at the sector level posed challenges that few nations could surmount.

By allowing developing nations to focus on one part or one stage at a time, the global value chain revolution made knowledge absorption easier. The requisite technology and skills base for making a product could be digested bit by bit. By the same token, advanced-technology firms could feel more comfortable in passing on the knowledge since they were not really setting up a competitor for themselves. They were improving the quality and productivity of their supplier base. Elements of these points can be seen in the case of Tabasco in Colombia (Box 13).

From Theory to Policy

Having looked at some case studies and briefly formulating an analytic framework to understand how and why globalization's impact on industrialization changed, it is time to turn to the policy implications and rethink industrialization policy.

As illustrated by the auto case, the sales-scale problem molded industrialization thinking for generations. It was why developing nations pursued activist policies aimed at kick-starting virtuous cycles of spreading industrialization and rising competitiveness. But given limited human resources, it was clear that not every industry could be pushed at the same time. This raised the key issue of the proper sequencing of sector-specific pushes.

The Traditional Development Ladder: Putting Sectors in Order

To make the big push easier, industrialization before the second unbundling was done in discrete steps. Indeed, pre-unbundling thinking was that there was something of a "development ladder." Nations would start with simple industries where they could be competitive without much of an industrial base. The experience in these starter industries—clothing, textiles, footwear, furniture, and the like— would then foster the accumulation of industrial competencies that would prove useful when it came to making more sophisticated products. A classic rendition of this process can be found in the writings of Bela Balassa.

In his 1985 collection of essays, *Change and Challenge in the World Economy,* he described the sequencing problem in this way: "The first stage of this import substitution involved replacing the imports of non-durable consumer goods, such as textile fabrics and leather, by domestic production. It has also been called the 'easy' stage of import substitution." The manufacturing processes in these sectors mostly involved unskilled labor, and scale economies were modest. For these goods, "efficient operations do not require the availability of a network of suppliers of parts, components and accessories." In other words, there was not much of a chicken-and-egg problem for sectors that formed the lowest rungs of the development ladder.

"The second stage of import substitution," Balassa continues, "involves the replacement of the imports of intermediate goods, and producer and consumer durables, by domestic production." This stage is much more difficult due to large economies of scale, and organizational and technical challenges.[6]

The Taiwanese Example

Something of this progression of industries, from simple to more complex, can be seen in the experience of Taiwan—one of the few developing nations to industrialize before the global value chain revolution.

In the early postwar years, Taiwan was quite closed. It exported mostly sugar and tea. In terms of Figure 58, the agriculture side of the Taiwanese seesaw was definitely down in the 1950s. The nation's development strategy consisted of a focus on promoting agriculture and promoting industry via import substitution.

The island's import substitution policy was maintained until the end of the 1950s when it was replaced by a policy that promoted the exports of unskilled-labor-intensive manufactured goods. This switch from an inward search for demand to an outward search for demand met with success in simple, labor-intensive goods. As Table 8 shows, the share of agricultural goods in exports dropped rapidly from almost 100 percent in 1952 to under 50 percent by 1965 and under a 10 percent in 1975.

The first manufactured export goods to take off were textiles, followed a few years later by clothing and footwear. Electrical machinery was next. Nonelectrical machinery and transport equipment were on the rise by the mid-1970s. Readers will be familiar with the rest of the story. Taiwan is now a powerhouse exporter of high-tech, high-precision goods, especially electronics like Acer computers. Moreover, Taiwan is now a full member of the global value chain revolution with its firms, like Foxconn, playing central roles in the international production networks of U.S., European, and Japanese firms.

TABLE 8
Taiwan climbing the development ladder,
export pattern from 1952 to 1976.

	Percent of exports, major commodities						
	1952	1955	1960	1965	1970	1975	1976
Agricultural products	13.0	26.4	6.8	19.9	2.3	0.4	0.2
Processed agricultural products	74.4	58.5	52.5	25.5	10.0	8.1	4.2
Manufacturing products	2.4	4.0	21.3	34.7	64.6	65.1	66.5
Textiles	0.1	0.9	11.6	10.3	13.8	10.1	10.0
Clothing and footwear	0.8	1.4	2.6	4.9	16.8	20.4	20.7
Plastic articles	0.0	0.0	0.0	2.6	5.1	6.5	6.5
Electrical machinery and appliances	0.0	0.0	0.6	2.7	12.3	14.0	15.7
Plywood	0.0	0.1	1.5	5.9	5.5	2.5	2.3
Non-electrical machinery	0.0	0.0	0.0	1.3	3.2	4.4	4.0
Transport equipment	0.0	0.0	0.0	0.4	0.9	2.2	2.5
Metal products	0.0	0.0	0.6	1.1	1.9	2.6	3.0
Cement	0.7	0.0	0.7	1.9	0.7	0.1	0.2
Basic metals	0.8	1.6	3.7	3.6	4.4	2.3	1.6
Other	10.2	11.1	19.4	19.9	23.1	26.4	29.1
Total exports ($ millions)	13	12	164	450	1,481	5,309	8,166
Export to GDP (%)	8.5	8.2	11.2	18.4	29.5	41	51.9

Taiwan is a classic example of the "flying geese" pattern of development. It started with agricultural goods and stepped up to simple industry goods before commencing exports of more sophisticated manufactured goods. After taking each new step, it dropped the exports that had dominated the previous step.

SOURCE: T. H. Lee and Kuo-Shu Liang, "Taiwan," in *Development Strategies in Semi-Industrial Economies*, World Bank Research, ed. Bela Balassa (Baltimore and London: Johns Hopkins University Press, 1982), 310–350. Table 10.12.

Before the second unbundling the approach was focused on sectors, so the main question was: What sector should the country develop next? This changed with the second unbundling.

Sequencing Question Disrupted: From Sectors to Stages

The traditional sequencing of import substitution policies, and indeed the whole idea of a development ladder, became increasingly irrelevant when the ICT revolution made it feasible for developing nations to join international supply networks.

This new ability shifted the sequencing question from "what sector" or "what product" to "what stage" or "what part." The switch meant, as mentioned, that the big push could be done in small nudges for those developing nations that managed to join global value chains.

Switching the development paradigm from the big push to the small nudges had three key implications.

Comparative advantage became much more of a regional concept and less of a national concept. When considering the competitiveness of locations from a global value chain perspective, nations should not be viewed in isolation. Myanmar, for instance, should find it rather straightforward to join what I call "Factory Asia."[7] The region has an ongoing demand for low-cost labor in nations that are convenient to Japan, Korea, China, Taiwan, and Singapore in terms of moving goods, ideas, and people.

By contrast, consider a South American country trying to compete with Mexico as a location for production stages that are being offshored from the United States. The ICT revolution largely melted the binding power of the coordination constraint but it still takes time to ship parts and components, and it takes time for managers and technical staff to commute to the offshore facilities. These factors make it very hard for South American locations to be as attractive as Central American locations.

This is another of the multiple equilibrium situations at the geographical level. The presence of many suppliers makes a location attractive as a production spot and this in turn attracts more suppliers and the cycle continues. In this way, agglomeration economies tend to exaggerate the natural advantage of proximity to G7 nations. We can even put the point more directly.

Distance matters differently. Location was always important in industrialization efforts. Since the eighteenth century, Europeans had the advantage of a large and nearby market (each other), and this was surely a factor in Europe's takeoff. But distance before the ICT revolution generally referred to its impact on the cost of shipping goods.

After the global value chain revolution, the world is up against the face-to-face constraint, so the time cost of travel is an important factor. Distance matters differently than the way it mattered for trade in traditional, made-here-sold-there goods. (See the example in Box 14.)

Industrial policy is less risky. As the example of the car industries in Korea and Malaysia shows, the old-style, big-push industrial policies were massively expensive. They were also subject to massive political capture. By making the whole process less lumpy, the global value chain revolution has lowered the cost of policy mistakes.

From Geese to Starlings

The development ladder or sequencing perspective is thoroughly embedded in many people's thinking about industrialization. Many analysts, for example, routinely refer to "moving up" the value chain, as if there were some sort of linear ranking of sectors. To counter such misthinking, consider an illustration.

Before North-South production unbundling took off around 1990, the sequencing concern was aptly described with the "flying geese" model of development (first posited by Japanese economist Kaname Akamatsu and his students at Hitotsubashi University). This pattern of development envisages a fairly well-defined sequence of industries through which a nation should progress on the road to riches. It is, so to speak, an A-frame development ladder on its side.

BOX 14: LOCATION, LOCATION, LOCATION: THE AVIONYX CASE

The importance of travel costs for key personnel can be seen in the marketing material of the Costa Rican "near-shoring" firm Avionyx. "As with buying real estate, the three most important things to consider when going offshore are Location, Location, Location!" writes Avionyx President Larry Allgood, referring to the opportunity to offshore jobs in embedded software engineering. (Embedded software is important in many industries, including aviation.)

Allgood argues that while India (Costa Rica's main rival) has some advantages, the twenty-plus-hour flights are imposing, as is the one-day lag time in communications due to a twelve-hour time difference, "which makes it difficult—if not impossible—to include all the team members in weekly teleconference status meetings."

In his business, back-and-forth shipments also matter. This type of software is developed in parallel with the hardware that it is designed to run on. The hardware therefore needs to cross borders several times. While these shipments can be delayed by weeks and sometimes a month or more in India, Allgood notes, shipments to Costa Rica can make the door-to-door trip in one to two days (in a FedEx Letter), or three to five days for larger shipments.

The flying geese also depict an international specialization dimension. The lead country / goose, typically taken to be Japan, accumulates competencies that allow it to attain competitiveness in the next sector up the development ladder. The same process, however, raises Japanese wages, thus reducing its competitiveness in sectors on the lower rungs. This opens the doors for the next goose in line. The first wave of followers (Hong Kong, Singapore, Taiwan, and Korea) were called the newly industrializing countries or, more colorfully, the "four dragons." Countries in the second wave

(Thailand, Philippines, Indonesia, and Malaysia) were called the "four tigers."

The traditional view of import substitution and orderly development-ladder thinking became increasingly irrelevant with production un-bundling. All of a sudden, geese at the very back of the formation started exporting what used to be considered sophisticated parts. The evolution was not following a sector-by-sector logic but a stage-by-stage logic, so the strict sequencing of yesteryear broke down.

One way to express this changed sequencing is to think of the orderly flying geese formation as being replaced by something that looked more like a flock of starlings (Figure 61). The starlings do fly in formation, but the formation is ever transforming—beautiful and orderly but extremely difficult to predict.

The Illusion of Easy Gains

The fact that it became much easier to get into the manufacturing game via global value chains does not necessarily mean that it was easier to industrialize. This point deserves some attention before I move on to the new policy questions raised by the global value chain revolution.

While switching from the big push to the small nudges made it easier for some developing nations to get manufacturing jobs, it also made the result less meaningful in itself. The jobs came faster and with less intrusive industrial policy because the global value chain revolution made industry less lumpy and less interconnected domes-tically. Oversimplifying to make the point, all the developing nation had to do was be located near a supply chain, provide reliable workers, and establish a hospitable business environment. It was, so to speak, "instant" industry—just add labor and stir.

Global value chain industrialization, however, was less mean-ingful for exactly the same reasons. Korean car exports to the United

FIGURE 61: Geese versus starlings: the second unbundling disrupted the development ladder.

Before the second unbundling, industrialization had to happen sector by sector since a nation had to build up a domestic supply chain before it could become competitive abroad. The first steps on the development ladder involved final goods (e.g., clothing and footwear) that had simple supply chains. The experience gained in these "light" industries primed the nation for taking the next step to a more sophisticated industry (or at least that was how it was supposed to work). In Asia, this orderly sequence of industry is known as the "flying geese" model (left panel).

Since the second unbundling allowed nations to join international supply chains, the orderly progress is disrupted. Nations industrialize stage by stage, not industry by industry. For example, Vietnam makes parts (wire harnesses) for final goods ranging from refrigerators to aircraft. It did not have to master refrigerators before moving into automobiles and then into aircraft. A flock of starlings (right panel) is a better analogy for this development pattern than the geese's flying-V.

States were a trophy, a gold medal in the import substitution games. These exports were a testimony that Korean industrial firms had the full range of competencies necessary to make it on global markets. Vietnamese exports of car parts to Japan are surely to be applauded, but these exports are mostly a testimony to the country's place in an international supply chain. Broad swaths of the necessary competencies are not provided by Vietnamese firms.

Put differently, the ability to join an international supply created a new development trap—what might be called the Kaesong syndrome. North Korea's Kaesong Industrial Region is perhaps the perfect example of what not to do. Set up in the early 2000s, it allows

South Korean firms to tap into low-wage labor available in the North. While the North views it as a convenient hard currency "cash cow," Kaesong has done nothing to spur the North's manufacturing sector. Indeed, the country has done almost everything possible to prevent any sort of spillovers to the rest of its economy.

For other developing nations, the spillovers that North Korea tries so hard to stifle are exactly what is attractive about participating in the global value chain. The challenge is to leverage the global value chain factories to raise living standards and create a self-fueling industrialization process.

In short, the question is: How can policy ensure that global value chain participation benefits the domestic economy as a whole through more and better paid jobs, better living conditions, superior training, infrastructure, and the like? This is our next subject. But don't get your hopes up. I don't have the answers.

New Policy Questions

For policymakers, the critical issue is how to make global value chains work for their nation's development. It is not enough to draw in a few offshore production facilities that create a few new jobs in an export processing zone. Industrialization and broader development only come by densifying participation in these international production networks. This can happen far faster as global value chains remove bottlenecks, but global value chains are not magical. They are only door openers. Most of the hard work in pushing a nation into middle-income ranks and beyond still has to be done at home.

Development means getting more value added from a country's productive factors. This requires improvements in labor skills and technological capabilities as well as fixing domestic market failures and knitting social cohesion to ensure a consensus stays in favor of economic progress.

In a 2014 report from the World Bank, *Making Global Value Chains Work for Development,* Daria Taglioni and Deborah Winkler write that three new policy issues arise when it comes to global value chains.[8]

- How to enter global value chains.
- How to expand and strengthen participation in global value chains.
- How to turn global value chain participation into sustainable development.

The GVC Entry Question

In global value chains, like dancing, it takes two to tango. National governments cannot unilaterally dictate global value chain participation. They have to induce foreign partners to set up new production facilities or invite existing national firms into their network.

As discussed in Chapter 8, global value chain production requires two sets of policies. First are policies that convince the foreign firms that they can safely do business in the developing nation. When these firms set up production facilities—or even when they form long-term ties with suppliers—they are exposed to theft of their tangible and intangible property. If a nation hopes to attract global value chain production, it will need to find a way to provide assurances that property rights will be protected.

The second set of policies concerns hindrances to cross-border flows of the things that are needed to keep the international production network running as a network. Notably, these include world-class business services, easy movement of key people, and smooth and reliable movement of inputs into the nation and output out of the nation.

The general pro-global value chain policies that I have discussed are necessary, but more specific questions arise when looking at the question of how to enter a global value chain. For example, what sort of production stages should a developing nation encourage?

This is a complex question with many case-specific elements, but one point is worth stressing: the choice of stages should be informed by the developing nation's geographic location. When it comes to back-and-forth trade in parts and components, a faraway nation—say, Peru—has very little chance of competing with developing nations located near G7 nations—say, Mexico. This suggests that Peru may have to focus on sectors where physical distance is less important—for example, stages of production that involve services.

Another aspect of this question is an evaluation of the type of global value chain to join. A key distinction is between buyer-led and seller-led global value chains. The Bombardier case discussed in Chapter 3 is an example of what Duke sociologist Gary Gereffi calls "producer-driven value chains." Gereffi—the man who coined the phrase "global value chain" and was instrumental in getting economists to view global value chains as something more than foreign direct investment—notes that in producer-led networks, it is the manufacturer who is in charge of arranging the foreign production and coordinating it with domestic production, marketing, sales, after-sales services, and the like.

Other international production networks are of the buyer-driven type. Here the buyer—say, a large retailer like Tommy Hilfiger—is the one in charge. The buyer knows what will sell and then passes the order to an intermediary like Li & Fung Limited, which cooperates with a vast network of suppliers. Li & Fung owns no factories, but it has long-term relationships with over 15,000 suppliers in over sixty countries. The buyer feeds firm-specific knowledge into the chain by giving very specific instructions on colors, trimmings, textiles, types of zippers, and so forth.

The final product, say, a $150 pair of Tommy Hilfiger khakis, is a thorough mix of the sources of competitive advantage. It includes the market and retail knowledge of the U.S. retailer; the logistics, quality control, and supply management knowledge of the Hong

Kong intermediate; and the manufacturing capacities of, say, a Malaysian factory.

While more research needs to be done, it seems plausible that producer-driven value chains are likely to involve more transfer of know-how. While buyer-led chains often help developing nation firms conform to higher standards, the firms in such networks tend to be retailers rather than manufacturers. This limits the extent to which they can help with upgrading the developing nation's production, but this is just a conjecture.

The Expansion Question

To avoid the Kaesong syndrome—a few good jobs but no real spillovers—development policy needs to find ways of connecting the global value chain's initial activity to the broader domestic economy. With tighter connections, the participation is more likely to spark knock-on benefits, such as an expanding range of industrial competencies, diffusion of know-how, training of managers, and the like. The ultimate goal is to create more and better jobs for workers and to encourage new activity by local firms.

There is little new in terms of how a government goes about reaching those goals, since the transmission channels are just as they were before global value chains. The extra benefits tend to come from supply-side linkages (called forward linkages in the pre-unbundling development literature), demand-side linkages (or backward linkages), and skill formation.

The demand linkages were very much the focus of the old import-substitution approach. For instance, one of Korea's goals in exporting lots of cars to the United States was to achieve a large enough demand for engines to make local engine production economical. This was also the goal of the local content restrictions that Thailand imposed on Japanese carmakers.

The supply linkages are slightly more novel. If, say, Bangladesh all of a sudden gets a world-beating producer of textile dyes to supply the rapid production of shirts for Zara, then unrelated Bangladeshi clothing manufacturers may find they have an edge over other nations who face delays in importing such dyes.

The skill upgrading is easy to understand and it works through on-the-job experience. Managers and technicians get better at what they do by doing it. Thus experience in production facilities in the global value chain can pave the road to either higher paid jobs or a move to local firms. Enhancing quality is a related issue.

Quality upgrading was a theme that came through in many of the previous examples. Modern manufacturing has very little tolerance for hit-and-miss quality, but fortunately, achieving high quality standards is something that can be learned. The point is illustrated by the case of the Vietnamese company Hai Ha, which now supplies motorcycle parts and components to leading European producers (see Box 15).

BOX 15: EXPORTING MOTORCYCLE PARTS TO EUROPE

Consultants at the Dutch aid agency CBI implemented a program of continual improvement at the Hai Ha Company. To spiff up the production floor, the consultant Rolf Hoffmann used the five-S path to better quality. The first S, "sorting," involved a triage of tools on the shop floor. Everything that was nonessential was eliminated. Then came "stabilizing," which means a place for everything and everything in its place. "Shining" was the third S term used to enforce tidiness and good organization of the workspaces, leaving "standardizing" and "sustaining" as the last two S words. One refers to standardizing procedures across all workers; sustaining refers to getting supervisors to consistently enforce the first four S words.

These simple practices helped Hai Ha meet European standards for quality and reliability. They are a good example of what know-how means in the second unbundling. Know-how is far more than just technical knowledge or advanced management techniques. The most important things in poor nations may involve very basic practices that are taken for granted in G7 workplaces.[9]

The Sustainability Question

The last question is perhaps the easiest to write about but the hardest to do. It involves nothing less than transforming societies. Social upgrading means creating an equitable distribution of the opportunities and outcomes that global value chains create, supported by labor regulation and monitoring and occupational safety, health, and environmental rules and the like. There is really nothing global-value-chain-specific about the need for, or the mechanisms of actions of these critical policies.

Indeed, it is important to realize that global value chains opened a new pathway to prosperity, but they do not reduce the difficulty of the really hard things about development.

Old Problems Are Still with Us

One way to think of the New Globalization's impact on industrialization is to say it changed the nature of the "master plan." The grand sector-by-sector schemes pursued by Korean and Taiwan are no longer as important as they once were. But as readers who have experience with real-world "change management" will know, having the right master plan gets you only so far. The three hardest things about accomplishing something difficult are implementation, implementation, and implementation.

When it comes to development the first-order implementation problem concerns people. People need to have the basic skills that prepare them to acquire the specific skills they will need in new industrial jobs. They also have to move to where the jobs are, and this, in turn, requires new houses and schools and the provision of local services.

One step up, development requires the establishment of networks of suppliers and buyers among firms and smaller productive networks within firms. And the society needs to be ready for the jarring social, economic, political, and generational changes that arise when a nation shifts from a stagnant agrarian economy to a fast-changing industrial economy.

All sorts of other implementation problems must be tackled. There is physical infrastructure to set up—everything from roads and bridges to airfields and ports. Likewise, development requires a legal infrastructure that is conducive to the rapid accumulation of human, physical, and knowledge capital. The political challenges can be no less daunting, especially if the nation starts out with deep social, economic, or ethnic cleavages.

In short, there is nothing easy about development, but what is clear is that the world needs much more research on how developing nations can make global value chains work for them.

BOX 16: SUMMARY OF POLICY IMPLICATIONS
FOR A DEVELOPING ECONOMY

This chapter looked at the implications of the global value chain revolution for developing nations. The main message is that developing nations can now industrialize by joining a supply chain. Before the second unbundling, they had to build the whole supply chain at home to become competitive abroad. Now they can become competitive abroad by joining an international production network. The trick, then, is to expand their participation in these networks in a fashion that creates more good jobs and triggers self-sustaining growth. How this trick is to be accomplished in practice is still a phenomenally under-researched area. The chapter therefore relies heavily on examples and simple illustrations.

A few general points emerged. First, since industrialization can happen stage by stage in global value chains (rather than sector by sector as in the Old Globalization world), industrialization policy is easier and less risky. Industry can be established with a series of small nudges rather than a few big pushes. Second, the sequencing question was blurred by the fragmentation implicit in the global value chain revolution. Developing nations may jump straight into exporting what may look like highly advanced sectors such as aerospace or automobiles. Instead, new questions arise: What global value chains should be joined? How can the country keep expanding and strengthening its participation in global value chains? And—most important—how can it turn global value chain participation into sustainable development?

The last key point is simply that global value chains are not magical. They open a new way to industrialize, but they do not solve the hardest development problems. Successful development requires a broad array of social, political, and economic reforms that are as difficult now as they ever were.

Encouragingly, the idea that global value chains require a re-thinking of development strategies is rapidly catching on. For instance, the World Bank has established a unit to help nations join global value chains and get more good jobs once they have joined. This unit has teamed up with institutional efforts at the Organization for Economic Cooperation and Development (OECD), the World Trade Organization (WTO), and several national think tanks such as Japan's Institute of Developing Economies (IDE-JETRO).

It is an exciting area for scholars. Policymakers in East Asia, Central Europe, and Central America have been trying out various policies for a couple of decades. Now, new datasets are emerging to guide more systematic thinking about which of these policies works best.

PART V

Looking Ahead

Despite the best efforts of the smartest humans, no one has found a way to know the future. This ineluctable fact has caused many thinkers to shy away from making predictions. As the Confucian poet Lao Tzu put it: "Those who have knowledge, don't predict. Those who predict, don't have knowledge."

But this is wrongheaded. We have a duty to think hard about what may be so as to better prepare society for the changes that may come. As Henri Poincaré wrote in *The Foundations of Science,* "It is far better to foresee even without certainty than not to foresee at all."[1] Following his wise words, this book's closing chapter puts forth some conjectures about how globalization may change in the years to come. My guess is that the changes will be radical and disruptive.

CHAPTER 10

Future Globalization

Globalization is, I believe, in for a radical new transformation, but it will only happen if the cost of moving people falls in the future as much as the cost of moving ideas has in the recent past. The driving force is simple.

Despite the Great Convergence, salaries and wages are much higher in rich nations and there are billions of people who would like to earn those wages. They are, today, unable to do so, since they find it hard to get into the rich nations. If technology opens a sluice-gate that allows these people to offer their labor services in advanced economies without actually being there, the impact on jobs could be shocking. And the necessary technology is, I conjecture, not too far away.

The chapter's organization follows the advice of futurologist John Naisbitt: "The most reliable way to forecast the future is to try to understand the present." The first matter to deal with is thus an examination of the current trends in the cost of shifting goods, ideas, and people across borders. Weighing up the trends yields a set of conjectures about the likely trajectory of these three separation costs. Taking these guesses as data, the discussion then speculates about the future course of offshoring and the likelihood that the global value chain (GVC) revolution will continue to transform global manufacturing.

The chapter concludes with some simple hypotheses about the future of globalization that clarifies what I mean by "a radical new transformation."

Future Course of Separation Costs

The three-cascading-constraints view of globalization rests on bedrock made of three costs: the costs of getting goods, ideas, and people from one place to another. Since the timer on modern globalization started in 1820, these costs have generally been compressed by technological advances. Politics, however, have frequently trumped technology.

War-related disruptions caused trade costs to soar in World War I and II, and man-made barriers (tariffs) soared between the two wartime spikes. Since people move by the same means as goods, war disruptions also made the movement of people difficult. The most important difficulties in getting people from one nation to another, however, are related to government policies. There are episodes where migration was actively encouraged and others where it was absolutely forbidden.

To think carefully about globalization's future, it is thus imperative to think carefully about today's political and technological tendencies, starting with trade costs.

Will Trade Costs Rise or Fall Substantially?

The cost of moving goods could, in principle, be sharply increased by a 1930s-style protectionist surge. This seems unlikely to me. In reaction to the 2008 global crisis, world trade experienced a sudden, severe, and synchronized collapse in 2009. This was the sharpest drop in recorded history and deepest since World War II. Joblessness shot up and politicians were under pressure to do something.[1] Massive 1930s-style protectionism, however, did not materialize.

If protection was not triggered by this mammoth shock, it is hard to see what would trigger it. My view is that the rise of international production networks has deeply changed the politics of protection— at least for the nations that are involved in these networks. When a nation's factories are crossing borders, closing the borders no longer saves jobs even in the short run. Walling up the borders in the twenty-first century would destroy jobs as surely as putting up artificial walls inside factories would have done in the twentieth century. In short, protectionism is a really bad idea for nations hoping to get or keep industry.

Trade costs, however, could rise if oil prices shoot up. The future course of oil's price is unknowable. Recent expert opinions suggest the price will stay low for a long time, but just a few years ago the same experts were extrapolating triple-digit oil prices into the 2030s. Fortunately, oil prices are probably not that important anymore when it comes to helping or hindering the forward march of globalization. To see this point, it helps to look back.

The second unbundling started when falling oil prices provided a powerful tailwind (Figure 62). In inflation-adjusted prices, a standard barrel of oil halved from $40 in 1990 to $20 in 2000; this made it cheaper to move goods internationally. But the second unbundling continued to power ahead in its second decade of this century despite the strong headwind created by a fivefold rise in oil prices. Plainly, oil prices do affect the cost of moving goods, but they are not determinant.

Communication Costs

The trajectory of communication costs seems to be much easier to calculate. The "laws" driving the ICT revolution—Moore's, Gilder's, and Metcalfe's—are in the rising part of their S-curve (see Chapter 3 for details). This suggests that the cost of moving ideas is likely to continue to fall in the coming years—even without any new Star Trek-like technological breakthrough.

But technology is not the only determinate of international communication costs. Government policies could counteract the cost effects of advancing Information and Communication Technology (ICT). China, for example, has been fairly successful in suppressing cross-border communication for political ends, so it is technically

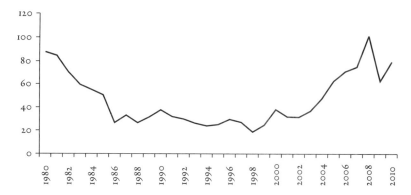

FIGURE 62: Falling oil prices facilitated the second unbundling during its early years but hindered it after 2000.

Taking 1990 as the beginning of the second unbundling, this chart shows that production unbundling started in an era of low energy costs. Oil prices were quite stable, falling gently for ten years. From the turn of the century, however, the second unbundling has progressed despite sharply rising oil prices.

SOURCE: U.S. Energy Information Administration (EIA) Annual Energy Outlook.

feasible. The key question then is whether governments will have an incentive to turn off the tap.

To put it differently, which governments would win from reducing the know-how that is flowing from the G7 nations to developing nations inside global value chains?

Issues are clarified by returning to the soccer team analogy from the Introduction. The analogy suggests that the Old Globalization was like two soccer teams swapping players, while the New Globalization was like the coach of the best team training the worst team's players in his / her spare time. In this analogy, cross-border knowledge flows are like the cross-team training. Plainly the owners of the best team have an incentive to stop this while the owners of the other team have an incentive to encourage it. Putting it directly, G7 governments are the only ones that have a clear incentive to disrupt the knowledge flows.

Given how antiglobalization sentiment is surging in many G7 nations, it is not inconceivable that a populist government might seek to stem the flow. But could they actually do that? It is very hard to know exactly how, for instance, American firms move essential knowledge to the Mexican factories. This point, illustrated by the Bombardier example in Chapter 3, suggests that it would take a truly radical closing of ICT borders to stop firms from leveraging their knowledge with low-cost labor abroad.

My guess is that, at least in G7 nations, the instinct for an open society is stronger than any protectionist instinct that is likely to arise. It seems likely, therefore, that the cost of moving ideas internationally will continue to fall.

Communication Technology (CT), however, is only one half of the ICT revolution. The other half concerns Information Technology (IT). As the discussion about production unbundling in Chapter 6 makes clear, both IT and CT affect the course of offshoring, but they work in opposite directions.

When thinking about the future of global supply chains, we must speculate about the possibility of truly revolutionary IT developments. One such possible development relates to computer-integrated manufacturing (CIM). This is not futurology. It has already had a big impact. It has already produced a tectonic shift in manufacturing in high-wage nations—moving manufacturing from a situation where machines helped workers make things to a situation where workers help machines make things.

The integration and automation of tasks, however, does not stop at the factory gate. Many design, engineering, and management tasks have been computerized. Computers have greatly boosted productivity and the speed of product design as well as greatly reduced the need for prototyping. Once designed, the production process can be outlined using computer-aided process planning systems and design programs can create instructions for numerically controlled machines. The basic manufacturing functions—machining, forming, joining, assembly, and inspection—are supported and integrated by computer-aided manufacturing systems and automated materials-handling systems. Inventory control is automated for tracking inventory movement, forecasting requirements, and even initiating procurement orders.

Given these recent trends, my guess is that the world will see rapid advances in the computerization and automation of manufacturing, at least in the G7 nations. These advances will extend far beyond using more robots in fabrication stages. It will lead to more computerization of the design and testing of new products as well as their distribution and after-sales service.

Face-to-Face Costs, the Virtual Presence Revolution and Telerobotics

The third separation cost—the cost of face-to-face interaction—is also likely to persist on its downward path. More specifically, really good ICT is creating reasonable substitutes for in-person meetings. This "virtual presence revolution" is based on high-quality video and audio systems on both ends of what can be thought of as "the telephone wire." It is—in essence—really, really good Skype.

An example is Cisco Systems' TelePresence. This combines full-size images of participants, using three plasma screens, sound channels, high-precision microphones, custom lighting, and high-definition cameras. Audio is arranged such that the voices of the participants on the "left" (who could be in Mumbai) sound like they are coming from the left.

The result is much more information being passed among participants than is possible with audio or even standard video conferencing. High-quality video allows a much better reading of faces. Psychological research shows that "microexpressions"—split-second facial changes lasting only a twenty-fifth of a second—can indicate whether a person is concealing an emotion, consciously or unconsciously. These reactions cannot be perceived over regular video calls or Skype and, indeed, these sorts of nonverbal messages are one of the reasons face-to-face meetings generally lead to better understanding and trust than calls or Skype.

Such systems are already deployed in high-end services sectors. They have reduced the need for face-to-face meetings in businesses such as consulting firms and financial services companies. However, they are still expensive and still limited to fixed facilities. If such systems became much cheaper and more mobile, they could significantly reduce the need for specialists and managers to travel to remote factories and offices. Of course, in-person meetings are likely to be part of coordination for a very long time, but the number of meetings could be greatly reduced.

The next step is "holographic telepresence." This projects real-time, three-dimensional holographic images of people (along with audio) in a way that makes it seem as if the remote person is right next to you. This allows the participants to gauge each other's full "body language" in an interactive way. This is the stuff of science fiction, but it is not unimaginable. Cisco has already demonstrated a beta version. Interested readers can find videos on this by browsing for "Holographic Video Conferencing."

Telerobotics is another important trend. After all, moving people is not just about people-to-people meetings, it is also about people-to-machine interactions. Keeping a complex production process running usually involves specialists manually engaging with various forms of hardware. If virtual presence technology were combined with human-controlled robots of the type used today in operating rooms, technicians could conduct inspections or undertake repairs from remote locations.

As with telepresence, the widespread use of telerobotics is constrained by high costs. But if it is possible to develop systems that allow surgeons to fix people at a distance, surely it is possible to develop systems that allow technicians sitting in Stuttgart to fix machinery in Brazil. Given the falling cost of manufacturing things, it would seem to be only a matter of time before human face-to-face and person-to-machine constraints are relaxed.

An important complement of this trend is the rapid development of computerized translation. When it comes to translating written words, amazing strides have been made in the last ten years or so. Google Translate, for example, was the source of great mirth to bilingual people in 2000. Now it is really quite good and getting better all the time. Even more recently, Apple released "iTranslate," which translates voice to and from dozens of languages. The language barrier, which has been an important separating force throughout human history, may soon be lowered or even dismantled.

The Future of Production Unbundling

What do these likely trends in separation costs mean for globalization? As discussed at length in Chapter 6, production unbundling is best thought of as a two-step process—fractionalization of the production process (breaking it up into finer stages) and international dispersion of stages (offshoring)—even though the two are decided concurrently.

The impact of lower trade costs and lower face-to-face cost quite clearly make it easier to separate production processes into finer stages while simultaneously making it easier to transfer more stages overseas. These trends thus suggest that the unbundling of G7 factories and the offshoring of an ever wider range of production stages is likely to continue.

The tendency has been slowed by rising wages in today's major offshoring centers (China, Mexico, Poland, etc.), but there are still billions of low-cost workers in the world who would love the chance to move out of agriculture and into international production networks. Many of their governments are working diligently on making this a reality (see discussion in the previous chapter). My guess is that the push of high Northern wages and the pull of low Southern wages will continue to drain manufacturing jobs from the G7 to an ever widening circle of developing nations.

The impact of improved IT, however, is less clear, as Chapter 6 explained. Fractionalization of the supply chain is determined by the interplay between the gains from specialization and costs that the extra coordination this requires. Some types of ICT—especially better communications technology (CT)—reduce the cost of specialization, in the sense that they make it easier to coordinate a finer division of labor. This pushes toward more fractionalization. Other types of ICT—especially robotics and computerization—reduce the benefit of specialization because they make it easier for one worker to deal with a wider range of tasks. In short, CT is pro-fractionalization, whereas IT is anti-fractionalization. Mobile, always-on, virtual presence would be an extreme example of better communication technology that pushes firms toward an ever finer division of labor.

A fascinating special report by *The Economist* in 2012 extrapolates these trends even further.[2] It notes that manufacturing may be going through a new industrial revolution due to the advent of "3D printing" (also called additive manufacturing), which bundles virtually all stages of manufacturing into a single machine. Combined with the virtual designing made possible by computer-aided design systems, 3D printing would take manufacturing very close to the Star Trek replicators. While it seems more than a few years away, we are clearly moving toward a reality where "if I can imagine it, the computer can make it for me."

Supply chain unbundling would be seriously undermined by radical advances in the direction of mass customization and 3D printing by sophisticated machines. Whether these machines end up in high-wage, high-skill nations or are distributed to be near every large customer base, the impact would be a very substantial reduction in supply chain trade. To put it sharply, the transmission of data would substitute for the transportation of goods.

Shifting the focus from fractionalization to the international dispersion of stages raises a different set of issues. As discussed in Chapter 6, the decision to relocate production stages abroad turns on the costs and benefits of doing so. Generally speaking, lowering any of the separation costs makes offshoring more attractive given the very large wage differences that exist around the world despite the Great Convergence. But this is not the only reason I expect offshoring to continue.

While it is very useful to stylize the offshoring decision as helped by wage gaps and hindered by separation costs, market size also matters. There is always a tendency to locate production near consumers. When the G7 markets were globally dominate, this was an argument for keeping manufacturing in G7 countries. As the Great Convergence proceeds, the force of the argument switches from anti-offshoring to pro-offshoring. The number of customers with the means to buy products is, after all, rising faster in the developing world than it is in the developed world.

The reasoning has so far ignored the question of where new offshoring will go to next. As this is a critical question—especially to developing nations trying to join the GVC revolution—it is the next topic for consideration.

Destination of Future Offshoring

To formulate conjectures on the destination of future offshoring, it is useful to recall that, as Chapter 6 explained, the geographical unbundling of stages of production is governed by a balance between dispersion forces and agglomeration forces. Agglomeration forces make clusters attractive and this has two implications. First, it discourages offshoring in the first place as firms prefer to colocate with their customers and suppliers in G7 nations. Second, if stages are offshored, they tend to head for pre-existing clusters. That is why the nations that have already received offshore production stages will tend to continue getting them going forward. It is the old chicken-

and-the-egg logic whereby having a chicken usually results in more chickens. Countermanding this, however, are trends in wages.

Wages are critical on the dispersion force side of the balance. The movement of production stages from the North into developing-nation factories—especially into Chinese factories—was at first met with little or no increase in local wages. The reason, according to three-cascading-constraints reasoning, is that the knowledge was not, in some sense, moving into China. It was moving into particular factories in particular sectors in particular cities. While some wage-raising spillovers occurred, G7 firms sought to limit or delay such spillovers. Moreover, the offshoring sector was initially quite a small proportion of the overall local economy. In the words of Nobel Prize–winning economist Arthur Lewis, this was "economic development with unlimited supplies of labor."[3]

More recently, however, labor markets in the rapidly industrializing nations have begun to enjoy higher wages. As a result, the most unskilled-labor intensive stages have started moving to lower-wage developing nations. The basic logic of production unbundling suggests that this trend will continue, creating a twenty-first-century version of the pattern suggested by the "flying geese model" (see the previous chapter for details). However, I conjecture that the pattern will probably happen only with respect to the least skill-intensive stages. It has already begun in East Asia, where new low-wage nations—like Vietnam and Bangladesh—have joined the GVC revolution. Once wages get high enough, the offshoring destinations may spread even further afield.

This development would be accelerated by the virtual reality revolution. By lowering face-to-face and face-to-machine interactions, such a revolution would make the geography of international production networks less sensitive to cartographical distance, and thus easier to spread to a wider range of developing nations.

My guess is that the geographical spread of the second unbundling is destined to move to the east coast of Africa. East Africa is close to Europe and closer to India and East Asia than is South America. Indeed, from the days of antiquity, East Africa was part of the trade pattern between the Middle East, India, and China (see Chapter 1).

Two Further Conjectures

As mentioned, incomes are converging between developed economies and rapidly industrializing developing nations. Since offshoring was initially motivated by the big wage gaps between these two groups of countries, one might think that narrowing the gaps would reduce trade between the two groups. I think this is wrong. Rather, I conjecture that trade between these two groups of nations will come to resemble the trade that occurs today among rich nations, namely lots of two-way trade in manufactured goods (also known as supply chain trade).

As Chapter 3 showed, supply chain trade was prevalent among nearby high-wage nations like Canada and the United States and within Western Europe even before the second unbundling, and it is still widespread today. This sort of trade is driven by extreme specialization that allows firms to become the low-cost supplier in particular varieties of intermediate goods (see Chapter 6). In other words, such trade is based on firm-level excellence rather than on wage gaps.

This tendency to shift from cost-competitiveness based on low-wage to cost-competitiveness based on firm-level excellence is already underway. Developing nations like China are producing more sophisticated intermediate goods domestically—parts that previously would have been imported. China, for example, is a major supplier of intermediate goods to nations around the world.[4] I believe this will continue, so that the extra specialization will more than compensate for any reduction in wage-driven trade.

The polarization of jobs is another important aspect of future globalization. To date, advancing IT has tended to polarize the landscape of work in rich nations. It produced occupations that involve a great deal of skill and high-tech machines, on one hand, and jobs that are quite menial, on the other hand. Chapter 3's example of the South Carolina factory illustrates this point quite precisely.

I expect this to continue. As routine, low-skill, and repetitive tasks are easier to computerize and automate, advancing IT is likely to continue eliminating occupations that involves such tasks. At the same time, the more intensive use of sophisticated production machines will make the remaining jobs more skill, capital, and technology intensive. This leads to a polarization of stages in terms of skill content. Routine low-skill tasks are bundled into high-skill occupations, while the remaining low-skill tasks will typically be highly labor intensive but less routine. The resulting broader stages will involve more capital-intensive, more technology-intensive, and more skill-intensive processes. This tends to favor their location in developed nations. Putting it crudely, this trend suggests that there will be factory jobs in G7 nations for high-skill workers and robots. Low- and medium-skill workers will see their jobs eliminated or offshored.

Deep down, this polarization stems from the fact that computers were substitutes for some workers but complements for others, as David Autor, Larry Katz, and Melissa Kearney pointed out in their 2006 paper, "The Polarization of the U.S. Labor Market."[5]

Globalization's Third Unbundling

One of this book's central premises is that understanding globalization requires a sharp distinction between three types of "separation costs"—trade costs, communication costs, and face-to-face costs. Globalization's first acceleration—or first unbundling—came when the cost of moving goods plummeted in the nineteenth century. Globalization's second unbundling came when the cost of moving ideas plummeted in the late twentieth century.

A third unbundling is likely to happen if the cost of moving people plummets. I am not talking about some sort of "Beam me up,

Scotty" technology that would make it cheap to literally move people across borders quickly and safely. I am talking about technologies that would create very close substitutes to being there in person. The two breakthroughs discussed might accomplish this. The first is really good substitutes for people traveling to be in the same room to exchange brain services (telepresence). The second is really good substitutes for people traveling to provide manual services (telerobotics).

Before looking at what the breakthroughs might look like, it is worth backing up a bit to think about what offshoring really is from an economic perspective.

Offshoring Is Arbitrage

The touchstone economics of North-South offshoring is based on arbitrage between high-wage and low-wage nations. To see the point, it helps to think about offshoring in an unusual way—to think of offshoring as a means of getting the labor services of low-wage labor out of low-wage nations.

Consider a firm that has excellent know-how and is based in a G7 nation, say the United States. To combine its technology with low-cost labor, say Mexican labor, the firm must either bring Mexicans to its U.S. factories, or move chunks of its factories to Mexico. If it brings Mexicans to its U.S. factories, Mexican labor services are embodied in goods that are sold directly, or used as inputs into goods that are sold. When it offshores production stages to Mexico, the Mexican labor services are embodied in goods that are exported to the United States (or other markets) for direct sales or further processing.

These options are equivalent in a very abstract economic model, but in the real world immigration is usually difficult, expensive, or forbidden, so firms often choose the offshoring alternative. Under either option, the big cost savings comes from the firm's ability to buy low-wage Mexican labor services instead of high-cost U.S. labor services. Offshoring, in other words, is a means of arbitraging international wage differences.

Telerobotics, Telepresence, and "Virtual Immigration"

Such arbitrage via offshoring is not possible for all activities. For the offshoring option to work, the firm needs some way of getting Mexican labor services out of Mexico. For many types of manufactured goods, this is easy since the labor services, as mentioned, are added to goods that are then exported. For many other types of activities— especially service activities—labor services cannot be separated from the laborers. For example, the only way to use Mexican labor services to tend to a U.S. garden is to have Mexicans in the garden.

Telerobotics could change all this for manual workers. It would allow workers based in developing nations to provide labor services inside developed nations without actually being there. Call it "virtual immigration" or telecommuting for manual workers. Hotel rooms in Oslo could be cleaned by maids sitting in Manila—or more precisely by robots in Oslo that were controlled by Philippine-based workers. Security guards in U.S. shopping malls could be replaced by robots driven by security guards sitting in Peru, or perhaps there would be one human security guard assisted by a dozen remotely piloted robots. The possibilities are only limited by the imagination.

The remote provision of labor services is likely to flow both ways. The general trend would be for low-skilled workers from developing nations to telecommute to rich nations, and high-skilled workers from rich nations to telecommute to developing nations. For example, experienced German technicians could fix German-made capital equipment in China by controlling sophisticated robots placed in Chinese factories.

Telepresence could do the same for brain workers living in developing nations. When telepresence meeting facilities are cheap and portable, and holographic telepresence is widespread, the need for face-to-face meetings will be greatly reduced, even if the need is not eliminated. This will make it much easier to coordinate the provision of brain power at great distances.

Given the vast North-South salary differences that exist for engineers, designers, accountants, lawyers, publishers (and let us not forget professors of economics), the ability to fractionalize the production of business services could lead to a great deal of "virtual offshoring." That is to say, telepresence would make it possible for developing nation professionals to work inside G7 offices and universities without actually being there.

This would be nothing more than an amplification of what is already happening. "Microwork" or "micro-outsourcing" is the ability to get individuals to perform small, disjointed tasks as part of a larger project with all the work taking place over the Web. Virtual presence will make the fractionalization and offshoring much easier to coordinate. Think of it as micro-outsourcing on steroids; for example, something like Amazon's Mechanical Turk but far more pervasive.

Of course, the offshoring of simple, modular services is an old story. All sorts of back-office tasks have been offshored or outsourced already. This could go much further. Leading providers of services ranging from banking to legal advice pay large numbers of expensive people to sit in expensive buildings in expensive cities since in-person interactions matter. Globalization's third unbundling could disrupt this.

In a nutshell, the next radical change in globalization is likely to involve workers in one nation undertaking service tasks in another nation—tasks that today require physical presence. Or to use the unbundling theme, globalization's third unbundling is likely to mean that labor services are physically unbundled from laborers.

Consequences

Relaxation of the face-to-face constraint via telepresence and telerobotics would make it much easier to separate the physical application of labor services from the physical presence of laborers. This is likely to produce two monumental changes. The first would stem from developed nation workers and managers applying their talents inside a wider range of developing nations without actually traveling to the nations.

The miracle of GVC industrialization has, so far, occurred only in a handful of developing nations—most of which are geographically close to Japan, Germany, and the United States. Yet the North-South imbalance in knowledge-per-worker is still quite extreme. Opportunities for arbitraging this imbalance are abundant. As wages rise in the nations that have benefited the most so far (above all China), and telepresence and telerobotics get better, firms with advanced know-how may increasingly leverage their knowledge with low-cost labor in, say, Africa or South America. Chinese firms may spearhead this new offshoring in an effort to offset the competitiveness losses that stem from rising Chinese wages.

If the geographic extent of the GVC revolution does widen, more developing nations could join the rapid-industrialization parade. This might reignite the commodity super-cycle and the Great Convergence would continue apace.

The second set of monumental changes would come from poor nation workers applying their talents inside rich nations without leaving home. For manufacturing sectors, this would be an evolution—a continuation of the unbundling and offshoring trend. But rather than sending production stages abroad to take advantage of lower cost labor, the labor would telecommute to factories that remained in advanced economies. All the impacts of the second bundling discussed in Chapter 8 would be amplified by this sort of virtual immigration.

For service sectors, the impact is likely to be more revolutionary. Many service sectors were only indirectly affected by the first and second unbundlings since they sold services that were essentially untradable. The heart of the un-tradability was the necessity for service providers and service buyers to be physically in the same place at the same time. Really cheap, reliable, and ubiquitous virtual presence technology and telerobotics would break the necessity. Nontraded services would become tradeable. In short, the third unbundling could do to the service sector what the second unbundling already did to the manufacturing sector.

In this speculative view of the future, all good and bad consequences of the second unbundling that showed up in manufacturing will carry over to services sectors. Because something like two-thirds of all jobs are in service sectors, the impact could be historic. In a broad swath of service sectors, rich nation workers could find themselves in direct wage competition with poor nation workers providing their labor services remotely. But of course, this challenge to rich nation workers would be an opportunity for poor nation workers.

To put these changes in perspective, it is worth drawing a parallel with the discussions of how disruptive Artificial Intelligence (AI) may be. According to Erik Brynjolfsson and Andrew McAfee, authors of *The Second Machine Age,* the near future will be marked by a very systematic use of AI to operate robots that replace humans in high-wage nations.[6] The authors point out that this would have large effects for workers ranging from truck drivers to investment managers. I would suggest that "Remote Intelligence" (RI) could end up as at least as transformative. After all, why go for computer operators when remote human operators would be so much more responsive (especially after the language barrier is demolished by costless, simultaneous translation)? In short, I suggest that we should all start thinking ahead about the impact of RI, not just AI.

Concluding Remarks

There is no proper way to end a book like this. A summary would be too long and I have already provided speculative conjectures about the future. Instead, I will end with an old quip: "Things have changed so much that not even the future is what it used to be."

I hope this book serves as a reminder that today's globalization does not resemble your parents' globalization. And tomorrow's globalization is very likely to be quite different from today's. The baseline reason is that the driving forces changed. Until the late twentieth century, the main driver was a massive cut in the cost of moving goods, which was ultimately triggered by the steam revolution. The main driver switched to phenomenal drops in the cost of moving ideas when the ICT revolution came along. In the future, the main driver may be transformative reductions in the cost of telepresence and telerobotics triggered by the virtual presence revolution.

If I am right, it will be important for governments and businesses to start rethinking globalization.

Notes

PART I. THE LONG HISTORY OF
GLOBALIZATION IN SHORT

1. Gerald M. Meier and Robert E. Baldwin, *Economic Development: Theory, History, Policy* (New York: John Wiley and Sons, 1957).

1. HUMANIZING THE GLOBE AND THE FIRST BUNDLING

1. Vincent Macaulay, et al., "Single, Rapid Coastal Settlement of Asia Revealed by Analysis of Complete Mitochondrial Genomes," *Science* 308, no. 5724 (2005): 1034–1036.

2. Jared Diamond, *Guns, Germs, and Steel: The Fates of Human Societies* (New York: W. W. Norton, 1997).

3. Ian Morris, *Why the West Rules—for Now: The Patterns of History and What They Reveal about the Future* (London: Farrar, Straus and Giroux, 2010).

4. William J. Bernstein, *A Splendid Exchange: How Trade Shaped the World* (New York: Atlantic Monthly Press, 2008).

5. Angus Maddison, *Contours of the World Economy 1–2030 AD: Essays in Macro-Economic History* (Oxford: Oxford University Press, 2007). See Chapter 3 for details.

6. Norman Cantor, *In the Wake of the Plague: The Black Death and the World It Made* (New York: Free Press, 2001).

7. Ronald Findlay and Kevin H. O'Rourke, *Power and Plenty: Trade, War, and the World Economy in the Second Millennium* (Princeton, NJ: Princeton University Press, 2007).

8. Stephen Broadberry, "Accounting for the Great Divergence," Economic History Working Papers 184-2013, London School of Economics, November 2013, http://www.lse.ac.uk/economicHistory/workingPapers /2013/WP184.pdf.

9. Edward L. Dreyer, *Zheng He: China and the Oceans in the Early Ming Dynasty, 1405–1433* (New York: Pearson Longman, 2007).

10. Felipe Fernández-Armesto, *Millennium: A History of the Last Thousand Years* (New York: Scribner, 1995).

11. David, S. Landes, *The Unbound Prometheus: Technological Change and Industrial Development in Western Europe from 1750 to the Present* (Cambridge: Cambridge University Press, 1969).

2. STEAM AND GLOBALIZATION'S FIRST UNBUNDLING

1. Kevin H. O'Rourke and Jeffrey G. Williamson, "When Did Globalization Begin?" *European Review of Economic History* 6, no. 1 (2002): 23–50.
2. Paul Bairoch and Susan Burke, "European Trade Policy, 1815–1914," in *The Cambridge Economic History of Europe,* vol. 8, *The Industrial Economies,* ed. Peter Mathias and Sidney Pollard (Cambridge: Cambridge University Press, 1989), 1–160. See also Bairoch, *Economics and World History* (London: Harvester Wheatsheaf, 1993); and Bairoch and Richard Kozul-Wright, "Globalization Myths: Some Historical Reflections on Integration, Industrialization, and Growth in the World Economy," Discussion Paper 113, United Nations Conference on Trade and Development, Geneva, 1996.
3. The quote comes from a speech Bismarck gave in 1879 supporting a protectionist law. Quoted in William Harbutt Dawson, *Protection in Germany: A History of German Fiscal Policy during the Nineteenth Century* (London: P. S. King & Son, 1904).
4. Simon Kuznets, *Economic Growth and Structure: Selected Essays* (London: Heinemann Educational Books, 1965).
5. Lant Pritchett, "Divergence, Big Time," *Journal of Economic Perspectives* 11, no. 3, (1997): 3–17; Kenneth Pomeranz, *The Great Divergence: China, Europe, and the Making of the Modern World Economy* (Princeton, NJ: Princeton University Press, 2000).
6. Charles P. Kindleberger, "Commercial Policy between the Wars," in *Cambridge Economic History of Europe,* ed. Mathias and Pollard, 161–196.
7. Gerhard Weinberg, "The World through Hitler's Eyes" (1989), in *Germany, Hitler, and World War II: Essays in Modern German and World History* (Cambridge: Cambridge University Press, 1995), 30–53.
8. I introduced the juggernaut concept in my book *Towards an Integrated Europe* (London: CEPR Press, 1994) and subsequently developed it with Frédéric Robert-Nicoud in Baldwin and Robert-Nicoud, *A Simple Model of the Juggernaut Effect of Trade Liberalisation,* CEP Discussion Paper 845, Centre for Economic Performance, London School of Economics and Political Science, London, UK, 2008.

9. Marc Levinson, *The Box: How the Shipping Container Made the World Smaller and the World Economy Bigger* (Princeton, NJ: Princeton University Press, 2006). See also Daniel M. Bernhofen, Zouheir El-Sahli, and Richard Kneller, "Estimating the Effects of the Container Revolution on World Trade," *Journal of International Economics* 58 (2016): 36–50.

3. ICT AND GLOBALIZATION'S SECOND UNBUNDLING

1. Paul Gallant, "How Bombardier's Experiment Became Ground Zero for Mexico's Economic Revolution," *Canadian Business,* April 15, 2014.
2. David L. Hummels and Georg Schaur, "Time as a Trade Barrier," *American Economic Review* 103, no. 7 (2013): 2935–2959.
3. For details, see Yuqing Xing, "How the iPhone Widens the US Trade Deficit with China," April 10, 2011, VoxEU.org.
4. See João Amador and Sónia Cabral, "Vertical Specialization across the World: A Relative Measure," *North American Journal of Economics and Finance* 20, no. 3 (2009): 267–280. Bottom panel: Baldwin and Lopez-Gonzales (2014).
5. Ibid., 267–280.
6. Robert C. Allen, *Global Economic History: A Very Short Introduction* (Oxford: Oxford University Press, 2011).
7. Paul Collier, *The Bottom Billion: Why the Poorest Countries Are Failing and What Can Be Done about It* (Oxford: Oxford University Press, 2007), 3.

PART II. EXTENDING THE GLOBALIZATION NARRATIVE

1. Karl Popper, *The Open Universe: An Argument for Indeterminism* (Totowa, NJ: Rowman and Littlefield, 1982); Stephen Hawking, *The Grand Design* (London: Bantam Books, 2011).

4. A THREE-CASCADING-CONSTRAINTS VIEW OF GLOBALIZATION

1. David Ricardo, *On the Principles of Political Economy and Taxation* (London: John Murray, 1817).
2. Andrew B. Bernard and Teresa C. Fort, "Factoryless Goods Producing Firm," *American Economic Review: Papers and Proceedings* 105, no. 5 (May 2015): 518–523.

3. Korea is something of an exception to this as its heavy industries did develop behind protectionist walls. Recently, however, it has set up international production networks of its own.

4. Full disclosure: Gene Grossman is my brother-in-law and he shared his Jackson Hole paper with me before the conference when we met at my mother's eightieth birthday in early August 2006; I wrote much of my own 2006 paper that same weekend.

5. WHAT'S REALLY NEW?

1. For details, see my 2015 paper with Javier Lopez-Gonzalez, "Supply-Chain Trade: A Portrait of Global Patterns and Several Testable Hypotheses," *World Economy* 38, no. 11 (2015): 1682–1721, and the longer 2013 version circulated as NBER Working Paper 18957 in April 2013.

2. Ibid.

3. See Pham Truong Hoang, "Supporting Industries for Machinery Sector in Vietnam," chap. 5 in *Major Industries and Business Chances in CLMV Countries,* ed. Shuji Uchikawa, Bangkok Research Center Research Report No. 2, Institute of Developing Economies, Japan External Trade Organization, 2009, http://www.ide.go.jp/English /Publish/Download/Brc/pdf/02_ch5.pdf.

4. Paul A. Samuelson, "Where Ricardo and Mill Rebut and Confirm Arguments of Mainstream Economists Supporting Globalization," *Journal of Economic Perspectives* 18, no. 3 (2004): 135–146.

5. National Board of Trade, "Made in Sweden? A New Perspective on the Relationship between Sweden's Exports and Imports," Stockholm, Sweden, 2011.

6. Robert Hall, "Macroeconomics of Persistent Slumps," in *Handbook of Macroeconomics,* vol. 2B, ed. John Taylor and Harald Uhlig (North Holland: Elsevier, 2016), http://web.stanford.edu/~rehall /HBC042315.pdf.

7. For details, see the website of Border Assembly Inc. at http://www .borderassembly.com/maquiladoras.html.

8. For details, see the website of QS Advisory at http://qsadvisory.com/.

6. QUINTESSENTIAL GLOBALIZATION ECONOMICS

1. Daniel Bernhofen and John C. Brown, "A Direct Test of the Theory of Comparative Advantage: The Case of Japan," *Journal of Political*

Economy 112, no. 1 (2004): 48–67; and Bernhofen and Brown, "An Empirical Assessment of the Comparative Advantage Gains from Trade: Evidence from Japan." *American Economic Review* 95, no. 1 (2005): 208–225.

2. Actually, Newton wrote: "Pigmaei gigantum humeris impositi plusquam ipsi gigantes vident," in a letter to Robert Hooke in the late 1600s. It can today be seen on the rim of £2 coins in the form: "Standing on the shoulders of giants." (Newton was warden of the Royal Mint for thirty years.)

3. The version of the endogenous growth theory is drawn from the Grossman and Helpman approach; see Gene Grossman and Elhanan Helpman, *Innovation and Growth in the Global Economy* (Cambridge, MA: MIT Press, 1991).

4. Ibid.

5. Nicholas Bloom, Luis Garicano, Raffaella Sadun, and John Van Reenen, "The Distinct Effects of Information Technology and Communication Technology on Firm Organization," NBER Working Paper 14975, National Bureau of Economic Research, May 2009.

6. Adam Davidson, "Making It in America," *Atlantic Magazine,* January/ February (2012).

7. ACCOUNTING FOR GLOBALIZATION'S CHANGED IMPACT

1. Paul Krugman and Anthony Venables, "Globalization and the Inequality of Nations," *Quarterly Journal of Economics* 110, no. 4 (1995): 857–880.

2. This is an old story to economic historians like Nicolas Crafts and Terrance Mills, who explicitly stress the importance of localized cumulative learning processes in their account of the Industrial Revolution (Terence C. Mills and N. F. R. Crafts, "Trend Growth in British Industrial Output, 1700–1913: A Reappraisal," *Explorations in Economic History* 33, no. 3 [July 1996]: 277–295). However, the formal connection between the logic of the New Economic Geography and the New Growth theory came much later. Specifically, the technicalities involved in integrating the Krugman-Venables logic with the Grossman-Helpman logic were first worked out in a paper on the geography of growth takeoffs that I wrote with Philippe Martin from the Paris School of Economics and Gianmarco Ottaviano from the London School of Economics (Richard Baldwin, Philippe Martin, and Gianmarco Ottaviano,

"Global Income Divergence, Trade, and Industrialization: The Geography of Growth Take-Offs," *Journal of Economic Growth* 6, no. 1 [2001]: 5–37).

3. Edward L. Glaeser, "Why Has Globalization Led to Bigger Cities?" Economix (blog), *New York Times,* May 19, 2009, http://economix .blogs.nytimes.com/2009/05/19/why-has-globalization-led-to-bigger -cities/?_r=o.

8. RETHINKING G7 GLOBALIZATION POLICIES

1. Reported in Pew Research Center article, "Faith and Skepticism about Trade, Foreign Investment," September 16, 2014, based a poll of forty-four nations, http://www.pewglobal.org/2014/09/16/faith-and-skepticism -about-trade-foreign-investment/.

2. See Paul Krugman, "Competitiveness: A Dangerous Obsession," *Foreign Affairs,* March/April 1994; this section draws on Richard Baldwin, "The Problem with Competitiveness," in *35 Years of Free Trade in Europe: Messages for the Future,* ed. Emil Ems (Geneva: European Free Trade Association, 1995).

3. Krugman, "Competitiveness: A Dangerous Obsession."

4. Richard Baldwin and Simon Evenett, "Value Creation and Trade in Twenty-First Century Manufacturing: What Policies for U.K. Manufacturing?" in *The U.K. in a Global World: How Can the U.K. Focus on Steps in Global Value Chains That Really Add Value?* ed. David Greenaway (London: Centre for Economic Policy Research, 2012).

5. Enrico Moretti, *The New Geography of Jobs* (Boston: Houghton Mifflin Harcourt, 2012).

6. I first made these points in a 2012 paper: Richard Baldwin, "WTO 2.0: Global Governance of Supply-Chain Trade," Centre for Economic Policy Research, Policy Insight No. 64, December 2012, http://www .cepr.org/sites/default/files/policy_insights/PolicyInsight64.pdf.

9. RETHINKING DEVELOPMENT POLICY

1. Richard Baldwin, "Trade and Industrialization after Globalization's Second Unbundling: How Building and Joining a Supply Chain Are Different and Why It Matters," in *Globalization in an Age of Crisis: Multilateral Economic Cooperation in the Twenty-First Century,* ed. Robert C. Feenstra and Alan M. Taylor, 165–212 (Chicago: University of Chicago Press, 2014).

2. See David L. Lindauer and Lant Pritchett, "What's the Big Idea? The Third Generation of Policies for Economic Growth," *Economía* 3, no. 1 (Fall 2002): 1–28.

3. See Paul Krugman, "The Fall and Rise of Development Economics," in *Development, Geography, and Economic Theory* (Cambridge, MA: MIT Press, 1995), chap. 1.

4. Dani Rodrik, *One Economics, Many Recipes: Globalization, Institutions, and Economic Growth* (Princeton: Princeton University Press, 2007), 55.

5. Harvey Leibenstein, *Economic Backwardness and Economic Growth* (New York: Wiley, 1957).

6. Bela Balassa, *Change and Challenge in the World Economy* (London: Palgrave Macmillan, 1985), 209.

7. Richard Baldwin, "Managing the Noodle Bowl: The Fragility of East Asian Regionalism," *Singapore Economic Review* 53, no. 3 (2008): 449–478.

8. Daria Taglioni and Deborah Winkler, "Making Global Value Chains Work for Development," Economic Premise No. 143 (Washington, DC: World Bank Group, 2014), http://documents.worldbank.org /curated/en/2014/05/19517206/making-global-value-chains-work -development.

9. Centre for the Promotion of Imports from developing countries (CBI), "How fast can you become part of the global motorcycle supply chain?" CBI Success Story, July 12, 2012, https://www.cbi.eu/success-stories /how-fast-can-you-become-part-of-the-global-motorcycle-supply-chain -/136079/.

PART V. LOOKING AHEAD

1. Henri Poincaré, *The Foundations of Science,* trans. George Bruce Halsted, Cambridge Library Collection (Cambridge: Cambridge University Press, 1902, 1905, 1908/2014).

10. FUTURE GLOBALIZATION

1. For details on this trade shock, see the 2009 eBook, Richard Baldwin, ed., *The Great Trade Collapse: Causes, Consequences and Prospects* (London: Centre for Economic Policy Research, November 2009).

2. "A Third Industrial Revolution," *The Economist,* April 21, 2012, 15.

3. See Arthur W. Lewis, "Economic Development with Unlimited Supplies of Labor," *Manchester School of Economic and Social Studies* 22 (1954): 139–191.
4. For details, see Richard Baldwin, and Javier Lopez-Gonzalez, "Supply-Chain Trade: A Portrait of Global Patterns and Several Testable Hypotheses," *World Economy* 38, no. 11 (2015): 1682–1721.
5. See David H. Autor, Lawrence F. Katz, Melissa S. Kearney, "The Polarization of the U.S. Labor Market," NBER Working Paper 11986, National Bureau of Economic Research, January 2006.
6. Erik Brynjolfsson and Andrew McAfee, *The Second Machine Age: Work, Progress, and Prosperity in a Time of Brilliant Technologies* (New York: W. W. Norton and Company, 2014).

Acknowledgments

This book was a very long time in the making. The original idea came from a paper I wrote in late 2006 for the Finnish prime minister's project "Globalization Challenges for Europe and Finland." The notion that something about globalization had fundamentally changed caught on quickly—for example, the *Economist* devoted a full page to my Finnish paper in January 2007. Eruption of the global financial crisis, however, pushed all such matters to the side for a few years in my mind and in the minds of the profession and policy makers. When globalization jumped back to the top of the policy agenda in the early 2010s, I started writing and speaking again on the topic. It was then that I realized that it deserved a book-length treatment.

I would like to thank my home institution, the Graduate Institute of International and Development Studies in Geneva, for granting me a sabbatical to get started in 2013. Many thanks go to the University of Adelaide where I laid out the main outlines of the book as the Geoff Harcourt Visiting Professor at the School of Economics in October and November 2013. The School of Economics provided an optimal atmosphere for this work and I want particularly to thank Richard Pomfret, Kym Anderson, and Mandar Oak for excellent discussions and hospitality.

I would also like to acknowledge the important intellectual contributions made by my coauthors in a few pure theory articles that outlined some of the basic mechanisms. (See the text for exact references.) Frédéric Robert-Nicoud and I showed how twenty-first-century trade could be integrated seamlessly into the classic twentieth-century trade framework known as the Heckscher-Ohlin model. Importantly, this crystalized my view that the second unbundling should be thought of as a phenomenon with two basic elements, namely fractionalization of the production process and within-firm technology transfers. Tony Venables and I looked at theoretical interactions between offshoring and agglomeration in a piece that predicted, among other things, the reshoring of offshored stages that has been observed in recent years. When it comes to globalization and growth takeoffs, Philippe Martin, Gianmarco Ottaviano, and I wrote down the first model of the agglomeration-competitiveness growth cycle that I use in this book to explain the Great Divergence. Philippe and I later developed a strand of theory where the interplay between trade costs and knowledge spillovers could result in the Great Divergence in the nineteenth century and the Great Convergence in the twenty-first century.

On the policy front, Simon Evenett, Patrick Low, and I worked out some of the policy implications for trade policy in a 2007 paper for the World Trade Organization. Simon and I subsequently worked out the key implications for industrial policy in a paper for the British government in 2012.

Index

Bronze Age, 27–28, 28f–29f, 121
Brown, John, 183–184f
bubonic plague (Black Death), 25,
35–36f, 45
build strategy, 250, 251–254

Cabral, Sónia, 98
Canada, 55, 58f, 59, 60f, 86–87, 139.
See also Atlantic economies; G7;
New World
canals, 62
Cantor, Norman, 35
capital: financial, 229f; growth and,
224–226; human, 231–232, 234–235;
knowledge, 192, 225–226; physical,
192, 225, 229f; policies and, 239, 240;
social, 225, 229f, 230
*Change and Challenge in the World
Economy* (Balassa), 263–264
China: BITs and, 104; bubonic plague
and, 35; cities over 100,000 and, 31f;
commodity super-cycle and, 135;
comparative advantage and, 149;
domestic value-added in export
growth by sector 1994-2008, 94f, 95;
European Renaissance/Enlighten-
ment and, 38; flourishing of, 37; G7
New Globalization policies and, 236;
GDP shares, 92f, 93, 209; ICT and,
139; income U.S. vs., 59; industrialization and, 55, 57, 58f, 59, 217; manufacturing and, 3, 87, 89, 90f, 91; poverty
and, 108, 242; pre-globalized trade
and, 116; production/consumption
clusters and, 30f; smile curve and,
159; tariffs and, 72; trade and, 31, 34,
55, 57; traditional mental models and,
244; urbanization and, 62–63t. *See also*
A7/global South/developing nations;
Asia; I6 (Industrializing Six); R11
(Rising Eleven); Silk Road

cities and urbanization: Americas/
China and, 62–63t; Asian dominance and, 31f–32f; 1820-1913, 47;
free trade/agglomeration and, 129,
194–196; human capital and,
234–235; New Economic Geography
and, 186–191; New Globalization
(second unbundling) and, 132, 141,
236; Old Globalization (first
unbundling) and, 78, 212–213;
policies and, 236, 240; pre-globalized
trade and, 116; rise of, 18–19, 25,
26–27; summary, 113; as twenty-first
century factories, 234–235
civilization, 26–27
climate change (global warming),
21–22, 22f, 24, 25, 45
Cline, Eric, 27
Clinton, Bill, 17
coal, 49, 51, 113
Cohen, Daniel, 84
Collier, Paul, 107
colonialism, 42, 209–210
colonies, 55
Columbia, 262
Columbian Exchange, 38, 40, 41f, 46
Columbus, 39
"Commercial Policy Between the
Wars" (Kindleberger), 64–65
commercial revolution, 43
commodity super-cycle, 7, 110, 135,
215–216
communication. *See* moving ideas
communication technology (CT), 287.
See also IT (Information Technology); moving ideas
comparative (competitive) advantage:
A7/developing nations and, 149,
217–218; cities as factories and,
234–235; defined, 179–180;
denationalized, 145–154; Dyson and,

comparative (competitive) advantage *(continued)*
136; exports and, 147–148; finer-resolution and, 257; global value chains and, 145–146, 217–218, 242, 273–274; high/low tech/wages and, 216; industrialization, 254; market fragmentation and, 184–185; measures of, 201; Meiji Japan example, 183–184f; migrations and, 138; national perspective and, 175–176; New Globalization (second unbundling) and, 147–148, 170–171, 175, 179–185, 221–222, 225–228, 231, 240, 257–262, 260f; offshoring and, 135, 168; Old/New Globalization compared, 166f–168, 171–172, 176, 179–185; policies and, 240; production networks and, 278; as regional/national concept, 266; Ricardo and, 125–129, 128, 138–139, 196; services and, 232; smuggling example of, 179–183; staged development strategy and, 259; stickiness and, 229; workers and, 168–169. *See also* development strategies; New Economic Geography; tariffs
complete knock-down kits (CKDs), 244–246
computer growth rate, 82
Constantinople, fall of, 37
consumers, 70, 185
containerization, 75–76
Contours of the World Economy, 1–2030 ad. (Maddison), 34
controllability, 176
coordination, 198–206, 203f, 217, 239–240, 266, 289
Crafts, Nick, 40

Davidson, Adam, 205
"deep" disciplines, 238–240

demand-side/supply-side circular causality, 174, 187–188, 208–209
developed nations. *See* G7/global North/developed nations
developing nations. *See* A7/global South/developing nations; development strategies
development strategies, 13, 241–277. *See also* global value chain; policies
Diamond, Jared, 24
diesel, 53
disease, 40, 41f. *See also* bubonic plague
dispersion. *See* agglomeration (industrial clustering)/dispersion
"The Distinct Effects of Information Technology and Communication Technology on Firm Organization" (Bloom, Garicano, Sadun and Van Reenen), 200
Doctrine of Universal Economy, 119, 121, 127
domestic value-added in export growth by sector 1994-2008, 94f, 95
Dreyer, Edward, 37
Dutch trade, 34–35, 40, 42
Dyson, 134–135, 135–136, 233–234, 237–240

Economic Development (Baldwin and Meier), 17
Economic Growth and Structure (Kuznets), 55
education and training, 13, 99, 186–187, 222, 225, 229–230
Egypt, 26f, 27, 30f, 31f, 72. *See also* A7/global South/developing nations
Eichengreen, Barry, 65
1177 BC: The Year Civilization Collapsed (Cline), 27
The End of Globalization (James), 64

endogenous growth theory, 179, 191–196, 193–196, 194f
energy, 19
Enlightenment, 38–39, 46
epidemics, 41f. *See also* Columbian Exchange
Estevadeordal, Antoni, 49
Eurasia, 40
Eurasian Integration, 25, 32–35, 45
Europe: Age of Discovery and, 38, 46; cities over 100,000 and, 31f; free trade (1846-1879) and, 54; incomes, 43f, 44f, 117–118f; industrialization and, 55–57, 59, 60f; innovation and, 118f; Investor State Dispute Settlement provisions and, 103; migrations to New World, 62t; Old Globalization (first unbundling) and, 128, 138; per capita industrialization (1750-1913), 58f, 59; population/output shares 1500 CE, 37f; protectionism and, 64, 66; rise of, 25, 35–44, 45–46; tariffs and, 56t, 72; trade and, 30–35, 39, 55, 57; urbanization and, 62–63t. *See also* Britain *and other countries;* European Union (EU); World Wars I and II
European Union (EU), 72, 75, 240
exchange rates, 65
exports, 138–139, 150, 151, 157, 183–184f, 237. *See also* comparative (competitive) advantage; sectors, economic; smuggling

face-to-face costs. *See* moving people
factories, 236
factoryless goods producer, 136
"The Fall and Rise of Development Economics" (Krugman), 243
Fernández-Armesto, Felipe, 38
Fertile Crescent, 21, 27

Finley, Moses, 118
Florida, Richard, 141
food. *See* agriculture and food
foreign direct investment (FDI), 102–103, 239, 249, 250. *See also* bilateral investment treaties (BTIs)
The Foundations of Science (Poincaré), 281
fractionalization (fragmentation) of production, 137, 142, 168, 175–176, 196–206, 203f, 231, 232, 290, 291
France, 188. *See also* Europe; G7
Frantz, Brian, 49
free trade, 101, 125, 129, 161, 166, 190–191, 193–196, 194f, 209. *See also* GATT; liberal policies; Washington Consensus
Friedman, Thomas, 142
Fujita, Masahisa, 127, 179
future (third unbundling), 8–10, 281–301

G7/global North/developed nations, 5–7; agglomeration and, 129, 188; BITs and, 104; communication and, 286–287; domestic value-added in export growth by sector 1994-2008, 94f, 95, 96; exports and, 151–154, 153f; GATT and, 101; global GDP share and, 48f, 81f, 89–, 92f, 93, 186; global income share of 1500-2020, 2f–3; Great Convergence and, 136; ICT/comparative advantage and, 139, 144; ideas and, 124; income divergence and, 57, 59; industrial clustering and, 124; industrialization and, 5, 55–56, 59–60, 60f, 61, 109; manufacturing and, 3f, 86–87, 88f, 89, 90f, 91, 133; national vs. corporate interest and, 169–170; New Globalization and, 12, 110, 143–144,

policies and, 237, 240, 267, 271–277; poverty and, 108; as regional, 141; smile curve and, 158; Thailand and, 250; value-added statistics and, 93–94. *See also* comparative (competitive) advantage; fractionalization; smile curve

Golden Fetters: The Gold Standard and the Great Depression (Eichengreen), 65

gold standard, 49

goods, rethinking, 238

Great Convergence, 1–2f, 3f, 110, 135f–136, 193–196, 194f, 215–216. *See also* New Globalization (Phase Four) (second unbundling)

Great Depression, 47

Great Divergence: cause of, 124; growth takeoffs and, 211–213; ICT and, 132; industrialization and, 19; knowledge spillovers and, 193–196, 194f; moving goods and, 121–124, 136; Old Globalization (first unbundling) and, 135, 140; separation costs and, 5; summaries, 1–2, 57–59, 58f, 78. *See also* Old Globalization (Phase Three) (first unbundling) (1820 to about 1990); steam revolution

Great Divergence (Pomeranz), 59

Greece, 27, 29, 208. *See also* A7/global South/developing nations

Grossman, Gene, 127, 137, 193, 211

Group of Seven nations. *See* G7/global North/developed nations

Guns, Germs, and Steel (Diamond), 24

GVCs. *See* global value chains

Haberler, Gottfried, 99

"Haberler Report" (Haberler), 99

Hai Ha company, 275–276

Hall, Bob, 162

Hawking, Stephen, 111

"headquarter" economics, 104

Heckscher, Eli, 127

Helpman, Elhanan, 127, 193, 211

Hengduan Shan Mountains, 27

"high development theory," 243

Hirschman, Albert, 187

Hobson, John, 38

home market effect, 190–191

Honda, 145–146

Hong Kong, 86, 151

Hoover, Herbert, 65–66

Hopkins, Anthony, 38

"How Bombardier's Experiment Became Ground Zero for Mexico's Economic Revolution" (Gallant), 79–80

humanization (globalization Phase One), 18, 21–44, 22f, 109

Hummels, David, 85

I6 (Industrializing Six), 2–3f, 86–89, 90f, 91–96, 110, 136, 151–154, 153f, 162

ICT (information and communication technology), 6–7; Africa/Latin America and, 98; comparative advantage and, 139; fractionalization and, 199–201; future and, 285–286, 291; G7 comparative advantage and, 139; G7 production and, 143; Great Convergence and, 193–196, 194f; growth figures, 81–82, 84f; incomes and, 162; Indian and, 96; industrial clustering and, 143; laws underpinning, 82–85; less controllability and, 174–175; migration compared, 139; moving people and, 288–290; national governments and, 174–175; Netherlands an, 235; New Globalization (second unbundling) and, 8, 19, 79–110, 85–109, 133f; parts and

ICT (information and communication technology) *(continued)*
    components exports and, 153f, 257, 258–259; policies and, 285–286; sectors sequencing and, 266; skilled vs. unskilled workers and, 205; staged development strategy and, 256–257; three-constraints view and, 131; workers and, 168–169. *See also* moving ideas; New Globalization (Phase Four) (second unbundling); North-South differences; offshoring; technology; telecommunications
The ICT Revolution (Cohen, Garibaladi and Scarpetta)by, 84f
IIT (intra-industry trade), 96, 97
imperialists, 43, 209
import substitution, 243–249, 248f, 263–269, 265t, 270, 274
incomes: 1 to 1820, 42–43f; Atlantic vs. Asia, 44; competitive advantage and, 147–148; 1500 CE, 37f; Great Divergence and, 59; industrial clustering and, 124; moving ideas and, 5, 161–165; New Globalization and, 162, 163f; North and, 2f–3, 57, 59–61, 60, 60f, 63; pre-globalized world and, 117–118f; trade and, 51; urbanization and, 63. *See also* GDP (income) shares; Great Convergence; Great Divergence; "shocking share shift"
India: BITs and, 104; bubonic plague and, 35; cities over 100,000 and, 31f; communication/urbanization and, 213; corporate brands and, 142; domestic value-added in export growth by sector 1994-2008, 94f, 95–96; face-to-face constraint and, 216; GDP and, 81f; globalization Phase 1 and, 27, 29; industrialization and, 55–56; Krugman-Vanables

abstraction and, 209; manufacturing and, 87; people-moving costs and, 7; per capita industrialization (1750-1913), 57, 58f, 59; poverty and, 108; production/consumption clusters and, 26f, 30f; tariffs and, 72; urbanization and, 62–63t. *See also* A7/global South/developing nations; Asia; I6 (Industrializing Six); R11 (Rising Eleven)
Indonesia, 72, 87, 89, 90f, 94f, 95, 96, 159. *See also* I6 (Industrializing Six); R11 (Rising Eleven)
industrialization (manufacturing). *See* A7; agglomeration; comparative (competitive) advantage; development strategies; G7; globalization, industrialization and trade; global value chains; New Economic Geography; production/consumption clusters; smile curve; steam revolution; workers and jobs
Industrial Revolution, 4, 19, 40–42, 46, 59–60, 61
information storage, 82
innovation: agglomeration and, 128f, 129; cities and, 26–27; Europe and, 118f; falling cost of, 191–192; industrial clustering and, 123–124f; industrialization and, 59; New Globalization (second unbundling) and, 193–196, 194f; North-South differences and, 55, 211–212; Old Globalization (first unbundling) and, 78, 193–196, 194f; pre-globalized world and, 116, 116–117f; South and, 210–211; transportation and, 77. *See also* spillovers
Innovation and Growth in the Global Economy (Grossman and Helpman), 193

International Monetary Fund (IMF), 99

Internet, 83–84, 84f, 130. *See also* ICT (information and communication technology)

In the Wake of the Plague (Cantor), 35

intra-industry trade (IIT), 96, 97

Investor State Dispute Settlement provisions, 103

Iron Age, 27, 28f–29f, 29, 31

Irwin, Doug, 119

Islam, Golden Age of, 33, 34, 37f

Islamic World, 35, 38, 43. *See also* Silk Road

IT (information technology), 79; future and, 287–288, 291; polarization of jobs and, 294–295

Italy, 29, 43, 180–182, 208. *See also* Europe; G7

Italy/Greece. *See also* A7

ITC (information and communication technology): speed and, 12

IT (information technology). *See also* technology

James, Harold, 64

Japan: cities over 100,000 and, 31f; comparative advantage example, 183–184f; competitive advantage and, 167; economy-wide smile curve and, 157; industrialization 1000-1913, 59, 60f; industrialization and, 55; manufacturing and, 86–87, 90f, 91; Meiji example, 183–184f; North-South back-and forth-trade and, 96, 97f, 98; offshoring and, 133; per capita incomes year 1 to 1820, 42–43f; per capita industrialization (1750-1913), 57, 58f, 59; railroads and, 51; smile curve and, 159; tariffs and, 72; urbanization and, 62–63t. *See also*

advanced-technology nations; G7; North, global; Uniqlo; World Wars I and II

jobs. *See* workers and jobs

join strategy, 250

Jones, Ronald, 137

juggernaut effect, 69–71, 73–74

Kaesong syndrome, 270–271, 274

"Kaleidoscopic globalization," 11

Katz, Larry, 295

Kearney, Melissa, 295

Kenya, 72

Kindleberger, 66

Kindleberger, Charles, 64–65

Knöpfel, Adrian, 181

know-how (knowledge), 78. *See also* innovation; moving ideas

knowledge, tacit, 229f, 230

"knowledge arbitrage," 12

Korea, 72, 87, 94f, 95, 151, 159, 246–250, 248f, 269–271, 274. *See also* A7; I6; R11

Krugman, Paul, 127, 179, 195, 208–211, 225–226, 243

Kuznets, Simon, 55

Kuznets cycles, 61–62

labor services, 10

land, 120, 124, 138–139

Landes, David, 42

land transport, 211

Lao Tzu, 281

Latin America, 30f, 98, 99–101, 100f, 118f, 243. *See also* developing nations

Leibenstein, Harvey, 256

Levinson, Marc, 76

liberal policies, 55, 56t, 131, 160, 184–185, 218. *See also* free trade

Lindauer, David, 243, 244

livestock, domestication of, 30

local competition, 186–188, 188–189,
191–192
local market size, 184–185
location. *See* agglomeration (industrial
clustering)/dispersion; geography,
physical; New Economic Geography;
offshoring
Lorde, Audre, 83
luck, 247
Lyons, Roger, 233

Macaulay, Vincent, 21–22
Maddison, Angus, 34, 37, 43f
made-here-sold-there goods, 143, 150,
151, 173, 267
*Making Global Value Chains Work for
Development* (Taglioni and
Winkler), 272
Malaysia, 72, 159, 245, 246, 251–254,
253f
Malthusian level, 43f
management, 83–84
Mankiw, Greg, 221–222
manufacturing and. *See* industrialization
market access, 211
market fragmentation, 184–185
market research, 173
Meier, Gerald, 17
Meiji Japan example, 183–184f
Melitz, Marc, 127
mental models, 111–112, 119, 137–138,
172, 177, 229f, 243–244, 263–266,
269. *See also* abstractions; national
perspective; Ricardo, David;
three-cascading-constraints view
mercantilism, 119–120
Mesoamerica, 26f, 27
Mesopotamia, 27, 31
Metcalfe's Law, 83, 285
Mexico, 41f, 72, 79–80, 86–87, 94f, 95,
97f, 102. *See also* Border Assembly

Incorporated; Latin America; R11
(Rising Eleven)
MFN principle, 68–69
Mianovic, Branko, 162–163
Middle Ages, 119–120
Middle East, 26f, 27, 30f, 31f, 37–38,
62–63t, 100f. *See also* Silk Road
migrations, human, 10, 21–23, 23f, 62t,
126, 138–139, 188–189, 284. *See also*
moving people
*Millennium: A History of the Last
Thousand Years* (Fernández-
Armesto), 38
Ming Dynasty, 36
minimum critical effort, 255f, 256, 258f
Modelski, George, 31–32
Mongolian Empire, 33, 34, 35
Moore, Gordon and Moore's Law, 83
Moore's Law, 83, 131, 285
Moretti, Enrico, 228, 233, 235
Morris, Ian, 25, 38
moving goods: future and, 284–285,
291; globalization and, 109; Great
Divergence and, 121–124, 136;
manufacturing and, 122–124, 123f;
moving ideas compared, 174; New
Globalization and, 13; Old Globalization (first unbundling) and, 140;
politics and, 12; Ricardo and,
124–126; U.S. and, 61–62. *See also* air
cargo; commodity super-cycle;
containerization; Old Globalization
(Phase Three) (first unbundling)
(1820 to about 1990); railroads; steam
revolution; tariffs and protectionism;
three-cascading-constraints view
moving ideas (knowledge) (know-how)
(communication): agglomeration
and, 129; Bombadier and, 80; cities
and, 212–213, 234; competitive
advantage and, 146; five-S path and,

and, 97f; pace of change and, 170; parts and components exports and, 151–154, 152, 153f; policies and, 237–240; poverty and, 106–108f, 242; predictability and, 171–172; resistance to, 148–149; rich nation/poor nations trade and, 161; summaries, 4–5, 4–5, 6, 9f, 18, 19, 47–48, 53–78; tariffs and, 101; trade and, 161; urbanization and, 63, 132; workers and, 162, 168. *See also* cities and urbanization; global value chains; Great Divergence; moving goods; policies; steam revolution; three-cascading-constraints view

One Economics, Many Recipes (Rodrik), 244

On the Principles of Political Economy and Taxation (Ricardo), 125–126

The Open Universe (Popper), 111

O'Rourke, Kevin, 5, 53

Pakistan, 30f, 57, 58f, 59, 72. *See also* A7

parts and components trade, 150–154, 153f, 238, 248f, 249, 257, 258–259. *See also* import substitution

Pax Britannica, 54, 57, 68, 122

Peru, 41f. *See also* South America

Philippines, 72, 159

Poincaré, Henri, 281

Poland, 87, 89, 90f, 94f, 95, 97f. *See also* I6; R11

polarization of jobs, 294–295

"The Polarization of the U.S. Labor Market" (Autor, Katz and Kearney), 295

policies: comparative advantage and, 149; development nations and, 98–105; development strategies and, 241–277; global value chains and, 237, 240, 267, 271–277; ICT and,

285–286; industrialization and, 98–99; migration, 138; New Globalization (second unbundling) and, 11, 13–14, 110, 217–218, 221–223, 225–241, 262–277; servification and, 160; social, 236–237; summary, 278–279; supply chain assurances, 217–218; trade/transportation, 54; value chain revolution and, 271–277. *See also* development strategies; education; foreign direct investment (FDI); GATT *and other agreements;* tariffs and protectionism

politics, 69–71, 284

Polo, Marco, 114, 115

Pomeranz, Ken, 59

Popper, Karl, 111, 201

population, 24–25, 26, 27–30, 28f–29f, 30f, 41f, 44, 57. *See also* agriculture and food

Portuguese exploration, 39

poverty, 105, 108f, 162–163, 242

predictability, 171–173, 176

pre-globalized world, 4–5, 9f, 114–120, 116f. *See also* production/consumption clusters

premature deindustrialization, 134

prices, 19, 53

primary sector, 157

Pritchett, Lant, 59, 243, 244

production: internationalization of, 132–133, 134, 135; modularization of, 83; as national, 232; networks, 101–102, 103, 105–107, 106t–107t, 158; New Globalization and, 142–147, 176; Old Globalization mental models and, 225; trade and, 149–165; unbundling of, 132, 196–197. *See also* fractionalization (fragmentation) of production; offshoring; specialization; TOPS framework

"Where Ricardo and Mill Rebut and Confirm Arguments of Mainstream Economists Supporting Globalization" (Samuelson), 147–148

Why the West Rules—For Now (Morris), 25

Williamson, Jeff, 5, 53

Wilson, Charles Erwin, 169–170

Wilson, Woodrow, 64

Winkler, Deborah, 272

wire harnesses examples, 79, 260, 261, 270

workers and jobs: cities and, 235; future and, 164–165, 284–285, 294–295; global value chains and, 230–231; manufacturing and, 232–234; New Globalization (second unbundling) and, 162, 164–170, 166f, 175, 176, 225, 236; Old/New Globalization compared, 166f–169; textile-mill, 236–237. *See also* capital, human; education and training; fractionalization; offshoring; productivity; wages; work skills

work skills (skilled and unskilled labor): Britain and, 210; bundling of, 206; development strategies and, 276–277; fractionalization/offshoring and, 205; globalization and, 185; policies and, 228–231, 229f, 230, 231–237, 241, 271, 275; wages and, 186–187, 201–202

World Bank, 243, 272

World Economic Forum competitiveness index, 201

The World Is Flat (Friedman), 142

The World of Odysseus (Finley), 118

"The World through Hitler's Eyes" (Weinberg), 66

World Trade Organization (WTO), 68, 70, 101, 105, 106t–107t, 279

World Wars I and II, 47, 51, 64–67, 65f, 68, 77, 85, 284

writing, 27, 29, 117

Zheng He: China and the Oceans in the Early Ming Dynasty (Dreyer), 37